Cupcakes!

320 amazing designs that you can make!

It's Always A Great Time For *Cupcakes!*

Cupcakes are coming up everywhere! You'll find them at all kinds of occasions and events: from backyard barbecues, to celebrations at work, school events and even engagement parties. And regardless of the event, it's always the same reaction. Everyone's face literally lights up when cupcakes are served. Cupcakes are the perfect treat for kids, grandkids and adults too. And with Wilton, they're so easy to make!

Wilton "Cupcakes!" helps you to create the most smile-worthy treats around with sensational designs, complete instructions and great products. You'll find cupcake ideas that are unexpected and fun. Just wait until everyone sees the amazing cupcakes you've made!

We'll even show you how to decorate the inside of your cupcakes, so there's a special surprise in that first bite. Mix in a rainbow of colors using jimmies and nonpareils. Or, add layers of colored batter for fun effects. It's the newest way to make your cupcakes a very special treat!

Get ready to "wow" your family and friends with all the delightful designs inside. At Wilton, it's our goal to make it easy for you to make it amazing!

CREATIVE DIRECTOR
Daniel Masini

SENIOR DIRECTOR OF CAKE & VISUAL DESIGN
Steve Rocco

ASSISTANT CUPCAKE DESIGNERS
Ella Buitrago, Emily Easterly, Kim Feledy, Kathy Krupa, Mark Malak, Andrea Nickels, Valerie Pradhan, Kim Zarobsky

DECORATING ROOM MANAGER
Cheryl Brown

SENIOR CUPCAKE DECORATORS
Mary Gavenda, Susan Matusiak

CUPCAKE DECORATORS
Ella Buitrago, Renee Campagna, Emily Easterly, Kim Feledy, Jenny Jurewicz, Rachelle Kerwin, Diane Knowlton, Kathy Krupa, Mark Malak, Andrea Nickels, Valerie Pradhan, Tracey Wurzinger, Kim Zarobsky

DIRECTOR OF EDITORIAL
Jo-El M. Grossman

EDITOR/WRITER
Jeff Shankman

COPY EDITOR
Ivan Rioja-Scott

WRITERS
Mary Enochs, Barbara McHatton, Jane Mikis, Marita Seiler, Ann Wilson

PRODUCTION MANAGER
Challis Yeager

ASSOCIATE PRODUCTION MANAGERS
Sandy Peterson, Mary Stahulak

SENIOR GRAPHIC DESIGNER/PRODUCTION
Courtney Porter

PREPRESS MANAGER
Dennis Trojan

PREPRESS TECHNICIANS
Brian Block, Greg Boone, Paul Christon

PHOTOGRAPHY MANAGER
Dale DeBolt

PHOTOGRAPHY
Holly DeGarmo, Alan Rovge, Cindy Trim

PHOTO STYLIST
Carey Thornton

FOOD STYLISTS
Carol Parik, Susie Skoog

CREATIVE SERVICES ASSISTANT
Judi Graf

PRODUCT DEVELOPMENT/PUBLICATIONS
Joanne Winston-Spencer

For photography purposes, many cupcakes in this book were decorated (by right- and left-handed decorators) with royal icing. Printed in U.S.A.

Wilton Industries, Inc.
2240 West 75th Street, Woodridge, IL, 60517 USA
www.wilton.com

Retail Customer Orders:
Phone: 800-794-5866 • Fax: 888-824-9520
Online: www.wilton.com

Class Locations: www.wilton.com/classes

IN CANADA
Wilton Industries Canada Company
98 Carrier Drive, Etobicoke, Ontario M9W5R1 Canada
Phone: 416-679-0790

Class Locations:
Phone: 416-679-0790, ext. 200
E-mail: classprograms@wilton.ca

¡SE HABLA ESPAÑOL!
Para mas informacion, marque 800-436-5778
In Mexico: www.wiltonenespanol.com

Table of Contents

CUPCS...

... Are Coming Up
Everywhere For Everyone!

Cupcake Basics

Cupcakes are fun, easy and delicious! Follow our kitchen-tested steps, and your cupcakes will look and taste fantastic each and every time.

Even if you've baked dozens of cupcakes before, the Wilton Test Kitchen can show you how to bake them better. Here's how we turn out cupcakes that are ready for their close-up. See how everything comes together—quality ingredients, careful mixing and precise baking—to create a delicious, great-looking treat that is worthy of any celebration.

Preparing the Pan

Cupcakes are traditionally baked in a paper or foil baking cup for neat and stylish serving and a moist texture. You can also bake right in muffin pan cavities without a cup.

1 BAKING WITH CUPS

For perfectly shaped cupcakes, place your cups in muffin pan cavities. Baking in cups on a cookie sheet may create uneven shapes. Be sure to spread cups evenly in pan cavities and check that cups are level before filling. You don't need to spray the pan or your baking cups with vegetable pan spray—cups are pleated to prevent sticking.

When using foil cups, remove paper liners, if included, before filling and baking. The liners are included to help separate the thin foil cups in the package.

2 BAKING WITHOUT CUPS

Even non-stick pans must be prepared before baking. Prepare pan cavities by spraying with Wilton Bake Easy! non-stick spray or non-stick vegetable pan spray. You can also brush cavities with Wilton Cake Release pan coating, or coat with vegetable shortening and flour for perfect release without sticking.

TIP: For even heating and a rich, golden color, Wilton recommends baking cupcakes in aluminum muffin pans. If you choose to bake without a baking cup, consider our non-stick muffin pans for easy cleanup. Look for aluminum and non-stick aluminum pans in standard, mini and jumbo sizes on p. 158.

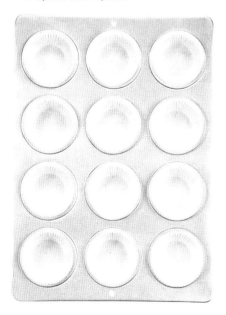

Preparing the Batter

As a general rule, most cake recipes or mixes will work for cupcakes. Simply adjust the baking time for the smaller portion, and test by inserting a Cake Tester (p. 159) during baking.

Proper measuring of ingredients is key to perfectly baked cupcakes—especially when you're making them from scratch. (See our recipes, starting on p. 132.) Measure liquids at eye level in standard liquid measuring cups. Measure dry ingredients by spooning into nesting measuring cups and spoons, then leveling off the top.

Time the mixing carefully, beating only for the length of time and at the mixer speed specified in recipe instructions.

TIP: For best results, and moister cupcakes, use large-size eggs (about ¼ cup each).

Filling Cups with Batter

The way you transfer batter into your baking cup makes a difference in the way your cupcakes look. Fortunately, Wilton has products that help you fill your cups consistently.

The Perfect Fill Batter Dispenser (p. 159, available April 2013) gives you excellent control, especially when filling mini baking cups. Just attach to a cut 16 in. disposable decorating bag, fill halfway with batter and squeeze. Its built-in valve helps control the flow and keeps batter from spilling over into the cavities. When you stop squeezing, the batter stops flowing.

Using Scoop-It Batter Spoons (p. 159) helps you bake cupcakes the same size. Most cupcake projects call for cups to be filled ⅔ full with batter The Scoop-It set includes mini, regular and jumbo spoons, for a foolproof way to fill any size cup ⅔ full with batter every time.

PERFECT FILL
BATTER DISPENSER

SCOOP-IT
BATTER SPOON

Baking Your Best Cupcakes

Know your oven! Inaccurate oven temperatures account for the majority of baking problems. If your cupcakes have indications of underbaking, try raising the oven setting about 25°F. If the problem appears to be overbaking, lower the oven setting about 25°F. If baking in dark bakeware, you'll need to lower temperature 25°F as well. Use an oven thermometer to check for accuracy.

Place the muffin pan as near to the center (both vertical and horizontal center) of the oven as possible. Make sure the oven rack is level. If you use two oven racks, rotate the pans midway through baking for even browning.

Time your baking accurately. If you are baking in several pans at the same time, you may need to add a few minutes to baking time. Test your cupcakes for doneness while they're still in the oven by inserting a cake tester into the center of a few cupcakes. Your cupcakes are done when the tester comes out clean.

Cool cupcakes in the pan on a cooling grid for 5 minutes before removing. Cool completely on a cooling grid before filling and icing.

TIP: Bake your cupcakes immediately after mixing the batter. Letting batter stand can cause some of the air you've beaten in to escape and your leavening isn't as effective, making for a denser baked treat.

Commonly Used Cupcake Products

Even if you have some basic bakeware and tools, consider upgrading with our recommended Wilton products below. They're designed to help you bake and decorate your best cupcakes ever.

Recommended Wilton Baking Products

- Aluminum or Non-Stick Muffin Pans (Standard, Mini or Jumbo)
- 10 in. x 16 in. Cooling Grid
- Cookie Sheets or Pans
- Cupcake Spatula
- Tilt-N-Mix 3-Pc. Bowl Set
- Scoop-It Batter Spoons
- Scoop-It Measuring Spoons and Cups
- Paper or Foil Baking Cups
- Cake Tester

Commonly Used Decorating Items

When you're gathering the products listed in your project instructions, make sure you have the following items as well:

- Knife
- Spoon
- Aluminum foil
- Waxed paper
- Zip-close plastic bags
- Cornstarch
- Solid vegetable shortening
- Granulated sugar
- Confectioners' sugar
- Plastic ruler
- Tape (or double-stick tape)
- Scissors
- Toothpicks
- Facial tissue
- Cotton balls
- Vegetable peeler (for candy curls)
- Craft foam blocks

The Inside Story!

Your cupcakes can be colorful and fun inside and out! Take that first bite and discover unexpected flavors, cool shapes and color schemes and even a treat inside a treat. Best of all, it doesn't take a lot of time to create any of these amazing effects—and the results bring a new world of excitement to cupcakes!

SURPRISE CENTER TREATS

It's taste times two! Cookies, candy and even mini pies are perfect mates for cupcakes. Whether you add a store-bought goodie or make your own petite treats, everyone will love these delicious duos.

Store-bought Sweets

A standard baking cup is the perfect size for a sandwich cookie, vanilla wafer, ginger snap or peanut butter cup. Just fill the cup ⅓ full with batter and position your treat. Complete filling the cup ⅔ full with batter. Bake and cool cupcakes.

CHOCOLATE SANDWICH COOKIE

PEANUT BUTTER CUP

Mini Cheesecakes

This is a great combination with cupcake flavors, such as chocolate, orange, peanut butter and strawberry. Prepare your favorite recipes for graham cracker crust and a custard/egg-based cheesecake batter. Press 1 teaspoon of graham cracker crust mixture into bottom of mini baking cup placed in Mini Muffin Pan. Fill crust area with cheesecake batter. Bake and cool following recipe directions. Fill standard baking cup ⅓ full with cupcake batter. Remove the baking cup from cheesecake and position in standard baking cup. Complete filling cup ⅔ full with cupcake batter. Bake and cool cupcakes.

MINI CHEESECAKE

Mini Pies

Fruit filling turns cupcakes into a little slice of heaven! For crusts, use the smallest cutter from Circles Nesting Metal Cutter Set (p. 166) to cut circles from refrigerated pie crust. Place the crust in Mini Muffin Pan cavity and fill with cherry pie filling. Bake and cool. Next, fill standard baking cup ⅓ full with batter and position mini pie. Complete filling cup ⅔ full with batter. Bake and cool cupcakes.

MINI CHERRY PIE

Mini Brownies

No one can resist this fudgy delight! Bake your favorite brownie mix in Mini Muffin Pan cavities, about 1 in. high. Fill a standard baking cup ⅓ full with cupcake batter and position the brownie. Complete filling the cup ⅔ full with cupcake batter. Bake and cool cupcakes.

MINI BROWNIE

COLOR EFFECTS

Have fun with your cupcake batter! Look at the cool patterns you can bake just by piping different color batters in the baking cup using a cut disposable bag.

Layering

Go with the cool contrast of the Black & White Zebra pattern or our psychedelicious Rainbow Tie-Dye look! Either way, the process is easy. Start with white or chocolate cake mix, divide the batters and tint with Wilton Icing Colors (for zebra, tint chocolate batter black; for tie-dye, tint white batter violet/rose, royal blue, kelly green, lemon yellow, orange and red-red). Pipe layers of batter in baking cup, filling about ⅔ full. Bake and cool cupcakes.

BLACK & WHITE ZEBRA

Diagonal

We've used chocolate and white cake mix here, but this quick trick will work for any pair of colors or flavors. Holding pan at an angle, pipe first batter color in baking cup, filling to about ⅔ of cup height. Pipe second batter color on opposite side of cup, filling about ⅔ full. Bake and cool cupcakes.

RAINBOW TIE-DYE

DIAGONAL

CAKE SHAPES

How do you get a bear inside a cupcake? It's easy! Cut shapes from a sheet cake using cookie cutters (p. 166); add the cake shape to your baking cup along with your cupcake batter in a different color.

Start by baking a cake, 1 in. high, in the 10.5 in. x 15.5 in. x 1 in. Jelly Roll Pan (p. 158), using a different color batter from your cupcakes. (We used chocolate batter for the bear, white batter tinted red-red for the star and rose for the heart.) Cut shapes using cutters. For the bear, use cutter from the Wilton Mini Noah's Ark Set. For the heart, use cutter from the Wilton Mini Romantic Set. For the star, use smallest cutter from the Wilton Star Nesting Plastic Set. Fill baking cup ⅓ full with cupcake batter and position your cake shape upright. Fill the cup ⅔ full, piping batter around cake shape. Bake and cool cupcakes.

TEDDY BEAR

HEART

STAR

MIX-INS

Stir a rainbow of colors right into your cupcake batter! Wilton Sprinkles create a dazzling confetti display that's perfect for parties.

FILLED CUPCAKES

Fillings are thrilling (and easy) additions to baked cupcakes! Just use a Wilton tip, such as the Bismarck tip 230, to pipe in whipped topping, pie filling, peanut butter and jelly, or flavored mousse.

LEMON MERINGUE

PURPLE NONPAREILS

Lemon Meringue

We've made this favorite pie portable! Use your favorite lemon pie filling in a disposable decorating bag fitted with tip 230. Insert the tip in the top of cupcake (we tinted the batter rose) and squeeze. For the top, prepare our Meringue Recipe (p. 143) and pipe a tip 1M swirl. Place cupcake in 375°F oven until top is light brown.

Raspberry Mousse

A great flavor match with chocolate cupcakes! Use your favorite raspberry mousse recipe in a disposable decorating bag fitted with tip 230. Insert the tip in top of cupcake and squeeze. Cover top with tip 1M swirl in raspberry mousse.

RASPBERRY MOUSSE

RAINBOW JIMMIES

Peanut Butter & Jelly

A flavor combination filled with memories. Attach tip 2A to two disposable decorating bags. Fill one bag with creamy peanut butter and one with your favorite jelly. Insert tip in top of cupcake, filling first with peanut butter, then with jelly. Cover top with tip 1A swirl in buttercream

Strawberry & Cream

It's a shortcake you can take anywhere, and it works just as well with blueberries or raspberries. For treat shown, wash and dry small strawberries and cut off tops with leaves and stem. Use a knife to cut a "v" shape in cupcakes. Pipe in whipped cream with tip 12; insert strawberry. Cover top with tip 1M swirl in rose-tinted whipped cream.

PEANUT BUTTER & JELLY

RAINBOW NONPAREILS

FRESH STRAWBERRY & CREAM

Covering a Cupcake

You can be as fancy as you want when covering your cupcakes. Just do it neatly for treats that look even more tempting! Use one of the easy methods below to serve cupcakes with a professional look. Or, try dipping cupcakes in melted icing, then topping with sprinkles.

USING A SPATULA

1. Place a dollop of icing at the center of the cupcake.

2. Spread the icing across the top, pushing toward the edges. For a smooth look, run the spatula edge across the top.

3. For a fluffier look, lightly touch the iced surface with the spatula blade and lift up.

USING TIPS

Another quick way to decorate your cupcakes is with Wilton Decorating Tips. It takes just minutes to pipe a fancy icing swirl on your cupcake top and it makes all the difference in eye appeal!

1. For a ridged swirl on a standard cupcake, hold tip 1M approximately ½ in. above cupcake top at a 90° angle to cupcake surface. Squeeze out icing to form a star.

2. Without releasing pressure, raise tip slightly as you drop a line of icing around the star in a tight, complete rotation.

3. After completing the first rotation, move tip toward center and up and around to make a second spiral around the inside edge of the first spiral.

4. Release pressure to end spiral at center of cupcake.

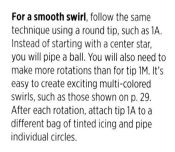

For a smooth swirl, follow the same technique using a round tip, such as 1A. Instead of starting with a center star, you will pipe a ball. You will also need to make more rotations than for tip 1M. It's easy to create exciting multi-colored swirls, such as those shown on p. 29. After each rotation, attach tip 1A to a different bag of tinted icing and pipe individual circles.

Cupcake Collections

A plain cupcake means something is missing: the excitement and fun! In these five cupcake collections, you'll see some of our favorite ways to decorate. Top your treats with classic techniques, colorful sprinkles, funny faces, lush flowers or fancy patterns. And start planning your next batch!

Top Billing

We've covered cupcake tops with fabulous flowers, swirls, stars, shells and more in a super-sized style. Just use a decorating tip and decorate with the buttercream icing color listed. See Basic technique instructions used here on p. 145-149.

Petal Canopy Lemon yellow. Pipe three layers of tip 104 petals, starting at edge of cupcake. Angle tip higher for each layer.

Teardrop Poppy Orange. Pipe a layer of tip 12 beads from edge of cupcake to center; overpipe with a second layer.

Winding and Weaving Rose. Pipe three layers of tip 125 ruffles, starting at edge of cupcake.

Flouncy Flower Sky blue. Pipe tip 402 ruffles, curved edge up, from edge of cupcake spiraling to center. Overpipe tip 402 tight ruffle center.

Shell Sunburst Rose. Pipe three layers of tip 32 pull-out stars from center to edge of cupcake.

Mum Fun Lemon yellow. Pipe tip 233 pull-out lines.

Connect The Dots Kelly green. Pipe tip 1A dots to cover top of cupcake.

Stars Collide Kelly green. Pipe tip 1E stars to cover cupcake.

Garden Beauty Orange. Pipe three layers of tip 150 ruffles, starting at edge of cupcake. Pipe five tip 150 petals at center.

Waving In The Breeze Violet with Rose. Pipe a layer of tip 125 ruffled petals around edge of cupcake. Pipe a second row ½ in. from edge of bottom row. Pipe tip 125 rosebud center.

Sapphire Starburst Sky blue. Pipe four rows of tip 1M pull-out stars from center of cupcake to edge.

Rose Reflection Violet with rose. Pipe tip 125 ribbon rose, wide end down, starting at center of cupcake and spiraling to outer edge.

Lush Leaves Rose. Pipe three layers of tip 366 pull-out leaves, starting at center of cupcake, positioning leaves between previous layers.

Petals in Profile Orange. Pipe tip 125 upright petals from edge of cupcake to center. Pipe tip 125 center upright petals.

Compelling Shells Kelly green. Pipe tip 32 reverse shells from edge of cupcake to center.

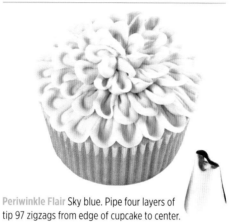

Periwinkle Flair Sky blue. Pipe four layers of tip 97 zigzags from edge of cupcake to center.

Bright Bouquet Lemon yellow. Pipe tip 1M rosettes from edge to center of cupcake.

Orange Blossom Special Orange. Pipe tip 150 tri-level rosebud (p. 148).

Remembered Rose Violet with Rose. Pipe rose using tip 402, curved side facing in. Follow Wilton Rose techniques but continue adding petals.

Beady Blossom Rose. Pipe tip 2A beads from edge to center of cupcake. Pipe tip 2A dot center.

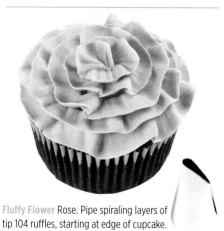

Fluffy Flower Rose. Pipe spiraling layers of tip 104 ruffles, starting at edge of cupcake.

Spellbinding Circles Lemon yellow. Pipe tip 2A spiral starting at center of cupcake.

Rippling Tide Sky blue. Pipe tip 79 ruffles, curved edge down from center of cupcake spiraling to edge.

Strategic Sprinkles!

Show off your sprinkles skills! Start with an iced cupcake top in white or tinted buttercream icing. Let icing crust. Then, pipe your design using piping gel. Cover the piped area with the sprinkle shapes and colors suggested here (see our Sprinkles selection on p. 156-157).

Fluttering Flower White. Attach jumbo confetti for petals and center; insert jumbo confetti at angle for border.

Hypnotic Treat Royal blue. Pipe tip 2A swirl. Outline swirl with piping gel; sprinkle with sapphire pearlized sugar.

Argyle Style White. Pipe center diamond with piping gel. Sprinkle with orange nonpareils. Repeat for left and right diamonds with pink and red nonpareils. Pipe diagonal lines in piping gel; position chocolate jimmies.

Bursting On The Scene White. Pipe starburst lines with piping gel. Sprinkle with lavender sugar.

The Art Of The Heart White. Use piping gel to pipe around edge of cupcake and center heart. Attach hearts from flowerful medley assortment in blue around heart and seven to eight in other colors around edge.

Coiling Cupcake White. Pipe tip 1A swirl. Attach pink Sugar Pearls.

Bright Spots White. Imprint circles with wide end of tip 2A. Position green, blue, red and pink Sugar Gems in circle areas.

Ornate Orange White. Pipe scrolls with piping gel. Sprinkle with orange sugar.

Color Cartwheels White. Pipe curling teardrops from center with piping gel. Sprinkle with blue, yellow, orange, pink and lavender sugars.

Pearled Posies White. Pipe tip 1A swirl. Spray icing with Pearl Color Mist food color spray. Attach green, yellow, pink, and blue jumbo daisies with piping gel. Attach white Sugar Pearls for flower center.

Violet Delight White. Imprint icing with dogwood cutter from gum paste flower cutter set. Pipe in with piping gel; sprinkle with lavender sugar. Attach jumbo confetti center.

Reach For A Rainbow Royal blue. Pipe one rainbow curve at a time with piping gel; immediately sprinkle each curve with colored sugars in red, orange, yellow, light green, blue and lavender. Pipe cloud shapes with piping gel; attach white nonpareils.

Lines Shine White. Pipe lines one at a time in various widths with piping gel; immediately sprinkle each line with orange, lavender, pink, yellow and blue sugars.

Magic Number White. Position number cutter from 101 Cutter Set on iced cupcake. Brush inside area with piping gel and sprinkle with red sugar; remove cutter. Attach jumbo stars around edge.

Color-Splashed White. Pipe tip 2A swirl. Immediately sprinkle with blue, yellow, pink, green, purple and orange crushed Cake Sparkles.

Juicy Melon White. Use piping gel to pipe around edge of cupcake; sprinkle with light green sugar. Fill in center with piping gel; sprinkle with red sugar. Attach chocolate jimmies.

Strong Lineup White. Spray icing with silver Color Mist food color spray. Pipe lines in various widths with piping gel. Sprinkle with black sugar.

Safari Stripes Pink. Pipe zebra stripes with piping gel; sprinkle with black sugar.

Ring Rounds Orange. Use Cut-Outs fondant cutters to imprint two small and one medium circle. Use wide end of tip 2A to imprint two circles. Outline three circles with piping gel; sprinkle with light green sugar; repeat for two with blue sugar.

Floral Sketch White. Imprint with large flower Cut-Out fondant cutter. Pipe outline with piping gel; sprinkle with rainbow nonpareils. Attach jumbo confetti center.

Garden Trio White. Spray icing with yellow Color Mist food color spray. Attach jumbo confetti for petals and center.

Intersections White. Pipe a line of piping gel across cupcake then sprinkle with gold Pearlized Sugar. Continue piping intersecting lines then sprinkling with sliver and blue sugars.

Bouncy Beachball White. Use edge of spatula to imprint lines for ball sections. Fill in one section at a time with piping gel; immediately sprinkle with yellow, orange, purple and pink nonpareils. Pipe a center dot; attach white nonpareils.

Put On A Happy *Face!*

Don't let those perfect round cupcake tops go to waste. Decorate them with a fun face! Just ice smooth with buttercream icing in the colors listed here, then add our tasty toppings, like sprinkles, crunches, candy eyeballs and more for the fantastic features shown. (Check out our colorful topping assortments on p. 156-157.) Try our ingenious ideas or use your noggin to come up with your own designs!

Blue Belle Royal blue. Large candy eyeballs, yellow jimmies for hair and jumbo hearts for bow and mouth, jumbo confetti for nose. Confetti for bow center/knot.

Keep One Eye Open Christmas red. Large candy eyeball, orange jimmies eyebrow, jumbo nonpareils freckles, black shoestring licorice mouth.

Wide-Eyed Guy Orange. Spice drops for hair (roll out and cut into strips), large candy eyeballs, jumbo confetti nose, black shoestring licorice eyebrows, confetti for cheeks, light cocoa Candy Melts candy mouth (trim to fit), jumbo hearts tongue (cut off point).

Shady Character Copper. Chocolate jimmies hair and mouth. Piping gel glasses sprinkled with black sugar.

Little Pig Me Up Rose. Jumbo hearts ears, jumbo confetti snout, chocolate jimmies mouth and nostrils, small candy eyeballs.

Roaring Success Lemon yellow with golden yellow. Small candy eyeballs, jumbo confetti ears, yellow Candy Melts candy cheeks. Pipe a line of melted yellow candy around edge of cupcake; attach chocolate jimmies for mane. Add chocolate chip nose, chocolate jimmies pieces for whiskers.

Mean and Green Leaf green. Cover with green Sugar Gems. Attach large candy eyeballs with icing. Roll a ⅝ in. ball of black ready-to-use fondant; shape into mouth and attach with icing. Roll two ¼ in. balls of black fondant; shape into logs for eyebrows and attach with icing.

Sweet Swashbuckler Copper. Piping gel bandana and eyepatch; sprinkle bandana area with red nonpareils and eyepatch area with black sugar. Jumbo heart bandana tie, chocolate jimmies eyepatch string and nose, small candy eyeball, jumbo confetti mouth (cut in half).

Tres Chick Lemon yellow with golden yellow. Small candy eyeballs, yellow jimmies for hair, orange Candy Melts candy beak (cut into triangle), pastel hearts feet. Tip 12 swirl wings sprinkled with yellow confetti.

Winking Woman Chocolate buttercream. Tip 12 bead hair; sprinkle with black sugar. Jumbo daisies flower barrettes with yellow confetti centers and green pastel heart leaves. Black shoestring licorice winking eyelid, chocolate jimmies eyelashes, small candy eyeball, jumbo heart mouth and confetti cheeks.

Dino Delight Orange. Large candy eyeballs, green confetti nostrils, pastel hearts teeth and spikes.

Pupcake Chocolate buttercream. Tip 12 ears; cover with turtle crunch. Large candy eyeballs, jumbo hearts nose and tongue (trim off one side), chocolate jimmies eyebrows, mouth and whiskers.

Fish Friend Royal blue. Jumbo hearts fins, tail and mouth, large candy eyeballs.

His Own Man Copper. Pipe tip 12 mounds on side edge and attach chocolate jimmies for hair. Add small candy eyeballs, jumbo confetti nose, rainbow jimmies mouth.

Crowned Head Copper. Crown with heart icing decoration, Sugar Pearls crown trim and earrings, jumbo confetti hair, jumbo hearts mouth, small candy eyeballs, chocolate jimmies eyelashes.

Look of Love Violet with rose. Orange jimmies hair, jumbo hearts eyes, confetti nose, red shoestring licorice mouth, blue nonpareil freckles.

Space Face Leaf green with lemon yellow. Blue confetti spots, spice drop mouth (roll out and cut crescent shape with tip 1A), large candy eyeballs, black shoestring licorice antenna with orange jumbo confetti tip.

Floral Finesse

A cupcake is the ideal garden spot for just about any flower you can imagine! Whether you make blossoms in advance using royal icing, gum paste or fondant, or pipe the petals right on top, you'll find that a 2 in. cupcake top, iced in a complementary color, provides the perfect showcase. Unless otherwise noted, see step-by-step flower-making techniques on p. 146-151 or visit wilton.com.

Rosette Romance Ice cupcake smooth in moss green. Use tip 18 to pipe rosette flower center in lemon yellow/golden yellow and six surrounding petals in rose.

Budding Beauty In advance, using royal icing, make tip 104 carnation in creamy peach. Let dry. Ice cupcake smooth in lemon yellow/golden yellow buttercream. Position carnation. Pipe tip 352 leaves in kelly green buttercream. Pipe tip 3 dots in white buttercream.

Definitive Dogwood In advance, make flower using ready-to-use gum paste. Use dogwood cutter and instructions from gum paste flower cutter set to make dogwood flower in white. Tint portion of gum paste moss green. Use flower impression set mat to make dogwood center in green. Use small rose leaf cutter and instructions from set to make two leaves in green. Brush dogwood petals with white Pearl Dust and curves of petals with orchid pink Pearl Dust/chocolate brown Color Dust mixture. Brush dogwood center and leaves with spruce green Color Dust. Ice cupcake smooth in creamy peach. Position leaves and flower.

Blue Bouquet In advance, make flowers using ready-to-use gum paste. Tint half of gum paste light sky blue, half dark sky blue. For each cupcake make five or six hydrangeas without wired centers in each color using hydrangea ejector and instructions from gum paste flower cutter set. Let dry. Brush with periwinkle blue Color Dust. Attach a blue sugar pearl center to each with piping gel. Ice cupcake smooth in white. Position flowers.

Charming Corsage Ice cupcake smooth in kelly green. Pipe white flower with bottom row of seven tip 104 elongated wild rose petals and top row of six tip 104 wild rose petals. Pipe tip 104 spiral center. Pipe tip 352 leaves in kelly green.

Sun Seeker Ice cupcake smooth in leaf green. Pipe tip 70 sunflower in golden yellow with tip 16 star center in brown.

Full Bloom Ice cupcake smooth in leaf green. Pipe tip 126 7-petal rose in rose.

Commune with Nature Ice cupcake smooth in white. Pipe tip 104 sweet pea petals in violet/rose in a cluster formation starting around outer edge continuing into center. Pipe tip 352 leaves in kelly green.

Standout Stem Ice cupcake smooth in white. Pipe tip 12 bead petals in violet/rose. Pipe tip 12 dot flower center in lemon yellow/golden yellow. Sprinkle center with yellow sugar.

Sizzling Sunburst Ice cupcake smooth in kelly green. Pipe tip 18 bachelor button in rose. Add tip 14 star center in lemon yellow/golden yellow.

Daisy Spotlight Make flower and accents using ready-to-use gum paste. Make a white daisy using medium daisy cutter and instructions from gum paste flower cutter set. Use flower impression set mat to make daisy center in lemon yellow/golden yellow. Attach center to daisy with gum glue adhesive. Use small rose leaf cutter and instructions from set to make three leaves in leaf green. Ice cupcake smooth in leaf green. Position daisy and leaves on cupcake.

Perky Daisy In advance, make flower and accents using ready-to-use gum paste. Make a single-layer daisy in lemon yellow/golden yellow using medium daisy cutter and instructions from gum paste flower cutter set. Use flower impression set mat to make daisy center in brown. Let dry. Ice cupcake smooth in leaf green. Use small rose leaf cutter and instructions from set to make three leaves in leaf green. Position daisy and leaves on cupcake.

Orange Appeal Ice cupcake smooth in white. Pipe tip 18 shell petals in orange. Pipe tip 12 dot center in lemon yellow/golden yellow.

Pansy Dance In advance, make flowers using royal icing. For each cupcake, on flower nail no. 7, make four tip 103 pansies in violet/rose and lemon yellow/golden yellow with tip 1 yellow center. Let dry on wave flower formers. Ice cupcake smooth in moss green. Position flowers. Pipe tip 352 leaves in moss green.

Romantic Ripples Ice cupcake smooth in leaf green. Pipe tip 125 daisy in rose. Pipe tip 12 ball center in lemon yellow. Position yellow sugar pearls.

Peeking Violets In advance, make flowers using royal icing. On flower nail no. 7, make three tip 59s violets in violet with tip 2 center dots in lemon yellow/golden yellow. Let dry on wave flower former. Ice cupcake smooth in white buttercream. Pipe tip 3 swirls in white. Position violets. Pipe tip 352 leaves in kelly green.

Robust Rose In advance, make flower using ready-to-use gum paste. Tint portions of gum paste violet/rose for flower and leaf green for leaves. Use large rose cutter and instructions from gum paste flower cutter set to make rose. Let dry. Use small rose leaf cutter and instructions from set to make two leaves. Let dry in wave flower former. Ice cupcake smooth in white. Trim off exposed wire. Position rose and leaves.

Cupcakes! 21

Strike Their *Fancy!*

These cupcake designs travel in sophisticated circles! Topped with elegant accents in fondant, candy, Sugar Sheets! edible decorating paper and Sugar Pearls, they combine high fashion with the fun indulgence of everyone's favorite childhood treat. Start with a buttercream-iced top in the color listed here, then add the dazzling details. See basic techniques and instructions used here on p. 145-151 and at wilton.com.

Island Blossom Chocolate buttercream. Use white fondant and folk fondant & gum paste mold to make five narrow leaves and one heart blossom. Paint with gold Pearl Dust/lemon extract mixture. Position to form flower.

Shell Elegance White. Use pink fondant and sea life fondant & gum paste mold to make shell; spray with pearl Color Mist food color spray. Position blue and white Sugar Pearls on cupcake. Position shell.

Strong Scroll Royal blue; spray with pearl Color Mist food color spray. Use white Candy Melts candy and dessert accents mold to make two swirls. Use hot knife to cut off ⅜ in. from one end of each swirl. Use white candy and jewelry fondant & gum paste mold to make round gem. Spray candy with gold Color Mist food color spray; let dry, then spray with pearl Color Mist food color spray. Position scrolls on cupcake in "S" shape. Attach gem with melted candy.

Winged Wedding Rose with black; spray with pearl Color Mist food color spray. Use white fondant and folk fondant & gum paste mold to make two birds and three small hearts. Paint birds with orchid pink and silver Pearl Dust/lemon extract mixtures. Paint hearts with lilac purple and silver Pearl Dust/lemon extract mixtures. Brush beaks with orange Color Dust. Pipe tip 1 dot eyes in black. Position birds and hearts.

Luxe Letter Moss green; spray with pearl Color Mist food color spray. Use white fondant and letters/numbers fondant & gum paste mold set to make letter. Use fondant and baroque fondant & gum paste mold to make large pearl chain border. Paint fondant with gold Pearl Dust/lemon extract mixture. Position on cupcake.

Style Underlined White. Use circle metal cookie cutter to cut a circle from black *Sugar Sheets!* edible decorating paper. Use knife to cut strips from white edible paper, ⅜ in. x 4 in.; spray with silver Color Mist food color spray. Attach strips to black circle with piping gel, trimming to fit. Use pink fondant and letters/numbers fondant & gum paste mold set to make letter. Spray with pearl Color Mist food color spray. Position circle and attach letter on cupcake with piping gel.

Lace Coverlet Ivory. Using white icing, pipe tip 2 outlines, swags, dots and fleurs de lis. Spray with pearl Color Mist food color spray.

Dew on Blue Delphinium blue. 1 day in advance, make puddle dots with white royal icing, from ¼ in. to ⅜ in. dia. (38 dots needed per treat). Let dry overnight. Position dots on cupcake. Spray with pearl Color Mist food color spray.

Formal Finish Delphinium blue; spray with pearl Color Mist food color spray. Roll out black fondant 1/16 in. thick. Use knife to cut two strips, 1/2 in. x 2 in.; fold ends together and attach with damp brush to form loops. Support with cotton balls and let dry overnight. Cut a black strip, 1/2 in. x 1 in., for knot; wrap around loops, securing with damp brush. Cut a black ribbon strip, 1/2 in. x 3 in. Position on cupcake; attach bow with damp brush.

All Buttoned Up Violet/rose. Roll out white fondant 1/8 in. thick. Cut a strip, 2 in. x 3 in. Gently fold pleats; pinch at center to shape bow tie. Use white fondant and fabric fondant & gum paste mold to make small button; attach to tie with damp brush. Position tie on cupcake. Spray with pearl Color Mist food color spray.

Regal Crest Ivory. Pipe two tip 4 fleurs de lis, one pointing up, one down; add tip 4 band in center. Score a line in center with edge of spatula . Add tip 1 scroll detail on one half. Pipe tip 4 bead border on cupcake. Paint border and fleurs de lis with bronze Pearl Dust/lemon extract mixture.

Gathering Interest Golden yellow. Cover top of cupcake with tip 127D ruffles. Use white fondant and fabric fondant & gum paste mold to make large button. Position at center. Spray top with pearl Color Mist food color spray.

Doily Delight Rose with black; spray with pearl Color Mist food color spray. Use fondant tinted gray and folk fondant & gum paste mold to make large medallion; use white fondant to make small medallion and fondant tinted light brown to make small heart. Spray large medallion with silver Color Mist food color spray; spray small medallion with pearl Color Mist and small heart with gold Color Mist. Attach pieces with damp brush; position on cupcake.

Peak Rose Rose with black; spray with pearl Color Mist food color spray. Use pink fondant and baroque fondant & gum paste mold to make rose. Paint rose with orchid pink Pearl Dust/lemon extract mixture. Position rose. Outline petals with tip 1 in black.

Butterfly's Berth Golden yellow. Spray with pearl Color Mist food color spray. Use white fondant and fern fondant & gum paste mold to make one each large butterfly, medium and small scroll. Fold butterfly wings up and let dry two to three hours, supporting with cotton balls. Paint butterfly and scroll details with orchid pink and leaf green Pearl Dust/lemon extract mixtures. Position scrolls and butterfly on cupcake.

Bracelet Mosaic Ivory; spray with pearl Color Mist food color spray. Use white fondant and jewelry fondant & gum paste mold to make square chain border and macrame mold to make small circle. Attach with piping gel. Paint with gold, silver and bronze Pearl Dust/lemon extract mixtures.

Focal Frame Violet with black. Mold two triangles using white Candy Melts candy and dessert accents candy mold; spray with silver Color Mist food color spray. Position on cupcake.

Party
Pleasers!

One great cupcake can pull your celebration together! It's the treat that lets guests hold a personal piece of the fun in their hands. See all a cupcake can be—from a caterpillar to a roller coaster, a stack of acrobats to a spaghetti dinner!

Ⓐ Constructing The *Cupcakes!*

Pans: Dimensions Large Cupcake, Cookie Sheet, 10 in. x 16 in. Cooling Grid, p. 158

Tips: 1, 1M, 2, 2A, 5, 8, 10, p. 162

Colors:* Rose, Brown, Red-Red, Christmas Red, Black, p. 163

Fondant: White Ready-To-Use Rolled Fondant (4 oz.), 9 in. Fondant Roller, Roll-N-Cut Mat, p. 164

Candy: White, Dark Green, Red Candy Melts Candy, Primary Candy Color Set (blue, yellow, orange), Peanut Butter Cups Mold, p. 163

Recipes: Buttercream Icing, Grandma's Gingerbread Cookie, p. 143

Also: Flowerful Medley Sprinkles (confetti), p. 167; Cinnamon Drops Sprinkles, Jumbo Confetti Sprinkles, Light Green Colored Sugar p. 156; Gingerbread Boy Metal Cutter, p. 166; 12 in. Rolling Pin, p. 159; 12 in. Disposable Decorating Bags, 15 in. Parchment Triangles, p. 161; candy sticks, spice drops

See p. 7 for a list of Wilton essential cupcake products and commonly used decorating items you may need.

INSTRUCTIONS

1 **Make chefs.** 1 day in advance, prepare and roll out gingerbread dough. Cut two cookies using gingerbread boy cutter. Use knife to cut two triangle easels for each, ¾ in. x 2 in. Bake and cool cookies. Reserve or freeze remaining dough for another design.

Pipe tip 5 dot and outline facial features. For aprons, roll out fondant ¹⁄₁₆ in. thick. Use knife and gingerbread boy cutter as a guide to cut full apron and half apron. Attach aprons to chefs with dots of icing. Attach confetti buttons with dots of icing. Attach two easels to backs with melted white candy.

For hat base, shape a fondant ball ¾ in. dia.; flatten slightly to 1 in. wide. Attach to head with melted white candy. For top, roll a 1 in. ball for small hat and a 1¼ in. ball for large hat. Flatten into an oval puff about 1½ in. wide; attach with melted candy.

2 **Make candy cups and cupcakes.** 1 day in advance, tint portions of melted white candy blue, yellow, and orange using candy

color. Use mold to make one candy shell cup (p. 151) each in blue, green, yellow, orange and red; and one solid candy cupcake in each color. On candy cupcakes, pipe tip 10 icing swirl. Position cinnamon drop.

3 **Make ingredients sacks and conveyors.** 1 day in advance, make two fondant logs, 1¼ in. dia. x 1½ in. high; flatten slightly. Shape into sacks, 1½ in. x 1½ in. Pinch top corners and pull out to shape. Pipe tip 1 ingredient names in black icing. Let dry overnight.

For conveyors, attach three candy sticks together using melted white candy in cut parchment bag. Chill until firm.

4 **Prepare 2-piece large cupcake.** Trim off peak from top section. On bottom section, use toothpick to mark door, 2¾ in. high x 2 in. wide, with round top. Mark window, 1½ in. high x 1¼ in. wide, 1½ in. from bottom. Mark a conveyor window on each side, 2 in. high x 2¾ in. wide, with rounded top 1 in. from bottom. Ice door smooth in dark rose and windows in brown.

Pipe tip 2A lines in rose to cover bottom section, piping indents first. Pipe tip 8 outline frames around door and windows in rose. Attach small confetti to frames and jumbo confetti for door window with tip 1 dots of icing.

Position top section on bottom section. Cover top with tip 1M swirl, following pan design. Position jumbo confetti. Tint 1 oz. fondant red. Roll a ball, 1½ in. dia., for cherry and position on cupcake top.

For door banner, roll out white fondant ¹⁄₁₆ in. thick. Cut a strip, ½ in. x 4½ in. Attach over door with dots of icing. Pipe tip 2 message in black.

5 **Assemble treats.** Sprinkle serving platter with green sugar, leaving walkway clear. Attach conveyors to windows and ingredients to conveyors with icing. Position chefs, candy cups and cupcakes. Position spice drops along walkway. Large cupcake serves 12; cookies and candy each serve 1.

*Combine Brown with Red-Red for brown shown. Combine Red-Red with Christmas Red for red shown.

Ⓑ Teddy Bear *Train*

Pans: Bar, 10 in. x 16 in. Cooling Grid, p. 158

Tips: 1, 2A, 5, p. 162

Recipe: Buttercream Icing, p. 143

Also: White Square Baking Cups, p. 154; Blue, Red, Green, Pink Sugar Gems, p. 156; Bear with Gum Drop Icing Decorations, Flowerful Medley Sprinkles (confetti), p. 157; Jumbo Confetti, Jumbo Nonpareils Sprinkles, p. 156; Cupcake Spatula, 12 in. Disposable Decorating Bags, p. 161; 9 in. Fondant Roller, p. 159; pinwheel candies, large and small spice drops

See p. 7 for a list of Wilton essential cupcake products and other commonly used decorating items you may need.

INSTRUCTIONS

1 **Prepare cupcakes.** Bake and cool seven square cupcakes; reserve two for train cab. Ice tops of remaining cupcakes smooth with spatula in white.

2 **Decorate train cab.** Trim tops of reserved cupcakes level; sandwich together with a thin layer of icing. Pipe tip 5 zigzags over seam. Attach confetti from Flowerful Medley assortment to zigzags. For side window, roll out spice drop ⅛ in. thick. Cut a rectangle, ½ in. x ¾ in. Attach to top cab cupcake with tip 5 dots. Attach jumbo nonpareils around window with tip 1 dots.

3 **Decorate engine.** Position large spice drop, narrow end down, for smokestack. Pipe tip 2A swirl smoke. For headlight, cut a small red spice drop in half. Attach to front with tip 5 dots.

4 **Decorate train cars.** Sprinkle each top with a different Sugar Gems color.

5 **Assemble train.** Position engine, cab and four cars. For wheels, attach pinwheel candies to sides with tip 5 dots. Attach jumbo confetti to center of each wheel. Attach bear decoration to cab and cars. Each serves 1.

C Complementing *Cupcakes*

Pans: Standard Muffin, 10 in. x 16 in. Cooling Grid, p. 158

Tip: 12, p. 162

Colors:* Sky Blue, Violet, Rose, Lemon Yellow, Golden Yellow, p. 163

Recipe: Buttercream Icing, p. 143

Also: Bright Rainbow Standard Baking Cups (blue, yellow, pink, purple), p. 155; Cupcake Icing Decorations, Flowerful Medley Sprinkles (confetti), p. 157; Cupcake Spatula, 12 in. Disposable Decorating Bags, p. 161

See p. 7 for a list of Wilton essential cupcake products and other commonly used decorating items you may need.

INSTRUCTIONS

1 **Prepare cupcakes.** Ice tops smooth with spatula in blue, yellow, rose or violet to contrast with baking cups.

2 **Decorate tops.** Outline cupcakes with tip 12 in white. Position cupcake icing decoration in center. Position a circle of confetti around decoration. Each serves 1.

*Combine Violet with Rose for violet shown. Combine Lemon Yellow with Golden Yellow for yellow shown.

Ⓐ Make A Big To-Do!

Pans: Dimensions Large Cupcake, 10 in. x 16 in. Cooling Grid, p. 158

Tips: 2, 12, p. 162

Colors:* Violet, Rose, Leaf Green, Orange, Sky Blue, Lemon Yellow, p. 163

Recipes: Buttercream, Color Flow Icings, p. 143

Also: White Ready-To-Use Rolled Fondant (21 oz.), Roll-N-Cut Mat, p. 164; Color Flow Mix, p. 160; 15 in. Parchment Triangles, p. 161; 11¾ in. Lollipop Sticks, White Candy Melts Candy, p. 163; 12 in. Disposable Decorating Bags, p. 161; 11 in. Straight Spatula, Brush Set, p. 165

See p. 7 for a list of Wilton essential cupcake products and other commonly used decorating items you may need.

INSTRUCTIONS

1　**Make dots for candy strips on cupcake sides.** 2 days in advance, make puddle dots (p. 149), ¼ in. dia. Make 54 each in rose, yellow and blue Color Flow. Let dry.

2　**Make lollipop toppers.** 2 days in advance, tint 3 oz. fondant each yellow, orange, rose, violet, green and sky blue. Reserve 3 oz. white. Make striped rope lollipops (p. 150). Let dry 48 hours.

　　Attach lollipop sticks with melted candy. Chill until firm.

3　**Prepare 2-piece large cupcake.** Pipe tip 12 candy backing strips in white buttercream on sides of cupcake bottom. Attach puddle dots with tip 2 dots of icing. Position top section on bottom section. Using spatula, ice top with rose buttercream. Insert lollipop sticks into cupcake top, trimming as needed. Serves 12.

*Combine Violet with Rose for violet shown. Combine Leaf Green with Lemon Yellow for green shown.

The more color the merrier! Why not cover your plain cupcakes with a rainbow?

Wilton

 B Brownie Swirl *Sundae*

Pans: Standard Muffin, p. 158; Round Pops Mold, p. 159; Cookie Sheet, 10 in. x 16 in. Cooling Grid, p. 158

Tips: 2A (6 needed), p. 162

Colors:* Violet, Sky Blue, Leaf Green, Lemon Yellow, Orange, Rose, p. 163

Recipes: Buttercream Icing, p. 143; favorite brownie recipe or mix

Also: Brown Dots Standard Baking Cups, p. 155; 12 in. Disposable Decorating Bags, p. 161; sour cherry candies

See p. 7 for a list of Wilton essential cupcake products and other commonly used decorating items you may need.

INSTRUCTIONS

1 **Prepare one cupcake and one brownie pop for each treat.** Attach brownie to cupcake with icing.

2 **Decorate icing rings.** Pipe tip 2A rings around edge of cupcake and around brownie in assorted colors, gradually decreasing size with each layer (p. 11). Position cherry candy on top. Each serves 1.

*Combine Violet with Rose for violet shown.

PARTY PLEASERS!

C Parfait *Perfection*

Pans: Standard Muffin, 10 in. x 16 in. Cooling Grid, p. 158

Tip: 1M, p. 162

Recipes: Buttercream Icing, Creamy Gelatin (3 or more batches in different flavors), p. 143

Also: White Standard Baking Cups, p. 155; 12 in. Disposable Decorating Bags, p. 161; Rainbow Sparkling Sugar, p. 156; maraschino cherries, 5 in. tall champagne flutes

See p. 7 for a list of Wilton essential cupcake products and other commonly used decorating items you may need.

INSTRUCTIONS

1 **Prepare gelatin.** Make three or more creamy gelatin recipes, using different gelatin flavors/colors. Chill until slightly thickened. Pipe three different colors into each flute, stopping ½ in. below rim. Chill until firm.

2 **Prepare cupcakes.** Remove baking cups; position cupcake in flute on top of gelatin. Cover tops with tip 1M swirl in white. Sprinkle with Sparkling Sugar. Position cherry on top. Each serves 1.

Ⓐ Party *Starters*

Pans: Standard Muffin, 10 in. x 16 in. Cooling Grid, p. 158

Tip: 3, p. 162

Colors:* Red-Red, Orange, Teal, Violet, Rose, Golden Yellow, Lemon Yellow, Moss Green, p. 163

Fondant: White Ready-To-Use Rolled Fondant (¾ oz. per treat), 9 in. Fondant Roller, Decorative Press Set (circle insert), Roll-N-Cut Mat, p. 164; Leaf Cut-Outs Fondant Cutters, p. 165

Recipe: Buttercream Icing, p. 143

Also: Rainbow Paint ColorCups Standard Baking Cups, p. 154; White Candy Melts Candy (¼ oz. per 6 to 8 treats), p. 163; Cupcake Spatula, 12 in. Disposable Decorating Bags, p. 161; black shoestring licorice

See p. 7 for a list of Wilton essential cupcake products and other commonly used decorating items you may need.

INSTRUCTIONS

1 **Make candles.** 1 day in advance, tint ½ oz. fondant each in red, violet, orange, teal, rose, green and ¾ oz. yellow to make seven assorted candles (reserve ¼ oz. yellow to make seven flames). For flames, roll out yellow ¹⁄₁₆ in. thick. Cut flames using smallest leaf Cut-Out. Let dry overnight on cornstarch-dusted board.

For each candle, use press set with circle insert to make one white and one colored fondant rope, 4 in. long. Twist together (p. 150). Cut to 3 in. lengths. Let dry overnight.

2 **Attach flames.** For wicks, cut licorice to 1¼ in. long. Insert ½ in. into top of candle, securing with melted candy; let set. Attach flame to wick with melted candy; let set.

3 **Prepare cupcakes.** Ice tops smooth with spatula in white. Pipe tip 3 e-motion design to match candle color. Insert candle in cupcake. Each serves 1.

*Combine Orange with Red-Red for orange shown. Combine Violet with Rose for violet shown. Combine Rose with Violet for rose shown. Combine Moss Green with Lemon Yellow for green shown.

Ⓑ Doubly *Delicious*

Pans: Standard Muffin, Mini Muffin, Cookie Sheet, 10 in. x 16 in. Cooling Grid, p. 158

Tip: 6, p. 162

Candy: Yellow (½ oz. for each mini cupcake), Pink (1 oz. for each standard cupcake) Candy Melts Candy, Garden Candy Color Set (pink), p. 163

Recipe: Buttercream Icing, p. 143

Also: Cake Boards, 9 in. Angled Spatula, 12 in. Disposable Decorating Bags, p. 161; Flowerful Medley Sprinkle Assortment (confetti), p. 157; Assorted Celebration Candles, p. 167; Parchment Paper, p. 159

See p. 7 for a list of Wilton essential cupcake products and other commonly used decorating items you may need.

INSTRUCTIONS

1 **Prepare cupcakes.** Bake and cool one standard and one mini cupcake for each treat without baking cups.

2 **Cover cupcake bottoms with melted candy.** Position cupcakes on cooling grid over parchment paper, top side down. Brighten melted pink candy with pink candy color. Cover mini cupcakes with yellow candy; standard cupcakes with pink. Let set on parchment paper-covered board.

3 **Add trims.** Ice cupcake tops smooth with spatula in white. Pipe tip 6 drips over sides with icing. Attach confetti to sides with melted candy; let set. Stack cupcakes and insert candle. Each serves 1.

C Cockeyed *Cupcakes*

Pans: Dimensions Large Cupcake, Jumbo Muffin, Standard Muffin, 10 in. x 16 in. Cooling Grid, p. 158

Tips: 1M, 2, 2A (2), 4, 5, 10, 12, 18, 22, p. 162

Colors:* Leaf Green, Lemon Yellow, Golden Yellow, Sky Blue, Orange, Rose, Violet, p. 163

Recipe: Buttercream Icing, p. 143

Also: Jumbo, Standard Baking Cups, p. 155; Circle Metal Cutter, p. 166; Leaf Cut-Outs Fondant Cutters, p. 165; 9 in. Fondant Roller, p. 164; Orange Candy Melts Candy, p. 163; Bamboo Dowel Rods, 12 in. Disposable Decorating Bags, Standard Coupler, p. 161; yellow spice drop, black shoestring licorice, candy stick (for candle)

See p. 7 for a list of Wilton essential cupcake products and other commonly used decorating items you may need.

INSTRUCTIONS

1 **Prepare cupcakes.** Bake and cool one each 2-piece large, jumbo and standard cupcakes. Trim and stack (p. 151).

2 **Decorate cupcake bottoms.** On large cupcake, pipe tip 2A vertical outlines in orange in recessed areas. Pipe tip 2A vertical outlines in green in raised areas. On jumbo cupcake, pipe tip 10 vertical outlines ¼ in. apart in yellow. Cover spaces with tip 10 vertical outlines in yellow. Pipe random dots in rose using tips 4 and 12. On standard cupcake, pipe tip 5 vertical outlines, ⅛ in. apart, in sky blue. Cover spaces with tip 5 vertical outlines in sky blue. Pipe tip 2 random swirls in violet.

3 **Decorate cupcake tops.** Pipe rosettes in white, using tip 1M for large cupcake, tip 22 for jumbo cupcake and tip 18 for standard cupcake.

4 **Make candle.** For flame, roll out yellow spice drop ¼ in. thick on waxed paper sprinkled with sugar. Cut flame using smallest leaf Cut-Out. For wick, cut a black licorice piece, ¾ in. long. Insert in bottom of flame. Attach wick to candy stick with melted orange candy. Let set.

Insert candle in cupcake, angled slightly. Large cupcake serves 12; jumbo and standard cupcakes each serve 1.

*Combine Lemon Yellow with Golden Yellow for yellow shown. Combine Violet with Rose for violet shown.

D Your Claim to *Flame*

Pans: Standard Muffin, 10 in. x 16 in. Cooling Grid, p. 158

Tip: 5, p. 162

Colors:* Lemon Yellow, Golden Yellow, Orange, Red-Red, p. 163

Fondant: White Ready-To-Use Rolled Fondant (2 oz. makes 10 treats), 9 in. Fondant Roller, Roll-N-Cut Mat, p. 164; Leaf Cut-Outs Fondant Cutters, Deluxe Brush Set, p. 165

Recipes: Buttercream, Chocolate Buttercream Icings, Thinned Fondant Adhesive, p. 143

Also: Pink/Purple/Orange Stripes, Yellow/Blue/Orange/Green Dots ColorCups Standard Baking Cups, p. 154; 4 in. Lollipop Sticks, p. 163; Cupcake Spatula, Cake Boards, p. 161

See p. 7 for a list of Wilton essential cupcake products and other commonly used decorating items you may need.

INSTRUCTIONS

1 **Make flames.** 1 day in advance, tint 1 oz. fondant each yellow and orange; roll out ⅛ in. thick. Cut yellow flame using largest leaf Cut-Out and orange inner flame using smallest. Attach with damp brush. Let dry overnight on cornstarch-dusted board. Attach flames to lollipop sticks with thinned fondant adhesive. Let dry.

2 **Prepare cupcakes.** Ice smooth with spatula and chocolate icing. Pipe tip 5 drips in white icing; pat smooth with finger dipped in cornstarch. Insert flames in cupcakes. Each serves 1.

*Combine Lemon Yellow with Golden Yellow for yellow shown. Combine Orange with Red-Red for orange shown.

Other cupcakes can't hold a candle to ours! Start with a bright, bouncy baking cup, ice in chocolate, then add drips of white icing and a flickering fondant flame.

Ⓐ Up, Down And All *Around!*

Pans: 8 in. x 2 in. Round, Standard Muffin, 10 in. x 16 in. Cooling Grid, p. 158

Tips: 1, 10, p. 162

Colors:* Leaf Green, Lemon Yellow, Golden Yellow, Teal, Orange, Rose, Brown, p. 163

Fondant/Gum Paste: White Ready-To-Use Rolled Fondant (12 oz.), Ready-To-Use Gum Paste (1 pk.), 9 in., 20 in. Fondant Rollers, 20 in. Fondant Roller Guide Rings, Roll-N-Cut Mat, Storage Board, p. 164; Brush Set, p. 165; Fine Tip Primary Colors FoodWriter Edible Color Markers (black), p. 163

Recipes: Buttercream Icing, Gum Glue Adhesive, p. 143; favorite crisped rice cereal treats

Also: Upper and Lower Flat Track Patterns, p. 152; Color Wheel Standard Baking Cups, p. 155; 4-Pc. Circles Nesting Metal Cutter Set, 50-Pc. A-B-C & 1-2-3 Plastic Cutter Set, p. 166; 9 in. Angled, 9 in. Tapered Spatulas, p. 161; 23-Ct. Cupcakes-N-More Dessert Stand, p. 167; 4 in. Lollipop Sticks, p. 163; 15 in. Parchment Triangles, Cake Boards, p. 161; Pastry Wheel, Bake Easy! Non-Stick Spray, p.159; round candy discs

See p. 7 for a list of Wilton essential cupcake products and other commonly used decorating items you may need.

INSTRUCTIONS

1 **Make tracks.** 2 days in advance, tint 3 oz. gum paste green. Roll out ¹⁄₁₆ in. thick. Use pastry wheel to cut arched track strips, four ¾ in. x 3½ in. for top row, five ¾ in. x 4½ in. for bottom row. Stand strips on cut edge on cornstarch-dusted board, curving top row strips with a 2⅝ in. opening, 1 in. high and bottom row strips with a 3¼ in. opening, 1¼ in. high. Let dry 24 hours.

Cut flat track strips. Use pastry wheel and patterns to cut four strips for top row and five strips for bottom row. Let dry 24 hours on cornstarch-dusted boards.

2 **Make letters.** 2 days in advance, tint 1½ oz. gum paste each rose, orange and teal. Roll out ⅛ in. thick. Cut letters using cookie cutters. Let dry 24 hours on cornstarch-dusted boards. Reserve remaining gum paste.

Attach lollipop sticks to letters with a strip of gum paste in matching color, securing with adhesive and leaving 2½ in. extended to insert in cereal treat top.

3 **Complete tracks.** 1 day in advance, roll out white gum paste ⅛ in. thick. Cut two rail strips for each track strip, ¼ in. wide x length of track. Attach one strip to edge of track with adhesive, aligning bottom edges. Store second rail strips under storage board flap until needed.

Roll out remaining white gum paste ¹⁄₁₆ in. thick. Cut six or seven railroad tie strips for each track, ¾ in. x ¼ in. Attach to tracks with adhesive, ⅜ in. apart. Trim as needed. Attach second rail. Let dry 24 hours.

4 **Make cars and riders.** 1 day in advance, use reserved tinted gum paste to make four cars in each color. Roll out colors ½ in. thick. Cut rectangles, ⅜ in. x 1 in. For seats, use round candy disc edge to make two imprints in each car.

Roll out remaining gum paste ⅛ in. thick. Cut four wheels per car using narrow end of tip 10. Attach to cars with adhesive.

For riders, use black edible marker to draw faces on candy discs. Insert in cars.

5 **Prepare 18 cupcakes and cereal treats mixture.** Press cereal treat mixture into prepared 8 in. round pan, 1½ in. high. Use second largest round cutter to cut circle. Position on cake board cut to fit.

Tint 7 oz. fondant green. Roll out ⅛ in. thick. Cover cereal treats circle.

For cereal treats circle, tint 1 oz. portions of fondant each teal, rose, orange and yellow. Roll out colors and 1 oz. white ⅛ in. thick. Use pastry wheel to cut six strips in each color, ¼ in. x 1½ in. Attach to sides of cereal treats circle with damp brush, ¼ in. apart.

6 **Complete and assemble treats.** Ice cupcake tops smooth with spatula in green. Use tip of tapered spatula to pull up icing for grass look. Pipe tip 1 pull-out hair on riders in brown or yellow.

At party, position cupcakes on stand. Position tracks on cupcakes, adjusting as needed to fit. Insert letters in cereal treat circle, trimming sticks as needed. Attach circle to top of stand with icing. Position cars on track. Cereal treats serve 6; each cupcake serves 1.

*Combine Leaf Green with Lemon Yellow for green shades shown. Combine Lemon Yellow with Golden Yellow for yellow shown.

Ⓐ

Ⓑ

Wilton

B Turning Colors

Pans: Standard Muffin, 10 in. x 16 in. Cooling Grid, p. 158

Tip: 8, p. 162

Colors:* Golden Yellow, Lemon Yellow, Violet, Rose, Orange, Teal, Burgundy, p. 163

Recipe: Buttercream Icing, p. 143

Also: Rainbow Dots ColorCups Standard Baking Cups, p. 154; Cupcake Spatula, 12 in. Disposable Decorating Bags, p. 161, sour cherry candies

See p. 7 for a list of Wilton essential cupcake products and other commonly used decorating items you may need.

INSTRUCTIONS

1   **Prepare cupcakes.** Ice smooth with spatula in yellow, violet, orange, teal or rose.

2   **Decorate cupcakes.** Pipe tip 8 white swirl from edge to center of cupcake, forming a pinwheel design. Position cherry candy on top. Each serves 1.

*Combine Golden Yellow with Lemon Yellow for yellow shown. Combine Violet with Rose for violet shown. Combine Rose with Burgundy for rose shown.

C Fun's In The Balance

Pans: Standard Muffin, Non-Stick Cookie Pan, 10 in. x 16 in. Cooling Grid, p. 158

Candy:* White (2 pks. makes 4 treats), Orange (7 oz.) Candy Melts Candy, Primary (yellow, blue, orange) and Garden (green, pink, black) Candy Color Sets, Decorator Brush Set, p. 163

Recipe: Favorite crisped rice cereal treat mixture

Also: Standard White Baking Cups, p. 155; Jumbo Confetti Sprinkles, p. 156; Small Candy Eyeballs, p. 157; 15 in. Parchment Triangles, p. 161; 4-Pc. Circles Nesting Metal Cutter Set (second largest used), p. 166; Cupcake Spatula, Cake Circles, p. 161

See p. 7 for a list of Wilton essential cupcake products and other commonly used decorating items you may need.

INSTRUCTIONS

1   **Make candy shell bottoms.** 1 day in advance, melt one package white candy. Divide into fourths and tint portions yellow, pink, blue and green. For each shell, spoon 1 to 2 tablespoons candy into baking cup. Brush candy up sides, keeping an even top edge. Chill until firm. Repeat until shell is ¼ in. thick. Let set completely.

2   **Make base.** In advance, add orange candy color to melted orange candy to brighten. Position second largest cutter on cookie pan; fill ⅝ in. deep with melted candy. Tap to settle; chill until firm.

Attach jumbo confetti, ¼ in. apart, around outer edge using melted candy in cut parchment bag.

3   **Prepare cereal treats mixture.** When cool enough to handle, gently press mixture into prepared candy shells; reserve remainder for tops. Carefully peel off baking cups. Shape four treat tops, 2¾ in. dia. x 1½ in. high, with flat bottom. Let cool completely.

4   **Cover with melted candy.** Ice bottom with melted white candy; let set. Position tops on cooling grid, flat side down. Cover with melted white candy. Tap to settle; chill until firm. Attach tops to filled shells using melted candy; chill to set.

5   **Add trims.** Tint a portion of melted white candy black. Use cut parchment bag to pipe 1 in. wide smiles. Attach candy eyeballs with melted candy. Chill until firm.

6   **Assemble treats.** Attach treats in a stack with melted candy. Hold each treat in position until candy sets completely before adding next treat. Each treat serves 1.

*Combine Yellow with Green for green shown.

D Capture The Rainbow

Pans: Mini Muffin, Cooling Grid, p. 158

Colors: Sky Blue, Kelly Green, Rose, p. 163

Recipe: Buttercream Icing, p. 143

Also: White Mini Baking Cups, p. 157; Cupcake Spatula, 12 in. Disposable Decorating Bags, p. 161; Blue, Green, Red Sugar Gems, White Nonpareils, p. 156

See p. 7 for a list of Wilton essential cupcake products and other commonly used decorating items you may need.

INSTRUCTIONS

Prepare cupcakes. Bake and cool 57 mini cupcakes; Ice tops smooth with spatula, 24 in white, 14 in rose, 11 in green and eight in blue. Sprinkle white tops with nonpareils. Sprinkle colored tops with matching Sugar Gems.

Assemble rainbow. Position rose, green and blue cupcakes in an arch. Position white cupcakes at ends of arch. Each serves 1.

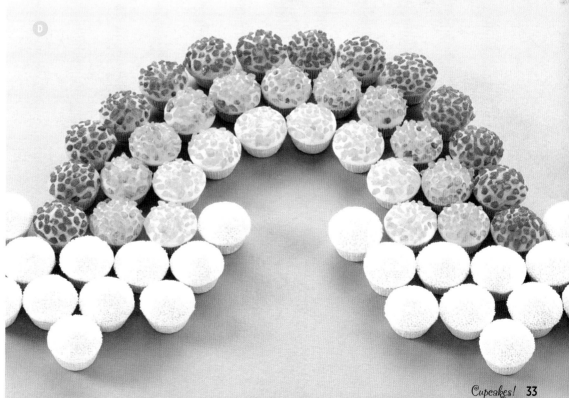

 Having Fun is the *Point!*

Pans: Standard Muffin, 10 in. x 16 in. Cooling Grid, p. 158

Tip: 2A, p. 162

Colors:* Red-Red, Rose, Teal, Orange, Violet, Golden Yellow, Lemon Yellow, p. 163

Fondant: White Ready-To-Use Rolled Fondant (24 oz. makes 12 treats), Gum-Tex, 9 in. Fondant Roller, Roll-N-Cut Mat, Fondant Trimmer, p. 164; Brush Set, p. 165

Recips: Buttercream Icing, Thinned Fondant Adhesive, p. 143

Also: Exclamation Point Pattern, p. 152; Rainbow Dots ColorCups Standard Baking Cups, p. 154; Cupcake Spatula, p. 161; Red Colored Sugar, p. 156; White Candy Melts Candy, p. 163; Piping Gel, p. 156; 4 in. Lollipop Sticks, p. 163; 8 in. Cookie Treat Sticks, p. 167; 10 in. x 14 in. Cake Boards, p. 161

See p. 7 for a list of Wilton essential cupcake products and other commonly used decorating items you may need.

INSTRUCTIONS

1. **Make fondant streamers.** 1 day in advance, tint 4 oz. portions of fondant each rose, orange, violet, teal, yellow. Knead ¼ teaspoon Gum-Tex into each color. Roll out ⅟₁₆ in. thick as needed. Cut strips, ⅟₁₆ in. x 3 in. long. Wrap loosely around cookie treat stick; let set for 30 minutes. Slide streamers off stick and place on cake board. Make six rose, 10 orange, four violet, seven teal and three yellow streamers for each cupcake. Let dry overnight.

2. **Make exclamation point toppers.** In advance, tint 4 oz. fondant red. Knead in ¼ teaspoon Gum-Tex. Roll out ⅛ in. thick. Use pattern and knife to cut top of point; use wide end of tip 2A to cut circle. Let dry on cornstarch-dusted boards.

   Attach top and circle to lollipop stick, ½ in. apart, with melted candy. Leave 1¼ in. extended at bottom to insert into cupcake. Brush exclamation point with piping gel; immediately sprinkle with red sugar. Let set.

3. **Prepare cupcakes.** Ice tops smooth with spatula in white. Position 30 assorted streamers on each cupcake. Insert exclamation point. Each serves 1.

*Combine Teal with Kelly Green for teal shown. Combine Orange with Red-Red for orange shown. Combine Violet with Rose for violet shown. Combine Golden Yellow with Lemon Yellow for yellow shown.

High-Rise *Surprise*

Pans: Standard Muffin, 10 in. x 16 in. Cooling Grid, p. 158

Tip: 2A, p. 162

Colors:* Teal, Golden Yellow, Lemon Yellow, Orange, Red-Red, Leaf Green, p. 163

Fondant: White Ready-To-Use Rolled Fondant (1½ oz. per treat), 9 in. Fondant Roller, Roll-N-Cut Mat, p. 164; Brush Set, p. 165; Fine Tip Primary Colors FoodWriter Edible Color Markers (black), p. 163

Recipe: Buttercream Icing, p. 143

Also: Yellow/Blue/Orange/Green Dots ColorCups Standard Baking Cups, p. 154; Cupcake Spatula, p. 161; 101 Cookie Cutters (small, medium round), p. 167; Cake Board, p. 161; Flowerful Medley Sprinkles Assortment (confetti), p. 157; White Candy Melts Candy (½ oz. per 8 treats), 4 in. Lollipop Sticks, p. 163; Gum-Tex, p. 164; Piping Gel, p. 160

See p. 7 for a list of Wilton essential cupcake products and other commonly used decorating items you may need.

INSTRUCTIONS

1. **Make toppers.** Tint 1½ oz. portions of fondant each teal, orange, yellow and green to make four treats. Knead ⅛ teaspoon of Gum-Tex into each color. Roll out ⅛ in. thick. Cut one large circle per treat using smallest round cookie cutter. Using wide end of tip 2A, cut one small circle per treat. Let dry overnight on cornstarch-dusted board. Reserve remaining colored fondant.

   Write message on large circle with black edible marker. Attach small circle to large circle with melted candy. Attach to lollipop stick with melted candy. Chill until firm.

2. **Prepare cupcakes.** Ice smooth with spatula in white. Roll out reserved fondant ⅛ in. thick. Cut circle using medium round cutter. Make cuts ⅝ in. deep in center of circle with knife. Brush top edge of cupcake with piping gel; attach fondant circle. Peel back cuts to expose icing. Pinch ends to create points. Attach confetti sprinkles to cupcake tops with piping gel. Insert topper in cupcake center. Each serves 1.

*Combine Golden Yellow with Lemon Yellow for yellow shown. Combine Orange with Red-Red for orange shown.

Wilton

⊙ Serving Up A *Surprise!*

Pans: Dimensions Large Cupcake, p. 159; Mini Muffin, 10 in. x 16 in. Cooling Grid, p. 158

Tips: 2A, 3, 5, 12 (6), p. 162

Colors:* Teal, Golden Yellow, Lemon Yellow, Orange, Rose, Burgundy, Leaf Green, p. 163

Candy: White, Light Cocoa Candy Melts Candy (4 oz. Light Cocoa and 2 oz. White makes head and arm), Garden Candy Color Set (black), Dessert Dome Candy Mold, p. 163

Recipe: Buttercream Icing, p. 143

Also: Hand Pattern, p. 152; Color Wheel Mini Baking Cups, p. 155; 8 in. Cake Circles, Cupcake Spatula, 15 in. Parchment Triangles, 12 in. Disposable Decorating Bags, p. 161; Hot Colors Rounds Candles, p. 167, sour cherry candy, pretzel rods

See p. 7 for a list of Wilton essential cupcake products and other commonly used decorating items you may need.

INSTRUCTIONS

1. **Make candy arm and hand.** In advance, mix 2 oz. melted white candy with 4 oz. melted cocoa candy. Dip 3 in. of pretzel rod into candy; let dry on waxed paper. Dip again and let dry.

   Cover hand pattern with a parchment triangle, tape down. Use melted candy in cut parchment bag to outline and pipe in hand. Chill until firm. Overpipe hand with melted candy; chill. Attach pretzel arm to hand on an angle with dots of melted candy.

2. **Make head.** In advance, use remaining white/light cocoa candy mixture to mold two large dessert dome halves. Run edges of halves on warm pan to smooth and immediately attach halves, positioning seam vertically. Let set.

   Use melted candy in cut bag to pipe dot nose. Tint a portion of light cocoa candy black. In cut bag, outline eyes and pipe-in mouth. Let set.

3. **Prepare cupcakes.** Bake and cool 2-piece large cupcake and one mini cupcake. On large cupcake, trim off peak of top half. On bottom half pipe tip 12 outlines in alternating colors of buttercream. Position top half. Ice top fluffy with spatula.

   Cover top of mini cupcake with tip 12 swirls; fluff with spatula.

4. **Complete arm.** Use tip 3 and desired buttercream color to pipe sleeve, 2 in. long, beginning 1 in. below hand.

5. **Assemble treats.** Position head on large cupcake, securing with icing. Pipe tip 2A swirl on head; position cherry candy. Insert arm into large cupcake. Attach mini cupcake to hand with a dot of melted candy. Insert candle. Pipe tip 5 name. Large cupcake serves 12; mini cupcake serves 1.

*Combine Golden Yellow with Lemon Yellow for yellow shown. Combine Rose with Burgundy for rose shown. Combine Leaf Green with Lemon Yellow for green shown.

Lift a friend's spirits with edible balloons! She'll love the way they burst out from the fondant-covered cupcake.

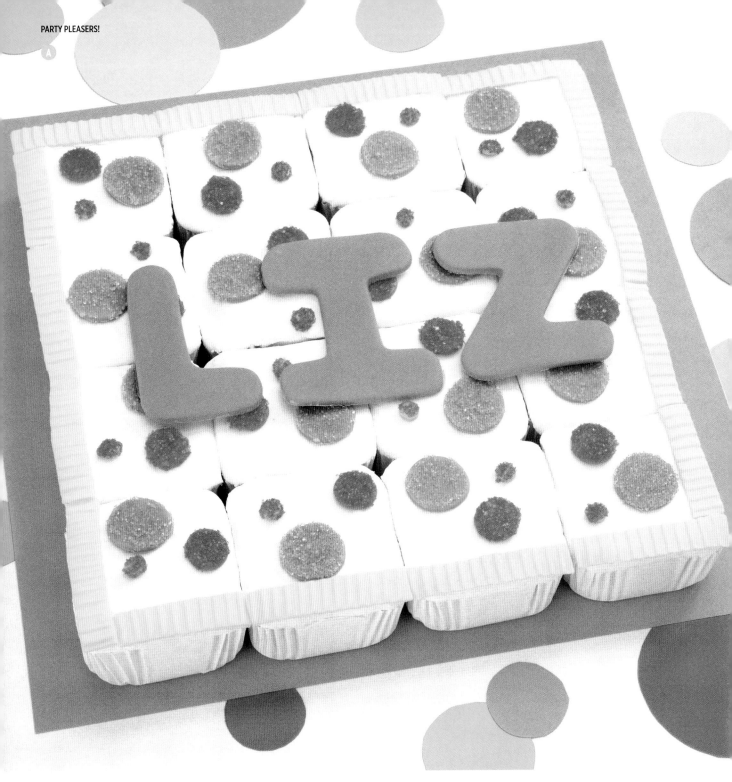

Ⓐ Poppin' Party Squares

Pans: Bar, 10 in. x 16 in. Cooling Grid, p. 158

Tips: 2A, 12, p. 162

Colors:* Leaf Green, Orange, Rose, Lemon Yellow, Golden Yellow, p. 163

Fondant: White Ready-To-Use Rolled Fondant (10 oz.), 9 in. Fondant Roller, Roll-N-Cut Mat, p. 164; Detail Embosser, Brush Set, p. 165

Recipe: Buttercream Icing, p. 143

Also: White Square Baking Cups, p. 154; 50-Pc. A-B-C & 1-2-3 Cutter Set, p. 167; Orange, Pink, Light Green Colored Sugars, p. 156; Pastry Wheel, p. 159; Cupcake Spatula, p. 161; Piping Gel, p. 160

See p. 7 for a list of Wilton essential cupcake products and other commonly used decorating items you may need.

INSTRUCTIONS

Prepare 16 cupcakes. Ice tops smooth with spatula in white. Position on cake plate in four rows of four treats each.

Make fondant trims. Tint 3 oz. fondant each in rose and yellow and 2 oz. each in green and orange. Roll out yellow ⅛ in. thick. Cut strips, 3 in. x 4 in. Imprint strips with straight wheel of detail embosser. Use pastry wheel to cut yellow strips, ½ in. wide. Position on edge of treat grouping. Use scissors to cut strips between treats.

For dots, roll out rose, orange, and green fondant ⅟₁₆ in. thick. Cut circles using wide end of tip 2A and wide and narrow end of tip 12. Brush tops with piping gel. Sprinkle with matching color sugar. Position randomly on cupcakes.

For name, roll out rose fondant ⅛ in. thick. Cut desired letters using cookie cutters. Position on cupcakes. Each serves 1.

*Combine Lemon Yellow with Golden Yellow for yellow shown.

Wilton

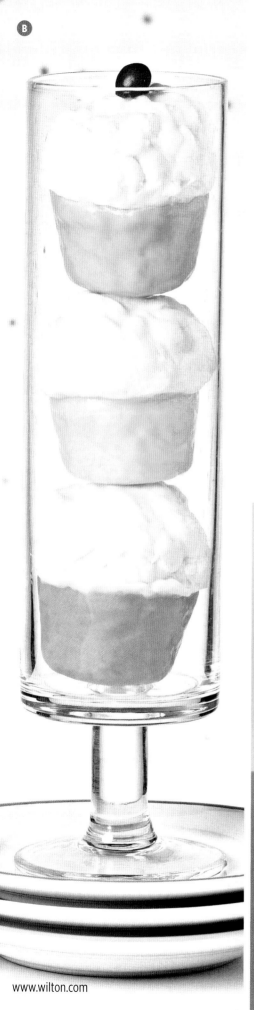

B Stack-Up Snacks

Pans: Mini Muffin, Non-Stick Cookie Pan, 10 in. x 16 in. Cooling Grid, p. 158

Candy: White Candy Melts Candy (6 oz. makes 3 treats), Garden Candy Color Set* (pink, yellow, green), p. 163

Also: White Mini Baking Cups, p. 155; Cinnamon Drops Sprinkles, p. 156; 10 in. x 14 in. Cake Boards, 15 in. Parchment Triangles, p. 161; mini marshmallows, parfait glass

See p. 7 for a list of Wilton essential cupcake products and other commonly used decorating items you may need.

INSTRUCTIONS

1 **Prepare cupcakes.** Remove baking cups. Position cupcakes bottom side up on cooling grid over cookie pan. Tint 2 oz. melted candy each pink, yellow and green. Cover cupcakes with candy; tap grid lightly to release air bubbles. Chill until firm. Repeat if needed.

2 **Make cupcake tops.** For each treat, coarsely chop 15 mini marshmallows. Combine 2 to 3 teaspoons of melted candy with mini marshmallows. On waxed paper-covered board, make mounds 1 in. high x 1¾ in. dia. Chill until firm.

3 **Position features.** Attach cinnamon drop to one cupcake top with melted candy. Chill until firm. Attach cupcake tops to bottoms with melted candy. Chill to set. Stack cupcakes in glass with cinnamon drop cupcake on top. Each serves 1.

*Combine Green with Yellow candy color for green shown.

C Wrap It Up!

Pans: Bar, 10 in. x 16 in. Cooling Grid, p. 158

Colors:* Orange, Kelly Green, Moss Green, Rose, Royal Blue, Lemon Yellow, p. 163

Fondant: White Ready-To-Use Rolled Fondant (1 oz. per treat), Gum-Tex, 9 in. Fondant Roller, Roll-N-Cut Mat, Fondant Trimmer, p. 164; Brush Set, p. 165

Recipes: Buttercream Icing, Thinned Fondant Adhesive, p. 143

Also: Warm Squares Square Baking Cups, p. 154; Cupcake Spatula, Cake Boards, p. 161

See p. 7 for a list of Wilton essential cupcake products and other commonly used decorating items you may need.

INSTRUCTIONS

1 **Make bow loops.** 1 day in advance, tint 1 oz. fondant each orange, yellow, rose and green. Knead ⅛ teaspoon Gum-Tex into each color. Roll out 1/16 in. thick. Use fondant trimmer to cut four strips in each color to make one bow, ⅜ in. x 3 in. Fold strips over to form loops; attach ends with damp brush. Let loops dry on sides on cornstarch-dusted, waxed paper-covered board. Reserve remaining fondant.

2 **Prepare cupcakes.** Ice tops smooth with spatula in white.

3 **Decorate cupcakes.** Roll out reserved fondant 1/16 in. thick. Use fondant trimmer to cut two ribbon strips, ⅜ in. x 3½ in. Position across cupcake, securing with damp brush.

4 **Assemble bows.** Attach four loops to center of ribbon strips with thinned fondant adhesive. For knot, roll a matching fondant ball, ½ in. dia.; flatten slightly. Attach to bow with thinned fondant adhesive. Each serves 1.

*Combine Rose with Royal Blue for rose shown. Combine Kelly Green with Moss Green for green shown.

A Feeling *Groovy*

Pans: Standard Muffin, 10 in. x 16 in. Cooling Grid, p. 158

Tips: 2A, 7, 789, p. 162

Colors:* Rose, Violet, Leaf Green, Lemon Yellow, Black, p. 163

Fondant: Black (1½ oz. makes 3 treats), White (1 oz. makes 3 treats) Ready-To-Use Rolled Fondant, 9 in. Fondant Roller, Roll-N-Cut Mat, Fondant Shaping Foam, p. 164; White Pearl Dust, Brush Set, p. 165

Recipe: Buttercream Icing, p. 143

Also: Bright Rainbow Standard Baking Cups (purple, green, pink), p. 155; Cupcake Spatula, p. 161; Circle Metal Cutter, p. 166

See p. 7 for a list of Wilton essential cupcake products and other commonly used decorating items you may need.

INSTRUCTIONS

1 **Prepare cupcakes.** Ice smooth with spatula in white.

2 **Make records.** Roll out black fondant ⅛ in. thick. Cut record using circle cutter. Immediately place on thin foam, use tip 789 serrated side down to imprint grooves. Cut center hole with narrow end of tip 7.

3 **Make labels.** Tint ⅓ oz. fondant each violet, rose and green for three treats. Roll out 1⁄16 in. thick. Cut labels with wide end of tip 2A; cut a center hole with narrow end of tip 7. Attach labels to records with damp brush, lining up holes. Position record on cupcake. Brush record with Pearl Dust. Each serves 1.

*Combine Violet with Rose for violet shown. Combine Leaf Green with Lemon Yellow for green shown.

B Cone *Colossus!*

Pans: Standard Muffin, 10 in. x 16 in. Cooling Grid, Non-Stick Cookie Sheet, p. 158

Candy: White (2 pks.), Peanut Butter (3 oz.) Light Cocoa (1 oz.) Candy Melts Candy, Garden (pink, green) and Primary (yellow) Candy Color Sets, p. 163

Recipe: Favorite crisped rice cereal treat mixture

Also: 15 in. Parchment Triangles, Cake Boards, p. 161; shredded coconut, sour cherry candy, 2¼ in. dia. ice cream scoop

See p. 7 for a list of Wilton essential cupcake products and other commonly used decorating items you may need.

INSTRUCTIONS

1 **Make candy cone.** Make candy shell (p. 151) using melted peanut butter candy poured into muffin pan without baking cup; chill until outer shell begins to form (approx. 10 minutes). Pour out soft center. Repeat if needed to create a ¼ in. thick shell. Chill and unmold.

2 **Prepare cereal treats mixture.** When cool enough to handle, use scoop to make four balls for ice cream scoops. Flatten bottoms and tops of three scoops, bottom only on fourth scoop. Set on waxed paper to cool completely. Use additional treat mixture to fill candy cone, ending slightly below top edge. Seal with melted peanut butter candy; let set. Use melted candy in cut parchment bag to pipe diagonal lines on cone.

3 **Decorate scoops.** Tint melted white candy green, pink, yellow and ivory (use a small amount of yellow for ivory). Place scoops on cooling grid set over cookie sheet. Cover with melted candy; let set then repeat. Stack scoops on candy cone, securing with melted candy. Working one color at a time, add two or three drops of water to thicken candy. Immediatelty use cut parchment bag to pipe swirls around bottom edges of scoops. Pipe light cocoa candy drips on top scoop; let set. Mix 1 tablespoon coconut with 2 tablespoons melted white candy; mound on top for whipped cream. Position cherry candy on top. Chill until firm. Each treat serves 5.

Record-topped cupcakes are a pick to click with all ages! The fondant platters are imprinted with a serrated tip to create the groovy detail.

Wilton

They'll flip over double-decker burgers with all the fixings piped right on top of the cupcake.

ⓒ Burger *Builder*

Pans: Standard, Mini Muffin, 10 in. x 16 in. Cooling Grid, p. 158

Tips: 2, 2A, 3, 4, 46, 104, p. 162

Colors:* Brown, Red-Red, Christmas Red, Orange, Leaf Green, Golden Yellow, Lemon Yellow, p. 163

Recipes: Buttercream, Chocolate Buttercream Icings, p. 143

Also: Gingham Standard Baking Cups, p. 155; 6 in. Lollipop Sticks, p. 163; 12 in. Disposable Decorating Bags, p. 161; white cardstock, fine tip marker

See p. 7 for a list of Wilton essential cupcake products and other commonly used decorating items you may need.

INSTRUCTIONS

1 **Prepare cupcake.** You will need one standard and three mini cupcakes for each treat; bake minis without baking cups.

   Stack three mini cupcakes on standard cupcake with icing. Insert lollipop stick through stack leaving 1 ¾ in. extended at top.

2 **Decorate burgers.** Beginning at bottom, pipe ingredients around mini cupcakes as follows: tip 2A outline bun; tip 2A outline burger (use chocolate buttercream); four tip 4 outline and fill in cheese triangles; tip 104 ruffled lettuce; tip 46 outline onion. Repeat. Pipe tip 2A rounded top bun; smooth with finger dipped in cornstarch.

   Pipe tip 2 bead seeds on top bun. Pipe tip 3 ketchup and mustard drips.

3 **Make pick.** Cut triangle flag, 2 in. x 1 in., from cardstock. Print message with marker. Attach flag to stick with tape (stick inserted in step 1). Each serves 1.

*Combine Brown with Orange for light brown buns shown. Combine Orange with Golden Yellow for orange cheese shown. Combine Golden Yellow with Lemon Yellow for yellow mustard shown. Combine Christmas Red with Red-Red for red ketchup shown.

ⓓ Luxe *Leather*

Pans: Standard Muffin, 10 in. x 16 in. Cooling Grid, p. 158

Color: Black, p. 163

Fondant: White Ready-To-Use Rolled Fondant (1 oz. per treat), 9 in. Fondant Roller, Roll-N-Cut Mat, p. 164; Silver Pearl Dust, Brush Set, p. 165

Recipe: Buttercream Icing, p. 143

Also: Silver Foil Standard Baking Cups, p. 155; Pure Lemon Extract, p. 160; Cupcake Spatula, 6 in. Cake Circles, p. 161; 101 Cookie Cutters (medium circle), p. 167; Black Sparkle Gel, p. 163; Silver Pearlized Jimmies, p. 156

See p. 7 for a list of Wilton essential cupcake products and other commonly used decorating items you may need.

INSTRUCTIONS

1 **Make zipper pull.** In advance, roll out fondant ¹⁄₁₆ in. thick. Cut a strip, ¼ in. x ⅝ in.; use knife to trim two angled corners. Use end of brush to cut a hole at opposite end. Let dry on cornstarch-dusted circle.

2 **Prepare cupcakes.** Ice smooth with spatula.

3 **Make leather jacket.** Tint remaining fondant black; roll out ⅛ in. thick. Cut jackets using medium circle cutter from set. Cut out a triangle at top, 1½ in. wide x 1½ in. deep. Position jacket on cupcake. Use knife to cut a square of black fondant, ⅝ in. x ⅝ in.; attach with damp brush for pocket. Brush jacket with Sparkle Gel.

4 **Make zipper.** Paint zipper pull with silver Pearl Dust/lemon extract mixture (p. 151); let dry. Position jimmies for zipper teeth; position zipper pull. Each serves 1.

Fun In A Can

Pans: Standard Muffin, 10 in. x 16 in. Cooling Grid, p. 158

Tip: 8, p. 162

Colors:* Kelly Green, Leaf Green, Orange, p. 163

Fondant: White Ready-To-Use Rolled Fondant (1¾ oz. per treat), Gum-Tex, 9 in. Fondant Roller, Roll-N-Cut Mat, p. 164; Silver Pearl Dust, Brush Set, p. 165

Recipe: Buttercream Icing, p. 143

Also: 101 Cookie Cutters (medium crinkle cutter used), p. 167; Silver Foil Standard Baking Cups, p. 155; Pure Lemon Extract, p. 160; Cake Boards, Cupcake Spatula, p. 161

See p. 7 for a list of Wilton essential cupcake products and other commonly used decorating items you may need.

INSTRUCTIONS

1. **Make lid.** 1 to 2 days in advance, tint ¾ oz. fondant gray for each treat. Knead in ⅛ teaspoon Gum-Tex; roll out ⅟₁₆ in. thick. Cut using medium crinkle cutter from set. Imprint lid rings using bottom of Gum-Tex can. Let dry overnight on cornstarch-dusted board. Paint with silver Pearl Dust/lemon extract mixture (p. 151). Let dry.

2. **Make veggies.** 1 day in advance, tint ½ oz. fondant each green and orange for each treat. For peas, roll green into 35 balls, each ⅜ in. dia. For carrots, roll out orange ¼ in. thick. Cut into 14 squares, each ⅜ in. Let dry overnight.

3. **Prepare cupcakes.** Fill cups ⅓ full with batter. Bake and cool cupcakes. Pipe tip 8 zigzag in white to cover top; smooth with spatula.

4. **Position trims.** Position peas and carrots. Position can lid in icing; support with peas and carrots. Each serves 1.

*Combine Kelly Green with Leaf Green for green shown.

Eat your veggies and you'll get dessert—all in one! By baking a shorter cupcake, there's room for the fondant peas, carrots and lid.

Summer Sizzle

Pans: Standard Muffin, 10 in x 16 in. Cooling Grid, p. 158

Tip: 7, p. 162

Colors:* Brown, Black, Lemon Yellow, Golden Yellow, Leaf Green, Ivory, Red-Red, p. 163

Fondant: White Ready-To-Use Rolled Fondant ($3\frac{1}{2}$ oz. makes 6 to 8 treats), 9 in. Fondant Roller, Roll-N-Cut Mat, 10-Pc. Gum Paste/Fondant Tool Set, p. 164; Silver Pearl Dust, Brown Color Dust, Brush Set, p. 165

Recipes: Buttercream, Royal Icings, p. 143

Also: Monochrome Standard Baking Cups (black), p. 155; 12 in. Disposable Decorating Bags, 10 in. x 14 in. Cake Boards, p. 161; Meringue Powder, Pure Lemon Extract, p. 160; Cupcake Spatula, p. 161; Parchment Paper, p. 159; Candy Melting Plate, Fine Tip Primary Colors FoodWriter Edible Color Markers (black), p. 163; black licorice twists

See p. 7 for a list of Wilton essential cupcake products and other commonly used decorating items you may need.

INSTRUCTIONS

1. **Make grill top.** 1 day in advance, draw a 2 in. dia. circle pattern; cover with waxed paper. Using full-strength royal icing, pipe tip 7 outlines for grill rim and grates $\frac{1}{4}$ in. apart. Let dry. Paint with silver Pearl Dust/lemon extract mixture (p. 151). Let dry.

2. **Make fondant food.** Tint 1 oz. fondant red and $\frac{1}{2}$ oz. each light yellow, dark yellow and dark brown, $\frac{1}{4}$ oz. each green, light brown and ivory. Shape a 1 in. dia. hamburger patty in dark brown. Roll out dark yellow fondant $\frac{1}{16}$ in. thick. Cut a square, $\frac{3}{4}$ in., for cheese; attach to hamburger with damp brush.

   For corn, using light yellow fondant, shape a log, $\frac{1}{2}$ in. x 2 in.; taper ends. Use knife tool to score surface for kernel look. Roll out green $\frac{1}{16}$ in. thick; cut leaves, $\frac{1}{2}$ in. x 2 in. Attach leaves to corn with damp brush. Shape a $\frac{1}{4}$ in. log for stem; attach to corn.

   For steak, shape a red triangle, $1\frac{1}{4}$ in. wide on each edge and $\frac{3}{8}$ in. thick. Round corners and indent side. Roll out ivory $\frac{1}{16}$ in. thick. Cut a strip, $\frac{3}{8}$ in. wide, for fat. Attach around sides of steak with damp brush. Use knife tool to cut T-bone; attach. For hot dog, shape red fondant into a log, $\frac{3}{8}$ in. dia x $1\frac{1}{2}$ in. long, with rounded ends. Draw grill marks with black edible marker. For potato, shape light brown fondant into a log, $\frac{5}{8}$ in. x $1\frac{1}{4}$ in. Dimple with large ball and thick modeling tools from set. Brush with brown Color Dust. Let all dry on cornstarch-dusted board.

3. **Prepare cupcakes.** Fill cups $\frac{1}{3}$ full with batter; bake and cool cupcakes. Ice smooth with spatula in black buttercream.

4. **Finish treats.** Cut black licorice twists into $\frac{3}{8}$ in. long pieces for coals; position level with top of cup. Position grate and food. Each serves 1.

*Combine Brown with Red-Red and Black for dark brown shades shown. Combine Lemon Yellow with Golden Yellow for yellow shades shown. Combine Red-Red with Brown for red shades shown.

Here's your cue for a great cookout cupcake! Top it with licorice coals, a royal icing grate and temptingly detailed fondant food.

Wilton

ⒷSpaghetti's *Ready!*

Pans: Standard Muffin, 10 in. x 16 in. Cooling Grid, p. 158

Tip: 3, p. 162

Colors:* Golden Yellow, Brown, p. 163

Recipe: Buttercream Icing, p. 143

Also: Assorted Primary Baking Cups (red), p. 155; Cupcake Spatula, 12 in. Disposable Decorating Bags, p. 161; Chocolate Ready-To-Use Rolled Fondant (½ oz. per treat), p. 164; raspberry filling

See p. 7 for a list of Wilton essential cupcake products and other commonly used decorating items you may need.

INSTRUCTIONS

1 **Prepare cupcakes.** Ice smooth with spatula.

2 **Add trims.** For pasta, pipe tip 3 random outlines, covering top of treat. For meatballs, shape chocolate fondant into roughly textured balls, ½ in. dia.; make three per treat and position. For sauce, mix 3 tablespoons raspberry filling with 1 teaspoon cornstarch. Pipe on cupcake using a cut decorating bag; leave areas of meatballs exposed. Each serves 1.

Combine Golden Yellow with Brown for ivory shade shown.

Have the camera ready when you switch his favorite birthday meal for a saucy surprise!

Breakfast in bed is always a thrill, but the real surprise will be the fondant eggs and bacon, complete with crispy edges.

ⒶBakin' and *Eggs*

Pans: Standard Muffin, 10 in. x 16 in. Cooling Grid, p. 158

Colors: Golden Yellow, Ivory, p. 163

Fondant: White Ready-To-Use Rolled Fondant (1¼ oz. per combo), Primary (1 oz. red per combo), Natural (½ oz. dark brown per combo) Fondant Multi Packs, 9 in. Fondant Roller, Roll-N-Cut Mat, 10-Pc. Gum Paste/Fondant Tool Set, Fondant Shaping Foam, p. 164; Brown Color Dust, Brush Set, p. 165;

Recipe: Buttercream Icing, p. 143

Also: Round Comfort-Grip Cutter, p. 166; White Standard Baking Cups, p. 155; Piping Gel, p. 160; Cupcake Spatula, 10 in. x 14 in. Cake Board, p. 161

See p. 7 for a list of Wilton essential cupcake products and other commonly used decorating items you may need.

INSTRUCTIONS

1 **Make eggs.** 1 to 2 days in advance, roll out white fondant (½ oz. per egg) 1⁄16 in. thick. Use round cutter to cut a circle. Use cutting wheel from set to cut wavy edge for an egg white 3 in. to 3¼ in. dia.

For yolk, tint ¼ oz. fondant yellow per egg. Shape into a 1⅜ in. dia. yolk with flat bottom. Attach to egg white using damp brush. Let dry overnight on cornstarch-dusted board.

Brush edge of egg white with brown Color Dust and entire egg with piping gel.

2 **Make bacon.** 1 to 2 days in advance, tint ½ oz. fondant ivory. Knead 1 oz. red fondant with ½ oz. dark brown for brown shade on bacon. Roll one ivory log and two brown logs, ⅛ in. dia. x 3½ in. long.

Place side by side with ivory log at center and press together. Roll out 1⁄16 in. thick. Use knife to cut a strip, 1 in. x 5 in. Place on thin foam and ruffle edges with large ball tool. Repeat for two or three additional strips per treat. Let dry on cornstarch-dusted board.

3 **Prepare cupcakes.** Ice tops smooth with spatula in white.

4 **Position trims.** Position egg on top of cupcake and bacon on side. Each serves 1.

A 🅐 Name In *Neon*

Pans: Standard Muffin, Non-Stick Cookie Sheet, 10 in. x 16 in. Cooling Grid, p. 158

Tip: 3, p. 162

Colors:* Teal, Golden Yellow, Lemon Yellow, Leaf Green, Orange, Red-Red, p. 163

Recipes: Buttercream, Color Flow Icings, Roll-Out Cookies, p. 143

Also: Yellow/Blue/Orange Green Dots ColorCups Baking Cups, p. 154; 101 Cookie Cutters (letters), p. 167; Blue, Yellow, Light Green, Orange Colored Sugars, p. 156; Color Flow Mix, p. 160; 12 in. Disposable Decorating Bags, Cupcake Spatula, p. 161; 6 in. Lollipop Sticks, Decorator Brush Set, p. 163; 10 in. x 14 in. Cake Boards, p. 161; 12 in. Rolling Pin, Parchment Paper, p. 159

See p. 7 for a list of Wilton essential cupcake products and other commonly used decorating items you may need.

INSTRUCTIONS

1. **Make cookies.** 1 day in advance, prepare and roll out dough. Cut letters using cutters from set. Bake and cool cookies. Tint portions of Color Flow icing assorted colors to match baking cups. Place cookies on waxed paper-covered boards. Outline tops using tip 3 and full-strength Color Flow; flow in with thinned Color Flow. Let set 5 to 8 minutes and sprinkle with matching colored sugar. Let dry 24 hours. Cut lollipop sticks to 3 in. Attach sticks to cookie backs, using full strength Color Flow, leaving 1½ in. extended at bottom. Let dry.

2. **Prepare cupcakes.** Ice tops smooth with spatula in white.

3. **Insert cookies.** Each serves 1.

*Combine Golden Yellow with Lemon Yellow for yellow shown. Combine Orange with Red-Red for orange shown.

Here's the splashy special effect their paint party needs! Serve marshmallow paint cans that pour a coat of colorful candy on each cupcake top.

B 🅑 Start Spreadin' The *Hues!*

Pans: Standard Muffin, 10 in. x 16 in. Cooling Grid, p. 158

Tip: 4, p. 162

Fondant: White Ready-To-Use Rolled Fondant (1 oz. makes 4 treats), 9 in. Fondant Roller, Roll-N-Cut Mat, p. 164

Candy: White Candy Melts Candy (1 pk. makes 6 to 8 treats), Primary (blue, orange, red), Garden (green, black) Candy Color Sets, 6 in. Lollipop Sticks, p. 163

Recipe: Buttercream Icing, p. 143

Also: Rainbow Paint ColorCups Standard Baking Cups, p. 154; Silver Color Mist Food Color Spray, p. 163; 15 in. Parchment Triangles, 12 in. Disposable Decorating Bags, p. 161; Brush Set, p. 165; Cupcake Spatula, p. 161, marshmallows

See p. 7 for a list of Wilton essential cupcake products and other commonly used decorating items you may need.

INSTRUCTIONS

1. **Make paint cans.** 1 day in advance, trim lollipop sticks to 4½ in. long. Insert into marshmallows at an angle. Dip marshmallows into melted white candy. Chill until firm. Spray marshmallow with silver Color Mist food color spra[y]. Let dry.

For labels, roll out fondant ⅛₆ in. thick. Cut a strip for eac[h] can, ¾ in. x 1¼ in. Attach labels to marshmallows with a damp brush. Tint a portion of melted candy with black color. Pipe letters using black candy in cut parchment ba[g]. Chill until firm.

Using white icing, pipe tip 4 outline rim and handle; allow icing to crust. Spray silver Color Mist food color spray on waxed paper; use to paint rim and handle. Let dry.

2. **Prepare cupcakes.** Ice tops smooth with spatula in white[.]

3. **Create paint details.** Tint melted white candy green, orange, red and teal (combine blue with green candy color). Pipe melted candy on top of can and on lollipop stick, leaving 1½ in. at bottom clean. Chill until firm. Inser[t] stick into center of cupcake. Pipe paint puddle on top of cupcake using melted candy in cut parchment bag. Chill until firm. Each serves 1.

Wilton

ⓒ Painter's *Party*

Pans: Dimensions Large Cupcake, p. 159; Standard Muffin, 10 in. x 16 in. Cooling Grid, p. 158

Tips: 7, 10, p. 162

Colors:* Orange, Moss Green, Lemon Yellow, Rose, Royal Blue, Violet, Christmas Red, Golden Yellow, Red-Red, Black, Brown, p. 163

Fondant: White Ready-To-Use Rolled Fondant (24 oz.), Gum-Tex, 20 in. Fondant Roller, 20 in. Fondant Roller Guide Rings, Roll-N-Cut Mat, Fondant Trimmer, p. 164; Silver Pearl Dust, Pure Lemon Extract, p. 160; Brush Set, p. 165

Recipe: Buttercream Icing, p. 143

Also: Rainbow Paint ColorCups Standard Baking Cups, p. 154; 8 in. Lollipop Sticks, p. 163; 12 in. Disposable Decorating Bags, Cupcake Spatula, p. 161

See p. 7 for a list of Wilton essential cupcake products and other commonly used decorating items you may need.

INSTRUCTIONS

1. **Make paint brush.** 1 day in advance, tint ¼ oz. fondant black, 1¼ oz. brown; reserve ⅛ oz. white. For handle, roll a brown log, ½ in. dia. x 6 in. long. Insert lollipop stick in end for bristles, leaving 3 in. extended to insert in cake. Taper handle at end.

   For bristles, roll out black fondant ¹⁄₁₆ in. thick. Cut a 1¼ in. x 2 in. strip. Wrap around handle end at stick side. Use a toothpick to score bristle lines. Roll out reserved white fondant ⅛ in. thick. Cut a strip, ½ in. x 2 in.; wrap around stick to cover seam, securing with damp brush. Paint white area with silver Pearl Dust/lemon extract mixture (p. 151). Let dry 24 hours.

2. **Prepare 2-piece large and standard cupcakes.**

3. **Create fondant overlay applique for large cupcake bottom.** Tint ½ oz. portions of white fondant yellow, orange, green, teal, rose, violet and red. Roll out colors ¹⁄₁₆ in. thick. Use knife to cut two freeform paint splatters in each color in various sizes.

   Make applique (p. 150) on white fondant strip, placing paint splatters randomly in various positions. Re-roll and position strip following instructions.

4. **Decorate cupcakes.** Ice tops smooth with spatula in white. Pipe tip 7 names in buttercream tinted to match paint splatter colors.

5. **Assemble treats.** Position large cupcake top section on bottom section. Ice top smooth in white. Print tip 10 name in red. Insert paint brush. Position cupcakes around large cupcake. Large cupcake serves 12; each standard cupcake serves 1.

*Combine Moss Green with Lemon Yellow for green shown. Combine Rose with Royal Blue for rose shown. Combine Violet with Christmas Red for violet shown. Combine Golden Yellow with Lemon Yellow for yellow shown.

Ⓐ A Year In The *Making*

Pans: Dimensions Large Cupcake, p. 159; Non-Stick Cookie Sheet, 10 in. x 16 in. Cooling Grid, p. 158

Tips: 1A, 1M, 2, 3, 4, 8, 12 (2 needed), p. 162

Colors:* Sky Blue, Brown, Red-Red, Black, p. 163

Recipes: Buttercream, Color Flow Icings, Roll-Out Cookies, p. 143

Also: Bear Metal Cutter, A-B-C and 1-2-3 Plastic Cutter Set (#1), p. 166; Leaf Cut-Outs Fondant Cutters, Brush Set, p. 165; White Candy Melts Candy, 6 in. Lollipop Sticks, p. 163; Pure Lemon Extract, Color Flow Mix, p. 160; Jumbo Confetti Sprinkles, p. 156; 12 in. Disposable Decorating Bags, 10 in. x 14 in. Cake Boards, 8 in. Circles, Fanci-Foil Wrap, p. 161; White Standard Baking Cups, p. 155; 5 in. to 6 in. candy sticks, yellow spice drop, large marshmallows

See p. 7 for a list of Wilton essential cupcake products and other commonly used decorating items you may need.

INSTRUCTIONS

1 **Make cookies.** 2 days in advance, prepare and roll out dough. Cut bears using metal cutter; use knife to cut two triangular easel backs, 1¼ in. wide x 2½ in. high. Cut number using plastic cutter. Bake and cool cookies. Reserve or freeze remaining dough for another use.

2 **Decorate cookies.** Prepare and tint portions of Color Flow icing light brown, dark brown, black, light blue and dark blue; reserve ¾ cup white. Outline bears with tip 3 and full-strength dark brown icing; flow in with thinned dark brown icing. Outline number with tip 3 and full-strength dark blue icing; flow in with thinned light blue icing. Let dry on waxed paper-covered boards.

Complete cookies with full-strength Color Flow. For number, attach lollipop stick to back with Color Flow leaving 1 in. extended at top and 2½ in. extended at bottom to insert in cake. For wick, paint top of lollipop stick black using black icing color mixed with lemon extract. For flame, roll out yellow spice drop ¼ in. thick in granulated sugar. Cut flame using smallest leaf Cut-Out. Attach.

For bears, pipe tip 8 dot muzzle and tip 3 dot inner ears in light brown. Pipe tip 2 outline smile and dot eyes and nose in black. Outline and fill in apron with tip 4 in white; pat smooth with finger dipped in cornstarch. Pipe hats using tip 1A dot for base and tip 12 dots for top. Pipe tip 4 bead decorating bag in his hand. Let dry. Attach easel backs to standing bear with melted candy. Let set.

3 **Make candy ladder.** For rungs, cut candy stick into six pieces, 1 in. long with scissors. Attach between two candy sticks, 1 in. apart, with melted candy. Chill to set. Attach climbing bear; attach a confetti sprinkle to his hand. Let dry.

4 **Prepare 2-piece large cupcake.** Decorate with buttercream icing. Cover sides of bottom cake with tip 12 outlines, alternating light and dark blues. Cover top with tip 1M swirls in white. Attach confetti.

5 **Add trims.** For paint can, use tip 4 to pipe drips of blue buttercream paint on one end of marshmallow; let dry. Fill white baking cup with confetti. Position ladder, standing bear and trims. Insert number. Cake serves 12; each cookie serves 1.

*Combine Brown with Red-Red for brown shades shown.

B First Birthday *Feast*

Pans: Mini Muffin, Non-Stick Cookie Sheet, 10 in. x 16 in. Cooling Grid, p. 158

Tips: 2, 12, p. 162

Candy: Light Cocoa, White Candy Melts Candy (1 pk. each), Garden (pink, black) Candy Color Set, Decorator Brush Set, Dessert Dome Candy Mold, p. 163

Recipe: Buttercream Icing, p. 143

Also: Pink Party Mini Baking Cups, p. 155; Letters/Numbers Fondant & Gum Paste Mold, p. 165; 4- Pc. Circles Nesting Metal Cutter Set, p. 166; Rainbow Jimmies Sprinkles, p. 156; 12 in. Disposable Decorating Bags, 15 in. Parchment Triangles, Cake Circles, Fanci-Foil Wrap, p. 161; Cinnamon Drop Sprinkles, p. 156, large marshmallows, warming tray

See p. 7 for a list of Wilton essential cupcake products and other commonly used decorating items you may need.

INSTRUCTIONS

1 **Make candy bear.** 1 day in advance, mix 8 oz. melted light cocoa candy with 4 oz. melted white candy for lighter brown shown. Follow dessert dome mold instructions to make four half shells in large cavity. Chill until firm; unmold. Run edges over warming tray then attach halves, postitoning seams vertically, to make balls for head and body. For ears, pipe two circles, ¾ in. dia. on waxed paper-covered board; chill until firm. For arms and legs, cut two marshmallows in half. Dip in melted light cocoa candy; let set on waxed paper.

To assemble bear, flatten both ends of body ball by running lightly over warming tray; stand on waxed paper. Flatten bottom of head ball; attach to body, flat side down. Attach ears, arms and legs. Tint a portion of white candy black; place in cut parchment bag with tip 2 taped to the outside. Pipe dot and outline facial features.

2 **Make one candy shell cupcake for top of head.** 1 day in advance, tint 4 oz. white candy pink to match baking cups. Pour some into fondant mold to make number. Make candy shell ⅛ in. thick using mini baking cups in pan (p. 151). Pour remaining melted candy into largest round cutter set on cookie sheet to form base for bear, ¼ in. thick. Chill until firm.

3 **Prepare mini cupcakes.** Cover tops with tip 12 swirl. Sprinkle with jimmies; position cinnamon drop candy on top. Pipe tip 12 swirl to fill candy cupcake; sprinkle with jimmies. Use melted candy to attach bear to base; attach candy cupcake to head. Insert candy number. Position bear on foil-wrapped cake circle or plate. Surround with mini cupcakes. Each serves 1.

C Caterpillar *Thriller*

Pans: Standard Muffin, 10 in. x 16 in. Cooling Grid, p. 158

Tip: 16, p. 162

Colors: * Orange, Lemon Yellow, Golden Yellow, Royal Blue, Christmas Red, Violet, Rose, p. 163

Recipe: Buttercream Icing, p. 143

Also: Rainbow Standard Baking Cups, p. 155; Large Candy Eyeballs, p. 157; 12 in. Disposable Decorating Bags, p. 161; black shoestring licorice, small spice drops, mini candy-coated chocolates, small jelly beans, 1 in. high serving platter

See p. 7 for a list of Wilton essential cupcake products and other commonly used decorating items you may need.

INSTRUCTIONS

1 **Prepare cupcakes.** Cover head cupcake with tip 16 stars. Cover body cupcakes with tip 16 stars using light and dark shades in ⅝ in. wide stripes.

2 **Prepare licorice trims.** Cut 10 licorice pieces, 2 in. long for legs and three pieces, 1½ in. long for antennae and smile.

3 **Attach trims.** Attach licorice smile, jelly bean nose and candy eyeballs with icing. For antennae, attach mini chocolates to licorice pieces with icing; insert into head. Cut spice drops lengthwise in half for shoes. Use knife tip to poke a small hole in rounded side of shoe; insert licorice leg. Insert legs into body. Position cupcakes on their sides on edge of serving platter. Each serves 1.

*Combine Lemon Yellow with Golden Yellow for light and dark yellow shown. Combine Violet with Rose for light and dark violet shown.

Pans: Standard Muffin, Non-Stick Cookie Sheet, 10 in. x 16 in. Cooling Grid, p. 158

Tips: Zebra—2, 3, 104, 233; **Giraffe**—2, 3, 7, 104, 233; **Elephant**—2, 12, 126, 233; **Tiger**—2, 104, 233; **Lion**—2, 3, 16, 233; **Monkey**—3, 104, 233, p. 162

Colors: Zebra—Leaf Green, Black; **Giraffe**—Lemon Yellow, Golden Yellow, Brown, Christmas Red, Leaf Green; **Elephant**—Black, Leaf Green; **Tiger**—Orange, Black, Leaf Green; **Lion**—Lemon Yellow, Golden Yellow, Orange, Leaf Green, Black; **Monkey**—Brown, Christmas Red, Black, Ivory, Leaf Green, p. 163

Recipes: Buttercream, Royal Icings, Roll-Out Cookies, p. 143

Also: 12 in. Rolling Pin, p. 159; Round Cut-Outs Fondant Cutters, p. 165; Meringue Powder, p. 160; Small Candy Eyeballs, p. 157; Grass Standard Baking Cups, p. 154; 4 in. Lollipop Sticks, p. 163; White Candy Melts Candy (1 oz. makes 10 to 12 treats), p. 163; Cake Boards, p. 161; Decorating Nail Set, p. 162; Cupcake Spatula, p. 161

See p. 7 for a list of Wilton essential cupcake products and other commonly used decorating items you may need.

A Giraffe Has a *Laugh*

Pans: Bar, Non-Stick Cookie Sheet, 14.5 in. x 20 in. Cooling Grid, p. 158

Tips: 2A, 3, 12, 16, 366, p. 162

Colors:* Royal Blue, Lemon Yellow, Golden Yellow, Leaf Green, Black, Orange, p. 163

Recipes: Buttercream Icing, Roll-Out Cookies, p. 143

Also: Cool Squares Baking Cups, p. 154; 4-Pc. Circles Nesting Metal Cutter Set, p. 166; 12 in. Rolling Pin, p. 159; Flowerful Medley Sprinkles (confetti), Large Candy Eyeballs, p. 157; Cake Boards, Fanci-Foil Wrap, 12 in. Disposable Decorating Bags, p. 161

See p. 7 for a list of Wilton essential cupcake products and other commonly used decorating items you may need.

INSTRUCTIONS

1 **Make cookie head.** In advance, prepare and roll out dough. Cut head using largest circle cutter. For ears, use knife to cut two triangle cookies, 1 in. wide x 1½ in. high; attach to head, 3 in. apart, using damp brush. For horns, cut two rectangles, ½ in. wide x 1 in. high; attach 1 in. apart. Press edges together with finger. Bake and cool cookie.

   Using toothpick and second largest circle cutter as a guide, mark semi-circular muzzle ¼ in. from bottom edge. Outline with tip 3 in orange. Fill in with tip 16 orange stars. Pipe in ears using tip 2A in yellow; pat smooth with finger dipped in cornstarch. Pipe in horns with tip 12 in yellow. Pipe tip 12 orange ball on tips. Cover remainder of head with tip 16 stars in yellow. Pipe tip 3 outline smile and bead nostrils in black. Position candy eyeballs.

2 **Prepare 18 cupcakes.** Ice tops of 14 cupcakes smooth with spatula in blue for outside border. Attach confetti sprinkles to sky areas. For giraffe neck, pipe tip 16 orange stars on four remaining cupcakes to make random spots. Cover remainder with tip 16 yellow stars. Position cupcakes on foil-wrapped board in three rows of six each. Position cookie head. Pipe tip 366 leaves in green. Each serves 1.

*Combine Lemon Yellow with Golden Yellow for yellow shown.

B Hungry *Monkey*

Pans: Standard Muffin, 10 in. x 16 in. Cooling Grid, p. 158

Color: Leaf Green, p. 163

Recipe: Buttercream Icing, p. 143

Also: Grass Standard Baking Cups, p. 154; Leaf Cut-Outs Fondant Cutters, p. 165; Monkey with Banana Royal Icing Decorations, p. 157; Cupcake Spatula, p. 161; 9 in. Fondant Roller, p. 164; pretzel sticks, large green spice drops

See p. 7 for a list of Wilton essential cupcake products and other commonly used decorating items you may need.

INSTRUCTIONS

1 **Make trees.** Roll out spice drops ⅛ in. thick on waxed paper sprinkled with sugar. Use Cut-Outs to cut five medium leaves and five small leaves.

   Press leaves onto top end of pretzel stick with a layer of medium leaves on top and small leaves below. Secure with icing if needed.

2 **Prepare cupcakes.** Ice smooth with spatula in green.

   Insert tree in cupcake. Position monkey icing decoration, supporting with icing as needed. Each serves 1.

INSTRUCTIONS

Create cookie critters. In advance, prepare and roll out dough. Cut cookies using largest round Cut-Out. Bake and cool. Place cookies on cooling grid over waxed paper-covered cookie sheet. Cover with thinned royal icing. Let dry 24 hours.

Add cookie details. With full-strength royal icing, pipe tip 126 ears for elephant and tip 104 ears for all other animals, except lion, using flower nail covered with waxed paper square. For zebra and giraffe, pipe 1¼ in. petal shapes. For zebra, pinch edges slightly upward; for giraffe, fold one edge over with cornstarch-dusted spatula. For tiger and monkey, pipe 1⅛ in. semi-circles. For elephant, pipe 2 in. long scallops; shape center and edges with finger dipped in cornstarch. Immediately attach ears to back of cookies with icing. Attach all cookies to waxed paper-covered board and let dry.

Decorate animals as follows:

Zebra: Use tip 3 to outline and pipe in muzzle and tip 2 for stripes; pat smooth. Use tip 3 to outline ears and pipe pull-out hair. Pipe tip 2 outline nostrils and mouth.

Giraffe: Pipe in muzzle and spots with tip 3; pat smooth. Pipe tip 7 pull-out and dot horns and tip 3 pull-out hair tuft. Pipe tip 2 outline nostrils and tip 3 outline mouth.

Elephant: Pipe tip 2 outline mouth and eyebrows. Pipe tip 12 pull-out trunk. Indent tip of trunk with end of lollipop stick dipped in cornstarch.

Tiger: Pipe in nose and stripes with tip 2; pat smooth. Pipe tip 2 outline mouth and dot whiskers.

Lion: Use tip 2 to pipe outline mouth and dot whiskers; pipe tip 3 outline ears. outline and pipe in nose. Pat smooth. Pipe tip 16 pull-out star mane.

Monkey: Pipe in face with tip 3, piping eye area first, then muzzle; pat smooth. Pipe tip 3 dot nostrils and outline mouth.

Attach candy eyeballs to all cookies with icing.

Prepare cupcakes. Cover tops with tip 233 pull-out grass in buttercream. Peel off waxed paper from cookies. Trim lollipop sticks to 3 in.; attach to back of cookies with melted candy. Insert cookies in cupcakes.

*Combine Brown with Christmas Red for brown shades shown. Combine Lemon Yellow with Golden Yellow for yellow shades shown.

ⒶSnake Charmer

Pans: Standard Muffin, 10 in. x 16 in. Cooling Grid, p. 158

Tip: 3, p. 162

Colors: Black, Christmas Red, p. 163

Fondant: White Ready-To-Use Rolled Fondant (1 ½ oz.), 9 in. Fondant Roller, Roll-N-Cut Mat, p. 164; Brush Set, p. 165

Recipe: Buttercream Icing, p. 143

Also: Black Dots ColorCups Standard Baking Cups, p. 154; Pearl Color Mist Food Color Spray, p. 163; Large Candy Eyeballs, p. 157; Jumbo Confetti Sprinkles (2 bottles for treat shown), p. 156; Cupcake Spatula, p. 161; round candy wafers

See p. 7 for a list of Wilton essential cupcake products and other commonly used decorating items you may need.

INSTRUCTIONS

1. **Prepare cupcakes.** Ice smooth with spatula in white.

2. **Attach confetti sprinkles.** Position two double rows of blue, green or violet, single rows of yellow, pink and peach. Slightly overlap edges to look like scales. Spray with pearl food color spray.

3. **Attach features with icing.** Add candy eyeballs to round candy wafers with tip 3 dots of icing; position on cupcake. Tint ½ oz. fondant black, 1 oz. red. Roll a black log for mouth, ⅛ in. dia. x 2 in. long; attach with tip 3 dots of icing. Roll out red fondant 1⁄16 in. thick. Cut a strip for tongue, ¾ in. x 3 in. Cut v-shaped notch in one end; curl slightly and attach.

4. **Position cupcakes.** At party, arrange cupcakes in snake design. Each serves 1.

Get ready to chomp on the king of the swamp! Line up cupcakes topped with scales, then add fondant legs and a cookie mouth and tail.

C This Croc *Rocks!*

Pans: Standard Muffin, Cookie Sheet, 10 in. x 16 in. Cooling Grid, p. 158

Tips: 2A, 3, 16, 103, p. 162

Colors:* Kelly Green, Leaf Green, Lemon Yellow, Rose, Black, p. 163

Fondant: White Ready-To-Use Rolled Fondant (4 oz.), Gum-Tex, 9 in. Fondant Roller, Roll-N-Cut Mat, p. 164; Brush Set, p. 165;

Recipes: Buttercream Icing, Roll-Out Cookies, p. 143

Also: Bright Rainbow Standard Baking Cups (green), p. 155; 4-Pc. Football Colored Metal Cutter Set (football), p. 167; Large Candy Eyeballs, p. 157; 9 in. Straight Spatula, 12 in. Disposable Decorating Bags, p. 161; 4 in. Lollipop Sticks, Fine Tip Primary Colors FoodWriter Edible Color Markers (yellow), p. 163; Cake Boards, p. 161; 12 in. Rolling Pin, p. 159; candy corn, jelly spearmint leaves

See p. 7 for a list of Wilton essential cupcake products and other commonly used decorating items you may need.

INSTRUCTIONS

1 **Make cookies.** 1 day in advance, prepare and roll out dough. Use football cutter to cut three football shapes for each crocodile. For tail, press first football over a lollipop stick, leaving 1½ in. extended to insert into cupcake. For top jaw, cut 1¼ in. off one end of second football. For bottom jaw, cut ¾ in. off one end of last football. Bake and cool cookies.

2 **Make legs.** 1 day in advance, tint 4 oz. fondant green. Knead in ½ teaspoon Gum-Tex. Shape into four legs, 4 in. long, tapering from ¾ in. dia. at top to ½ in. dia. at bottom. Bend into position. Let dry 24 hours on cornstarch-dusted board.

3 **Prepare cupcakes.** Bake and cool five cupcakes for each crocodile. Cover four of the cupcakes and tail cookie with rows of tip 103 scales. Position cupcakes in a row on serving tray; insert tail. Ice fifth cupcake and two jaw cookies smooth in green. Ice reverse sides of jaw cookies with black icing. Use tip 3 to outline and fill-in rose tongue on bottom jaw, leaving ¼ in. uncovered at outer edge; smooth with finger. Trim white tips off candy corn; using icing to attach around top and bottom jaw cookies for teeth.

4 **Assemble crocodile.** Position fifth cupcake for head. Insert jaw cookies; secure with icing if needed. Pipe tip 2A ball eye sockets. Color whites of candy eyeballs with yellow edible marker; attach eyeballs. Pipe tip 16 stars over eye sockets, head, top and sides of jaws; overpipe eyelid for dimension.

5 **Make feet.** Cut spearmint leaves in half lengthwise. Roll between sheets of waxed paper sprinkled with granulated sugar to flatten. Use scissors to trim into two webbed back feet and two four-finger front feet. Attach feet to fondant legs with icing; attach legs in position next to body. Cover legs with tip 16 stars; overpipe thighs for dimension. Each cupcake and cookie serves 1.

*Combine Kelly Green with Leaf Green and Lemon Yellow for green shades shown.

B Tempting *Snakes*

Pans: Standard Muffin, 10 in. x 16 in. Cooling Grid, p. 158

Colors:* Leaf Green, Lemon Yellow, Orange, Black, p. 163

Recipe: Buttercream Icing, p. 143

Also: Jewel Standard Baking Cups (purple), p. 155; Cupcake Spatula, p. 161; White Ready-To-Use Rolled Fondant (1½ oz. per treat), Gum-Tex, p. 164; Brush Set, p. 165

See p. 7 for a list of Wilton essential cupcake products and other commonly used decorating items you may need.

INSTRUCTIONS

1 **Make snakes.** Knead ¼ teaspoon of Gum-Tex into each 1½ oz. fondant. Break off a small amount of white for eyes; divide this and tint half black for pupils. Tint remaining fondant light and dark shades of green and orange. Roll fondant into 4 in. ropes. Twist light and dark colors together. Roll into a log, ⅜ in. dia. x 15 in. long. Taper one end for tail. Slightly flatten opposite end for head. Coil to form seated snake. Roll white balls, ⅛ in. dia., for eyes, black balls, ¹⁄₁₆ in. dia., for pupils. Flatten slightly and attach with damp brush.

   Prepare cupcakes. Ice smooth with spatula in white, creating a flat top. Position snake on cupcake. Each serves 1.

*Combine Leaf Green with Lemon Yellow for green shown.

Ⓐ Dirt Dessert

Pans: Jumbo Muffin, Cookie Sheet, 10 in. x 16 in. Cooling Grid, p. 158

Tips: 1, 2, 3, 5, 6, 10, 12, p. 162

Colors:* Black, Brown, Red-Red, Moss Green, Creamy Peach, p. 163

Recipes: Color Flow, Chocolate Buttercream Icings, Roll-Out Cookies, p. 143

Also: 12 in. Rolling Pin, p. 159; 4-Pc. Garden Colored Metal Cutter Set (spade), p. 166; Color Flow Mix, p. 160; 12 in. Disposable Decorating Bags, p. 161; White Jumbo Baking Cups, p. 155; 4 in. Lollipop Sticks, White Candy Melts Candy, p. 163; chocolate wafer cookies

See p. 7 for a list of Wilton essential cupcake products and other commonly used decorating items you may need.

INSTRUCTIONS

1. **Make cookies.** 1 day in advance, prepare and roll out dough. Cut cookies using spade cutter from set. Bake and cool. Divide Color Flow in fourths and tint gray, brown, dark green, peach. Reserve green, peach and a small amount of gray. Outline spade with tip 3 and full-strength gray icing; let set. Flow in with thinned icing; let dry. Pipe in handle area with tip 5 and 10 lines in full-strength brown Color Flow; let dry.

   Attach lollipop stick to back of spade with melted candy, leaving 2 in. extended to insert in cupcake. Chill until firm.

2. **Make Color Flow bugs.** Decorate with full-strength Color Flow on waxed paper-covered surface. Pipe tip 12 worms in peach; pipe outline body starting at tail, then pull up for head, ½ in. high. For beetle, pipe tip 12 ball body and tip 6 dot head. Add tip 2 pull-out legs. Pipe tip 2 legs and tip 1 dot eyes. Let dry.

3. **Prepare cupcakes.** Fill jumbo cups ⅓ full with batter; bake and cool cupcakes. Pipe tip 12 swirl with chocolate buttercream. Place cookies in plastic bag and crush with rolling pin until crumbled. Cover cupcake tops with crumbs. Insert spade in cupcake. Position beetle and insert worm. Each serves 1.

*Combine Brown with Red-Red for brown shown. Combine Creamy Peach with Brown for peach shown.

Ⓑ Grab Some Grub!

Pans: Standard Muffin, 10 in. x 16 in. Cooling Grid, p. 158

Tips: 2, 3, 12, 233, p. 162

Colors:* Leaf Green, Lemon Yellow, Brown, Black, p. 163

Recipes: Buttercream, Royal Icings, p. 143

Also: Rainbow Standard Baking Cups (blue), p. 155; Meringue Powder, p. 160; 12 in. Rolling Pin, Parchment Paper, p. 159; 12 in. Disposable Decorating Bags, 9 in. Straight Spatula, Cake Boards, p. 161; chocolate sandwich cookies

See p. 7 for a list of Wilton essential cupcake products and other commonly used decorating items you may need.

INSTRUCTIONS

1. **Make slug.** 1 day in advance, tint portions of royal icing brown, light brown and black. On parchment paper-covered board, pipe tip 12 S-shaped body, 1¾ in. long, in brown. Pipe tip 2 pull-out legs in light brown and tip 3 pull-out antennae in black. Let dry 24 hours.

2. **Prepare cupcakes.** Cover top with tip 233 pull-out grass. Use side of spatula to push icing toward sides of cupcake to make a ridge for slug. Place cookies in plastic bag and crush with rolling pin until crumbled. Sprinkle into ridge for dirt. Position slug. Each serves 1.

*Combine Leaf Green with Lemon Yellow for green shown.

It's fun to mess things up a little! This icing insect will make their skin crawl as he stirs up the cookie crumb dirt.

○ Aliens Up In *Arms*

Pans: Mini Muffin, 10 in. x 16 in. Cooling Grid, p. 158

Tip: 6, p. 162

Colors: Leaf Green, Kelly Green, Moss Green, p. 163

Recipes: Buttercream, Royal Icings, p. 143

Also: Silver Mini Baking Cups, p. 155; Large Candy Eyeballs, p. 157; 9 in. Straight Spatula, p. 161; Meringue Powder, p. 160; Cake Boards, Circles, p. 161

See p. 7 for a list of Wilton essential cupcake products and other commonly used decorating items you may need.

INSTRUCTIONS

1. **Make arms.** 1 day in advance, pipe tip 6 S-curve arms, 2 in. long x ⅝ in. deep, in royal icing on waxed paper-covered boards. You will need eight for each treat in desired shade of green; make extras to allow for breakage. Let dry 24 hours.

2. **Prepare cupcakes.** Ice smooth with spatula in desired shade of green. Position eyeball, supporting with icing if necessary. Insert arms in icing. Each serves 1.

A Swimming Serpent

Pans: Standard Muffin, Cookie Sheet, 10 in. x 16 in. Cooling Grid, p. 158

Tips: 16, 352, p. 162

Colors:* Royal Blue, Orange, Violet, Rose, Leaf Green, p. 163

Recipes: Buttercream Icing, Roll-Out Cookies, p. 143

Also: 4-Pc. Circles Nesting Metal Cutter Set, p. 166; Round Cut-Outs Fondant Cutters, p. 165; Small Candy Eyeballs, p. 157; Blue Sparkle Gel, p. 163; 12 in. Disposable Decorating Bags, p. 161; Rainbow Standard Baking Cups (blue), p. 155; 9 in. Straight Spatula, p. 161

See p. 7 for a list of Wilton essential cupcake products and other commonly used decorating items you may need.

INSTRUCTIONS

1 **Make cookies.** In advance, prepare and roll out dough ⅛ in. thick. Cut two doughnut-shaped rings (make more for more than six cupcakes) using second largest nesting cutter for outside edge and largest Cut-Out for inside edge. Cut each doughnut shape in half. Use knife to shape one head; use knife to cut slit for mouth and shape one pointed tail. Bake and cool cookies.

2 **Prepare cupcakes.** Ice tops with spatula in blue, lifting up slightly to create wave effect.

3 **Add trims.** Position cupcakes on serving tray. Insert cookies. Pipe tip 352 pull-out violet spikes across top edges. Pipe tip 16 green star clusters for assorted spots on both sides. Cover remainder of body with tip 16 orange stars. Attach a candy eyeball to each side of head. Accent waves with Sparkle Gel. Each cupcake or cookie serves 1.

*Combine Violet with Rose for violet shown.

B Have Lunch On The *Fly*

Pans: Standard Muffin, 10 in. x 16 in. Cooling Grid, p. 158

Tips: 1, 2A, 3, 4, 5, 8, 12, p. 162

Colors:* Leaf Green, Kelly Green, Black, p. 163

Recipe: Buttercream Icing, p. 143

Also: Rainbow Standard Baking Cups (green), p. 155; Large Candy Eyeballs, p. 157; 9 in. Tapered, 9 in. Angled Spatulas, p. 161; red fruit roll candy

See p. 7 for a list of Wilton essential cupcake products and other commonly used decorating items you may need.

INSTRUCTIONS

1 **Prepare cupcakes.** Pipe tip 2A icing mound in green; smooth and shape in a 1¼ in. high dome with angled spatula.

2 **Make facial features.** For back of eyes, build up tip 12 dots. Press candy eyeballs on front. Pipe tip 8 outline eyelids; pat smooth with finger dipped in cornstarch.

For nostrils, pipe tip 4 outline rings, ⅜ in. dia. Dip tip of tapered spatula in cornstarch; insert in icing to create a 2 in. wide mouth. For tongue, use knife to cut a fruit strip, 1 in. x 3½ in., with rounded end. Insert in mouth.

3 **Make flies.** Pipe tip 5 bead body and dot head. Pipe tip 1 dot eyes. Pipe four tip 3 bead wings. Each serves 1.

*Combine Leaf Green with Kelly Green for green shown.

C Bronto *Bites*

Pans: Standard Muffin, 10 in. x 16 in. Cooling Grid, p. 158

Tips: 2A, 3, p. 162

Colors:* Teal, Rose, Violet, Golden Yellow, Orange, p. 163

Fondant: White Ready-To-Use Rolled Fondant (1 oz. makes 3 treats), Gum-Tex, 9 in. Fondant Roller, Roll-N-Cut Mat, p. 164

Recipe: Buttercream Icing, p. 143

Also: Head & Tail Patterns, p. 152; Small Candy Eyeballs, p. 157; Jewel Standard Baking Cups, p. 155; 12 in. Disposable Decorating Bags, 9 in. Angled Spatula, Cake Boards, p. 161

See p. 7 for a list of Wilton essential cupcake products and other commonly used decorating items you may need.

INSTRUCTIONS

1 **Make head and tail.** 2 days in advance, tint 4 oz. fondant (for 12 treats) each teal, violet and yellow. Knead ½ teaspoon Gum-Tex into each color. Roll out colors ⅛ in. thick. Use patterns and knife to cut heads and tails. Let dry 48 hours on cornstarch-dusted board. Reserve remaining fondant for spots.

2 **Prepare cupcakes.** Ice smooth with spatula in teal, violet or yellow in a mounded shape, about 1¼ in. high.

3 **Position features.** Attach candy eyeballs to both sides of head with tip 3 icing dots. Insert head and tail in cupcake.

4 **Cut spots.** Roll out reserved fondant colors ¹⁄₁₆ in. thick. Cut small spots with narrow end of tip 2A, large spots with wide end of tip 3. Position on cupcake top. Each serves 1.

*Combine Violet with Rose for violet shown. Combine Golden Yellow with Orange for yellow shown.

A

Ⓐ Hoppin' *Non-Stop!*

Pans: Jumbo, Standard Muffin, 10 in. x 16 in. Cooling Grid, p. 158

Tips: 3, 8, p. 162

Colors:* Juniper Green, Lemon Yellow, Black, p. 163

Recipe: Buttercream Icing, p. 143

Also: Vibrant Green Candy Melts Candy, p. 163; White Jumbo, Standard Baking Cups, p. 155; Large Candy Eyeballs, p. 157; 9 in. Fondant Roller, p. 164; 15 in. Parchment Triangles, 12 in. Disposable Decorating Bags, Cake Boards, p. 161; green spice drops, green licorice twists

See p. 7 for a list of Wilton essential cupcake products and other commonly used decorating items you may need.

INSTRUCTIONS

1 **Prepare hands and feet.** For hands, roll out spice drop ⅜ in. thick. Use knife to shape ⅝ in. wide hand; cut slits for fingers. For feet, pinch spice drops to shape ¾ in. long ovals. Cut four pieces of green licorice for arms and legs, each 2¼ in. long. Attach hands and feet with melted candy. Let set on waxed paper-covered board.

2 **Prepare eyes.** Cut two pieces of green licorice, each 2¼ in. long. Use melted candy in cut parchment bag to attach a whole green candy melts candy wafer to licorice pieces; attach candy eyeballs to wafers. Let set.

3 **Prepare one jumbo cupcake head and one standard cupcake body for each frog.** For positioning eyes, use knife tip to cut two holes through jumbo baking cup, 1¼ in. from bottom and ¾ in. apart. For positioning arms and legs, cut four holes through standard baking cup, ⅝ in. from bottom. Ice cupcake tops smooth with spatula in green.

4 **Add details.** Insert eyes, arms and legs, securing with icing. Pipe tip 3 dot nostrils and outline smile on head. Pipe tip 8 dark green dots on body; flatten with finger dipped in cornstarch. Each serves 1.

*Combine Juniper Green with Lemon Yellow for light and dark green shown.

Ⓑ Wackos *Waving*

Pans: Standard Muffin, 10 in. x 16 in. Cooling Grid, p. 158

Tip: 2, p. 162

Colors:* Leaf Green, Lemon Yellow, Sky Blue, Teal, Orange, p. 163

Recipe: Buttercream Icing, p. 143

Also: Color Wheel Standard Baking Cups, p. 155; 9 in. Fondant Roller, p. 164; 9 in. Straight Spatula, 12 in. Disposable Decorating Bags, p. 161; Parchment Paper, p. 159; Small Candy Eyeballs, p. 157; pretzel sticks, assorted spice drops, black shoestring licorice

See p. 7 for a list of Wilton essential cupcake products and other commonly used decorating items you may need.

INSTRUCTIONS

1 **Prepare cupcakes.** Ice smooth with spatula in green, orange or blue. Position candy eyeballs. Pipe tip 2 outline eyebrows and mouth, pipe-in teeth.

2 **Make arms and legs.** Roll out spice drops on parchment paper sprinkled with sugar. Use scissors to cut hands and feet. Attach hands to pretzel sticks with icing; insert in cupcake. Cut licorice pieces, 1½ in. long, for legs. Attach feet to licorice with icing; insert in cupcake. Each serves 1.

*Combine Leaf Green with Lemon Yellow for green shown. Combine Sky Blue with Teal for blue shown.

B

ⓒ The Cupcake *Creature*

Pans: Dimensions Large Cupcake, p. 159; Mini Muffin, 10 in. x 16 in. Cooling Grid, p. 158

Tips: 2A, 4B, 12, p. 162

Colors:* Leaf Green, Lemon Yellow, Violet, Rose, Black, p. 163

Fondant: White Ready-To-Use Rolled Fondant (9 oz.), 9 in. Fondant Roller, Roll-N-Cut Mat, Fondant Trimmer, p. 164; Brush Set, p. 165

Recipe: Buttercream Icing, p. 143

Also: Mouth Pattern, p. 153; Primary (red), Jewel (gold, teal) Mini Baking Cups, p. 155; Small Candy Eyeballs, p. 157; Piping Gel, p. 160; Plastic Dowel Rods, Cake Boards, Circles, Fanci-Foil Wrap, 12 in. Disposable Decorating Bags, p. 161

See p. 7 for a list of Wilton essential cupcake products and other commonly used decorating items you may need.

INSTRUCTIONS

1 **Make arms.** 1 day in advance, tint 1½ oz. fondant violet, 2½ oz. green. Roll out violet ⅛ in. thick. Use fondant trimmer to cut two strips, 2½ in. x 3 in. Cut two dowel rods to 5 in.; brush with piping gel; cover with violet strips. Leave ½ in. exposed on one end for hand, leave 1½ in. exposed on other end to insert into cake.

For hands, divide green fondant into two flattened wedges, 2 in. x 2 in., tapering from ¾ in. at wrist to ⅜ in. thick at fingers. Push narrow end onto dowel rod. Shape into hands; cut slits, ½ in. apart and 1 in. deep, for fingers. Use your hands to round edges. Let set on cornstarch-dusted boards.

2 **Prepare 2-piece large cupcake.** Cut off top two swirls from top cake and trim top of bottom cake level. Attach top half to bottom with icing. Cover bottom cake sides with tip 12 vertical outlines in violet. Insert arms into sides, angled downward so hands rest on table.

For eyes, roll white fondant balls, 1⅝ in. dia. Flatten backs and attach, 1½ in. apart, and 1 in. above center seam. Cover top cake with tip 4B pull-out stars in green.

3 **Add large cupcake details.** Tint 2½ oz. fondant black. Roll out fondant ⅛ in. thick. Use pattern to cut out mouth; push into icing to attach. Outline mouth with tip 12 in violet. Roll out black fondant ¹⁄₁₆ in. thick. Cut pupils using wide end of tip 2A; attach with piping gel. For eyebrows, cut two strips, ¾ in. x 1¾ in. Cut slits for eyelashes, ⅛ in. wide and ½ in. deep; attach strips around eyeballs. Reserve excess fondant.

For teeth, roll out white fondant ¹⁄₁₆ in. thick. Cut five triangles, ⅝ in. wide x 1 in. long. Attach to mouth with piping gel.

4 **Prepare mini cupcakes.** Cover tops with tip 2A swirl in white. Position candy eyeballs. Roll out reserved black fondant to ¹⁄₁₆ in. thick. Cut mouths using narrow end of tip 2A; attach with piping gel.

Position mini cupcakes around large cupcake. Cake serves 12; each mini serves 1.

*Combine Leaf Green with Lemon Yellow for green shown. Combine Violet with Rose for violet shown.

Ⓐ Fish For Compliments!

Pans: Mini Muffin, 10 in. x 16 in. Cooling Grid, p. 158

Tips: 6, 104, 125, p. 162

Colors:* Violet, Rose, Orange, Lemon Yellow, Golden Yellow, Leaf Green, Royal Blue, p. 163

Recipes: Buttercream, Royal Icings, p. 143

Also: White Mini Baking Cups, p. 155; Small Candy Eyeballs, p. 157; Cupcake Spatula, p. 161; Light Green, Orange, Lavender, Pink, Blue, Yellow Colored Sugars, p. 156; Meringue Powder, p. 160; Cake Boards, p. 161; clear wine glasses

See p. 7 for a list of Wilton essential cupcake products and other commonly used decorating items you may need.

INSTRUCTIONS

1 **Make fins and lips.** 1 day in advance, pipe royal icing trims in desired colors on waxed paper-covered boards. For lips, pipe two tip 6 beads side by side. Pipe tip 104 single petal side fins and 1 in. wide ruffle petal top fins. Pipe tip 125 ruffle petal tail fins, 1¼ in. wide. Let all dry 24 hours.

2 **Prepare mini cupcakes.** Ice smooth with spatula in desired buttercream color. Position candy eyeballs, lips and fins. Place sideways in wine glass filled with 1 to 2 tablespoons colored sugar. Each serves 1.

*Combine Violet with Rose for violet shown. Combine Lemon Yellow with Golden Yellow for yellow shown. Combine Leaf Green with Lemon Yellow for green shown.

B Let's Go Mini *Dipping!*

Pans: Mini Muffin, 10 in. x 2 in. Round, 10 in. x 16 in. Cooling Grid, p. 158

Tips: 2, 2A, p. 162

Colors: Royal Blue, Black, p. 163

Fondant: Natural Colors Fondant Multi Pack (black), 9 in. Fondant Roller, Roll-N-Cut Mat, p. 164; Brush Set, p. 165

Recipe: Buttercream Icing, p. 143

Also: Jewel (teal, purple), Primary (red, yellow) Mini Baking Cups, p. 155; Small Candy Eyeballs, p. 157; Piping Gel, p. 160; 9 in. Angled, 11 in. Straight Spatulas, 12 in. Disposable Decorating Bags, p. 161; blue, white construction paper, glue stick, craft foam block 4 in. x 3 in. x 3 in. deep

See p. 7 for a list of Wilton essential cupcake products and other commonly used decorating items you may need.

INSTRUCTIONS

1. **Make diving board.** In advance, insert blade of 11 in. spatula in craft foam block, 1 in. from top, pushing in until 3 in. of blade extends beyond block. Remove spatula. Wrap block with blue construction paper, securing with glue. Reinsert spatula through paper.

2. **Make pool.** Bake and cool 1-layer round cake in pan, using 4½ to 5 cups batter for a 1½ in. high cake; keep cake in pan. Ice top smooth with angled spatula in blue. Tint piping gel blue. Spread over icing, using spatula to create rippling look.

   For pool sides, cut three blue construction paper strips, each 1¾ in. x 12 in. Attach around outside of pan with glue stick overlapping excess. For vertical posts, cut white construction paper strips, ½ in. x 1¾ in. Attach 2 in. apart.

3. **Prepare mini cupcake swimmers.** Cover tops with tip 2A swirl in white. Outline and pipe in tip 2 smiles. Position candy eyeballs on some; pipe tip 2 outline eyes on remainder.

   For inner tube, roll a 1 oz. black fondant ball into a log, 2½ in. dia. Shape into a ring with a 1½ in. dia. opening. Position one swimmer in ring.

4. **Assemble treats.** At party, position diving board next to pool. Attach mini cupcake to blade with icing; adjust length of blade to balance. Position swimmers in pool by pushing into gel. Cake serves 14; each cupcake serves 1.

C Diving *Buddies*

Pans: Standard Muffin, 10 in. x 16 in. Cooling Grid, p. 158

Tips: 3, 5, p. 162

Colors:* Copper, Black, Golden Yellow, Lemon Yellow, Royal Blue, Brown, p. 163

Fondant: White (½ oz. per treat), Black (1 oz. per treat) Ready-To-Use Rolled Fondant, 9 in. Fondant Roller, Roll-N-Cut Mat, p. 164

Recipes: Buttercream, Royal Icings, p. 143

Also: Primary Standard Baking Cups (blue), p. 155; 12 in. Disposable Decorating Bags, p. 161; Fine Tip Primary Colors FoodWriter Edible Color Markers (black), p. 163; Cupcake Spatula, p. 161; Meringue Powder, Piping Gel, p. 160

See p. 7 for a list of Wilton essential cupcake products and other commonly used decorating items you may need.

INSTRUCTIONS

Make hair. 1 day in advance, decorate with full-strength royal icing on waxed paper-covered surface. Pipe tip 5 wavy lines, 1¼ in. long. You will need approximately 25 to 30 hair strands for each treat. Make extras to allow for breakage and let dry 24 hours.

Make diving gear. 1 day in advance, tint ½ oz. fondant blue for each treat. For goggles, roll out blue ⅛ in. thick. Use knife to cut a 2¼ in. curved bean shape. For goggles border, roll a ³⁄₁₆ in. dia. black log. Attach to edge of goggles with piping gel. For eyes, draw dots with black edible marker. For snorkel, roll a black rope, ¼ in. dia. x 3 in. long. Shape a curve at one end. For mouthpiece, roll a ⅝ in. black fondant ball. Let all dry 24 hours.

Prepare cupcakes. Ice smooth with spatula in copper or brown buttercream. Insert hair into cupcakes. Pipe tip 5 dot noses and tip 3 outline mouths. Attach diving gear to cupcake with icing. Each serves 1.

*Combine Golden Yellow with Lemon Yellow for yellow shown.

His pool pal looks just like him! He's going to love the hydrated hair, made of royal icing waves and inserted in the cupcake top.

A Full-Tilt *Half-Pipe!*

Pans: Standard Muffin, 10 in. x 16 in. Cooling Grid, p. 158

Tip: 2, p. 162

Colors:* Copper (for skin tone shown), Black, Christmas Red, Red-Red, Leaf Green, Violet, Rose, p. 163

Fondant: White Ready-To-Use Rolled Fondant (2½ oz. per treat), Gum-Tex, 9 in. Fondant Roller, Roll-N-Cut Mat, p. 164; Round Cut-Outs Fondant Cutters, Brush Set, Wave Flower Former Set, p. 165

Recipes: Buttercream Icing, Thinned Fondant Adhesive, p. 143

Also: Primary Standard Baking Cups (blue), p. 155; 6 in. Lollipop Sticks, p. 163; Small Candy Eyeballs, p. 157; 9 in. Angled Spatula, Cake Boards, p. 161, round hollow-center fruit-flavored candy

See p. 7 for a list of Wilton essential cupcake products and other commonly used decorating items you may need.

INSTRUCTIONS

1 **Make skateboard.** 2 days in advance, tint 2 oz. fondant green, ⅛ oz. violet. Add ⅛ teaspoon Gum-Tex to green. Tear off strips of violet and position on top of green; roll out ¹⁄₁₆ in. thick. Cut a strip, 2 in. x 4⅛ in. Shape rounded front end with fingers. Bend up one edge of cornstarch-dusted cake board; let skateboard dry with back end resting on bent edge of board.

2 **Make cap.** 2 days in advance, tint 1 oz. fondant red; shape a 1¼ in. ball into a dome, 1½ in. dia. x ½ in. high for base of cap. Divide into fourths and score four section lines with edge of spatula. For button, roll a ¼ in. ball; flatten slightly and attach to top with thinned fondant adhesive. For bill, roll out remaining red fondant ⅛ in. thick. Use medium Cut-Out to cut circle. Let dry on convex side of small flower former, dusted with cornstarch. Attach bill under base with thinned fondant adhesive.

3 **Prepare cupcakes.** Ice smooth with spatula in copper, in a mounded shape. Position eyeballs. Pipe in tip 2 mouth, eyebrows and hair. Smooth hair with finger dipped in cornstarch.

4 **Make arms and hands.** Cut lollipop stick in half. For hands, roll two ½ in. balls of fondant; flatten slightly. Cut ½ in. deep slits for fingers; trim ⅛ in. from thumb. Shape into fingers. Insert lollipop sticks in hands, securing with thinned fondant adhesive. Insert arms in cupcake sides. Position cap.

5 **Make wheels.** For each wheel, attach two hollow-centered candies together with thinned fondant adhesive. Roll small balls of fondant; press into hollow centers. Stack three hollow-centered candies under center of skateboard, securing with thinned fondant adhesive. Position skateboard and cupcake. Each serves 1.

*Combine Christmas Red with Red-Red for red shown. Combine Violet with Rose for violet shown.

B Connect The *Dots!*

Pans: Standard Muffin, 10 in. x 16 in. Cooling Grid, p. 158

Tip: 2A, p. 162

Fondant: Primary Colors Fondant Multi Pack (¾ oz. for each treat), 9 in. Fondant Roller, Roll-N-Cut Mat, p. 164; Brush Set, p. 165

Recipe: Buttercream Icing, p. 143

Also: Rainbow Standard Baking Cups (red, yellow, blue, green), p. 155; Circle Metal Cutter, p. 166; Cupcake Spatula, p. 161; Piping Gel, p. 160

See p. 7 for a list of Wilton essential cupcake products and other commonly used decorating items you may need.

INSTRUCTIONS

Prepare cupcakes. Lightly ice smooth with spatula in white.

Make fondant tops. Roll out primary fondant colors ¹⁄₁₆ in. thick. Cut a circle for each treat using metal cutter; position on cupcake. For posts, roll out fondant ½ in. thick. Cut six circles per treat using narrow end of tip 2A. Soften edges slightly with fingers. Attach posts to cupcakes with piping gel. Each serves 1.

Show your skater you know some tricks, too... like how to decorate a cupcake that will make him flip.

Wilton

⒞ Robots Serve *Man*

Pans: Bar, Jumbo Muffin, 10 in. x 16 in. Cooling Grid, p. 158

Tips: 2, 2A, p. 162

Colors:* Violet, Rose, Black, p. 163

Recipe: Buttercream Icing, p. 143

Also: White Jumbo, Square Baking Cups, p. 154; Cupcake Spatula, p. 161; 4 in. Lollipop Sticks, p. 163; 9 in. Fondant Roller, p. 164; Large Candy Eyeballs, p. 157; Animal Faces Sprinkles, p. 156; 12 in. Disposable Decorating Bags, p. 161; green candy jelly leaves, spice drops, round hollow-center fruit-flavored candy, mini candy-coated chocolates

See p. 7 for a list of Wilton essential cupcake products and other commonly used decorating items you may need.

INSTRUCTIONS

1. **Prepare cupcakes.** Bake and cool one jumbo and one bar cupcake per treat. Ice smooth with spatula in violet.

2. **Make arms, legs and antenna.** Cut five lollipop sticks to 3 in. long. Use knife to trim ⅜ in. off one long side of green candy leaves for two shoes. Insert a lollipop stick in top of each shoe; stack three hollow-center candies over stick. For hands, roll out two spice drops ⅜ in. thick. Use knife to cut hand shape and slits for fingers. Insert a lollipop stick in bottom of each hand; stack three hollow-center candies and slide on stick. For antenna, insert lollipop stick in a spice drop.

3. **Assemble treats.** Position jumbo cupcake head against bar cupcake body. Use tip of knife to poke two holes in bottom side of bar cupcake, ½ in. from top edge and ½ in. from side edge. Insert legs. Use tip of knife to poke a hole in right and left sides of bar cupcake, ½ in. from top and ¾ in. from side edge. Insert arms and antenna.

   Position candy eyeballs, chocolate candy nose. Use tip 3 and black icing to attach spice drop ears and pipe zigzag mouth. Position triangle and oval sprinkles from animal faces set for front panel. Each cupcake serves 1.

*Combine Violet with Rose for violet shown.

Cupcakes that connect with kids. The fondant tops are styled after their favorite building toys, so they can create their own tower of treats.

⒟ Whimsical *Whirlybirds*

Pans: Standard Muffin, 10 in. x 16 in. Cooling Grid, p. 158

Tip: 4, p. 162

Colors:* Red-Red, Christmas Red, Black, p. 163

Fondant: White Ready-To-Use Rolled Fondant (2 oz. per treat), Gum-Tex, 9 in. Fondant Roller, Roll-N-Cut Mat, p. 164; Brush Set, p. 165

Recipes: Buttercream Icing, Thinned Fondant Adhesive, p. 143

Also: 101 Cookie Cutters (L, X), p. 167; Primary Standard Baking Cups (red), p. 155; Cake Boards, 9 in. Angled Spatula, 12 in. Disposable Decorating Bags, p. 161; 4 in. Lollipop Sticks, p. 163, marshmallows and mini marshmallows

See p. 7 for a list of Wilton essential cupcake products and other commonly used decorating items you may need.

INSTRUCTIONS

1. **Make fondant propellers and tail.** 2 days in advance, knead ¼ teaspoon Gum-Tex into 2 oz. fondant for each treat. Tint half red, half gray. Roll out colors ³⁄₁₆ in. thick. Use letter L cutter to cut red tail. Gently press inner corner to widen tail. Use letter X cutter to cut two gray propellers. For main propeller, cut ⅛ in. slits on the top and bottom to widen separation between arms. For small propeller, cut ⅛ in. slits as above. Trim arms to ½ in. long x ⅜ in. wide. Let dry 24 hours on cornstarch-dusted cake board.

   Turn main propeller bottom side up. Roll a gray fondant ball ⅜ in. dia.; slightly flatten bottom. Trim lollipop stick to 3 in. and insert into ball. Attach ball to propeller with thinned fondant adhesive. Let dry 24 hours, supporting stick with crumbled tissue if needed.

2. **Prepare cupcakes.** Generously ice tops smooth with spatula and red icing, shaping into a mound. Pipe tip 4 windows in black; smooth with finger dipped in cornstarch.

3. **Assemble cupcakes.** Attach small propeller to tail with thinned fondant adhesive. Roll two gray fondant balls, ³⁄₁₆ dia., for axles. Attach to top of propellers with thinned fondant adhesive. Insert tail and main propeller into cupcake. Position regular and mini marshmallows around cupcakes. Each serves 1.

*Combine Red-Red with Christmas Red for red shown.

Take the easy approach to treat your favorite golfers. Cover cupcake tops with tip 233 grass and add a lollipop stick and paper flag.

Ⓑ Treats To Spare

Pans: Standard Muffin, 10 in. x 16 in. Cooling Grid, p. 158

Colors:* Red-Red, Christmas Red, Black, p. 163

Fondant: White Ready-To-Use Rolled Fondant (6 oz. makes 10 treats), Gum-Tex, 10-Pc. Gum Paste/Fondant Tool Set, 9 in. Fondant Roller, Roll-N-Cut Mat, p. 164; Brush Set, p. 165

Recipe: Buttercream Icing, p. 143

Also: Pin Top Pattern, p. 152; Monochrome Standard Baking Cups (black, white), p. 155; Piping Gel, p. 160; 4 in. Lollipop Sticks, p. 163; 9 in. Angled Spatula, Cake Boards, p. 161

See p. 7 for a list of Wilton essential cupcake products and other commonly used decorating items you may need.

INSTRUCTIONS

1 **Make pin tops.** 2 days in advance, knead ½ teaspoon Gum-Tex into 6 oz. white fondant. Roll out ⅛ in. thick. Use pattern and knife to cut pin tops. Let dry overnight on cornstarch-dusted boards.

For stripes, tint ½ oz. fondant red. Roll out ¹⁄₁₆ in. thick. Cut strips, ¼ in. x 1 in. Attach at narrowest point of pin top with damp brush, trimming ends as needed. Let dry. Attach a lollipop stick to back of pin top with thinned fondant adhesive, leaving 1½ in. extended for inserting in cupcake. Let dry.

2 **Prepare cupcakes.** Bake and cool 10 in white cups, one in black cup. After cooling white cupcakes, add second white baking cup around each cupcake; secure with dots of piping gel. Ice tops smooth with spatula, pins in white, ball in black.

Using small ball tool from set, dusted in cornstarch, imprint three finger holes in top of ball. Position pin tops in icing.

3 **Assemble treats.** At party, position pin cupcakes in triangle formation. Position ball. Each serves 1.

*Combine Red-Red with Christmas Red for red shown.

Wilton

Ⓐ Going for the Green

Pans: Standard Muffin, Mini Muffin, 10 in. x 16 in. Cooling Grid, p. 158

Tip: 233, p. 162

Color: Leaf Green, p. 163

Fondant: White Ready-To-Use Rolled Fondant (2 oz. makes 6 golf balls), 9 in. Fondant Roller, Roll-N-Cut Mat, p. 164

Recipe: Buttercream Icing, p. 143

Also: Standard and Mini Assorted Pastel Baking Cups (green), p. 155; 6 in. Lollipop Sticks, p. 163; 101 Cookie Cutters (small circle, 1¾ in.), p. 167; 9 in. Straight Spatula, 12 in. Disposable Decorating Bags, p. 161; colored construction paper, black marker

See p. 7 for a list of Wilton essential cupcake products and other commonly used decorating items you may need.

INSTRUCTIONS

Make flags. 1 day In advance, cut paper triangles, 1⅜ in. high (base) x 1¾ in. wide (base to tip). Print numbers. Tape to sticks.

Prepare cupcakes. For mini golf balls, ice tops smooth in white with spatula. Roll out fondant ⅛ in. thick. Cut circles using smallest round cutter. Indent dimples with end of lollipop stick. Position on cupcakes.

For standard cupcake greens, cover tops with tip 233 pull-out grass. Insert flags. Each serves 1.

Cupcakes have always been perfect team treats. You can make them an even bigger hit by personalizing the players with candy eyeballs and a dimensional fondant cap.

Ⓒ Rally Cups

Pans: Standard Muffin, Mini Muffin, 10 in. x 16 in. Cooling Grid, p. 158

Tips: 2, 3, 12, p. 162

Colors: Copper, Rose, Black, Brown, Royal Blue, Christmas Red, Red-Red, p. 163

Fondant: White Ready-To-Use Rolled Fondant (2 oz. makes 6 treats), 9 in. Fondant Roller, Roll-N-Cut Mat, p. 164

Recipe: Buttercream Icing, p. 143

Also: Pastel Standard and Mini Baking Cups (green), p. 155; Round Comfort-Grip Cutter, p. 166; Small Candy Eyeballs, p. 157; 12 in. Disposable Decorating Bags, Cupcake Spatula, p. 161

See p. 7 for a list of Wilton essential cupcake products and other commonly used decorating items you may need.

INSTRUCTIONS

1 **Prepare standard and mini cupcakes.** Ice smooth with spatula, using copper or brown for faces, white for baseballs. Pipe tip 2 outline stitching on baseballs.

2 **Make cap brims.** Tint 2 oz. fondant blue; roll out ⅛ in. thick. Use round cutter to cut a circle; move cutter down 1 in. and cut crescent shape 3 in. wide for brim. Curve to shape and position on face, ¾ in. from top edge. Outline and pipe in area above brim with tip 12; pat smooth with finger dipped in cornstarch. Pipe tip 3 section lines and dot button on caps.

3 **Make faces.** Attach candy eyeballs with tip 3 dots. Pipe tip 3 outline mouth. Pipe tip 3 dot cheeks; flatten and smooth with finger dipped in cornstarch. Each serves 1.

*Combine Red-Red with Christmas Red for red shown.

ⓐ Candy *Cutie*

Pans: Jumbo Muffin, Mini Ball, p. 158

Tip: 12, p. 162

Color: Rose, p. 163

Fondant: White Ready-To-Use Rolled Fondant (3 ½ oz. per treat), Gum-Tex, 9 in. Fondant Roller, Roll-N-Cut Mat, p. 164; Brush Set, p. 165

Candy: White (7 oz. per treat), Light Cocoa (1 oz. per treat) Candy Melts Candy, Primary (orange), Garden (pink, black) Candy Color Sets, p. 163

Also: White Jumbo Baking Cups, p. 155; Small Candy Eyeballs, p. 157; 15 in. Parchment Triangles, Cake Boards, p. 161; favorite candies

See p. 7 for a list of Wilton essential cupcake products and other commonly used decorating items you may need.

INSTRUCTIONS

1. **Make fondant bow.** 1 day in advance, tint 1 oz. fondant rose. Knead in ⅛ teaspoon Gum-Tex. Roll out ¹⁄₁₆ in. thick. Cut a strip, ¾ in. x 4 in. Fold ends to meet at center; secure with damp brush. Pinch center slightly.

   For knot, cut a strip, ⅜ in. x 2 in. Wrap around bow center and secure using damp brush. Support loop openings with tissue; let dry overnight on cornstarch-dusted board. Reserve excess fondant for dots.

2. **Make bottom candy shell.** (p. 151) Tint 2 oz. melted white candy with pink candy color. Spoon 2 or 3 tablespoons melted pink candy into jumbo baking cup. Brush up sides, keeping an even top edge. Chill until firm. Repeat until you have a ¼ in. thick shell. Carefully peel off baking cup.

3. **Make face shell.** Tint 5 oz. melted white candy with orange candy color. Fill one cavity of mini ball pan. Tap to settle; chill for 8 to 10 minutes. Pour out center, leaving a ¼ in. thick shell. Chill until firm; unmold onto soft cloth. Set edge-side down on waxed paper-covered board. Pipe hair using melted light cocoa candy in cut parchment bag; let set.

4. **Assemble shells and add trims.** Position face on bottom shell. Attach candy eyeballs with melted candy. Tint small amount of melted light cocoa candy with black candy color. Use cut parchment bag to pipe outline lashes and smile. Melt pink candy; pipe bead heart lips.

5. **Make spiral hat.** Roll 2½ oz. white fondant into a log, ½ in. dia. x 20 in. long. Begin with a 3 in. dia. circle and wrap around, securing rows with damp brush.

   Attach hat to head and bow to hat using melted candy.

6. **Make dots.** Roll out reserved rose fondant ¹⁄₁₆ in. thick. Use narrow end of tip 12 to cut dots. Use melted candy to attach dots for cheeks and to decorate hat. Fill treat with sweet surprises.

*Combine Red-Red with Christmas Red for red shown.

ⓑ Chic *Boutique*

Pans: Standard Muffin, 10 in. x 16 in. Cooling Grid, p. 158

Tips: 1, 1A, 2, 3, p. 162

Colors: Red-Red, Black, p. 163

Fondant: Black Ready-To-Use Rolled Fondant (½ oz. makes 4 treats), 9 in. Fondant Roller, Roll-N-Cut Mat, p. 164; Leaf Cut-Outs Fondant Cutters, p. 165

Recipe: Buttercream Icing, p. 143

Also: Flowers, Pink Zebra, Zebra, Pink/Purple/Orange Stripes, Pink Dots ColorCups Standard Baking Cups, Red Dots, Bright Rainbow (blue, purple), Monochrome (black) Standard Baking Cups, p. 155; Small Candy Eyeballs, p. 157; White, Blue Sugar Pearls, p. 156; Piping Gel, p. 160

See p. 7 for a list of Wilton essential cupcake products and other commonly used decorating items you may need.

INSTRUCTIONS

1. **Prepare cupcakes.** Use tip 1A to cover tops with swirl in white.

2. **Decorate faces.** Position candy eyeballs or pipe tip 2 outline eyes in black. Pipe tip 1 pull-out lashes on all except face with glasses.

   For black mouths, roll out fondant ¹⁄₁₆ in. thick. Use wide end of tip 1A to cut a curve; move tip up ¼ in. to cut out crescent shape. Position on cupcake. For red mouth, pipe tip 3 bead heart. For glasses, use small leaf Cut-Out to cut two shapes; reverse for second shape. Use knife to cut out inner leaf, leaving ³⁄₁₆ in. frames. Position over eyeballs. Cut a black strip, ⅛ in. x ¼ in. for bridge piece; position.

3. **Position jewelry.** For earrings, position blue Sugar Pearls. For necklace, attach white sugar pearls with dots of piping gel. Each serves 1.

Wilton

ⓒ Heaven-Scent *Treats!*

Pan: Standard Muffin, p. 158

Color: Rose, p. 163

Fondant: White Ready-To-Use Rolled Fondant (½ oz. per treat), 9 in. Fondant Roller, Roll-N-Cut Mat, 9 in. Fondant Roller, p. 164; Deluxe Brush Set, Silver Pearl Dust, Heart Cut-Outs Fondant Cutters, p. 165

Candy: White Candy Melts Candy (5 oz. per treat), Garden Candy Color Set (pink), Dessert Dome Candy Mold, Candy Melting Plate, 4 in. Lollipop Sticks, p. 163

Also: White Standard Baking Cups, p. 155; Pure Lemon Extract, p. 160; Cake Board, p. 161; large marshmallows, small candies or treats

See p. 7 for a list of Wilton essential cupcake products and other commonly used decorating items you may need.

INSTRUCTIONS

1. **Make candy shell cupcake top.** Tint 2 oz. melted candy light pink. Use large dessert dome to make shell, following package instructions. Chill until firm; unmold.

2. **Make candy shell cupcake bottom.** Tint 2 oz. melted candy bright pink. Spoon 2 tablespoons candy into baking cup. Brush up sides, keeping an even top edge. Chill until firm. Repeat until you have a shell ⅛ in. to ¼ in. thick. Carefully peel off baking cup

3. **Make bottle top.** Insert lollipop stick in marshmallow. Dip marshmallow in 1 oz. melted white candy. Remove stick and let set on waxed paper-covered board. Paint with silver Pearl Dust/lemon extract mixture (p. 151). Let set.

4. **Assemble treat.** Fill bottom shell with treats. Position top shell. Attach silver bottle top with melted candy.

5. **Make fondant trims.** Tint fondant rose; roll out ⅛ in. thick. Cut heart using medium Cut-Out. Attach top half of heart to cupcake top, 1 in. from bottom edge, with melted candy. For bow, cut a strip, ⁵⁄₁₆ in. x 4 in. Loop ends over and attach at center with damp brush. For knot, cut a strip, ⁵⁄₁₆ in. x 1 in.; wrap around bow loops and secure in back. Attach bow with melted candy. Each serves 1.

Each flower holds a fondant fairy, to make the day magical. Our petal baking cups transform the cupcakes into beautiful blossoms.

Ⓐ Stylized Butterflies

Pans: Standard Muffin, 10 in. x 14 in. Cooling Grid, p. 158

Colors:* Royal Blue, Violet, Rose, Kelly Green, Brown, Black, p. 163

Fondant: White Ready-To-Use Rolled Fondant (1 oz. makes 3 treats), 9 in. Fondant Roller, Roll-N-Cut Mat, Gum-Tex, p. 164; Brush Set, Oval Cut-Outs Fondant Cutters, p. 165

Recipes: Buttercream Icing, Thinned Fondant Adhesive, p. 143

Also: Black Dots Standard Baking Cups, p. 155; Cupcake Spatula, p. 161; White Pearl Dust, p. 165; 10 in. x 14 in. Cake Boards, p. 161

See p. 7 for a list of Wilton essential cupcake products and other commonly used decorating items you may need.

INSTRUCTIONS

1 **Make butterfly wings.** 1 day in advance, knead in ⅛ teaspoon Gum-Tex to each 1 oz. fondant. Roll out ¹⁄₁₆ in. thick as needed. Cut four wings using medium oval Cut-Out. Trim two ovals ¼ in. shorter for bottom wings using medium oval Cut-Out. Cut openings using smallest oval Cut-Out; position Cut-Out ¼ in. from bottom edge. Let dry 24 hours on cornstarch-dusted boards. Brush wings with dry white Pearl Dust. Attach head to body with thinned fondant adhesive.

2 **Make butterfly heads and bodies.** 1 day in advance, roll a ball ½ in. dia. for head. Roll a log, ½ in. dia. x 2 in. long, for body.

3 **Prepare and decorate cupcakes.** Ice cupcakes smooth with spatula in green, violet or blue. Position head and body. Insert wings in cupcake at an angle; support with additional icing if necessary. Each serves 1.

*Combine Violet with Rose for violet shown. Combine Royal Blue with a touch of Black for blue shown. Combine Kelly Green with Brown for green shown.

Ⓑ Garden Party Guests

Pans: Standard Muffin, 10 in. x 16 in. Cooling Grid, p. 158

Tip: 2A, p. 162

Colors:* Violet, Rose, Golden Yellow, Lemon Yellow, Copper (light skin tone shown), Brown (dark skin tone shown), Black, p. 163

Fondant: White Ready-To-Use Rolled Fondant (1½ oz. per treat), 9 in. Fondant Roller, Roll-N-Cut Mat, p. 164; Brush Set, Heart Cut-Outs Fondant Cutters, p. 165

Recipe: Buttercream Icing, p. 143

Also: Pink, Yellow, Lavender Petal Baking Cups, p. 154; White Sparkling Sugar, p. 156; Flower Stamen Assortment (glitter used), p. 165; Cake Boards, p. 161; Extra Fine Tip FoodWriter Edible Color Markers (black), p. 163

See p. 7 for a list of Wilton essential cupcake products and other commonly used decorating items you may need.

INSTRUCTIONS

1 **Make fondant fairies.** (p. 150) 1 to 2 days in advance, for each figure, tint 1 oz. dress color, ¼ oz. skin tone, ⅛ oz. hair color. For dress, reserve two ¼ in. balls for sleeves. Roll remainder into a cone 1¼ in. high with flat top and 1¼ in. dia. flat bottom. Using skin tone, roll a ⅝ in. ball for head. Attach to dress using damp brush.

For arms, roll logs, ³⁄₁₆ in. dia. x ¾ in. long. Flatten one end for hand; cut slits ¼ in. deep for thumb and fingers. Attach in position. Shape sleeves by cupping reserved balls. Attach. Roll out white fondant ¹⁄₁₆ in. thick. Cut two wings using smallest heart Cut-Out. Attach to back.

2 **Make hair.** 1 day in advance, roll out fondant ¹⁄₁₆ in. thick. For each treat, cut three hearts using medium Cut-Out; cut two hearts in half vertically. Place three heart halves on cornstarch-dusted mat, points facing up. Cut slits on wide end, ¾ in deep x ¹⁄₁₆ in. wide. Wrap ends around toothpick to form flip. Attach halves over back and sides of head, positioning pointed ends at top.

For bangs, cut ½ in. off bottom point of whole heart. Cut slits on wide end of cut point ⅜ in. deep x ¹⁄₁₆ in. wide. Attach bangs, point up. Fold one glitter stamen into a "V"; insert for antennae. Use edible marker to draw dot eyes and outline smile. Let dry overnight on cornstarch-dusted board.

3 **Prepare cupcakes.** Cover top with tip 2A swirl. Sprinkle with sparkling sugar. Position figures. Each serves 1.

*Combine Violet with Rose for violet shown. Combine Golden Yellow with Lemon Yellow for yellow shown.

ⓒ School's in Session!

Pans: Standard Muffin, 10 in. x 16 in. Cooling Grid, p. 158

Tip: 12, p. 162

Colors:* Royal Blue, Sky Blue, Orange, Pink, Lemon Yellow, Golden Yellow, Leaf Green, Kelly Green, p. 163

Fondant: White Ready-To-Use Rolled Fondant (12 oz.), Gum-Tex, 9 in. Fondant Roller, Roll-N-Cut Mat, 10-Pc. Gum Paste/Fondant Tool Set, p. 164; Brush Set, Round, Heart Cut-Outs Fondant Cutters, Sea Life Fondant & Gum Paste Mold, p. 165

Recipe: Buttercream Icing, p. 143

Also: 13-Count Cupcakes-N-More Dessert Stand, p. 167; Celebrate Blue ColorCups Standard Baking Cups, p. 154; Mini Doll Pick Set, p. 161; White Candy Melts Candy, 6 in. Lollipop Sticks, p. 163; Small Candy Eyeballs, p. 157; Jumbo Hearts Sprinkles, p. 156; Piping Gel, p. 160; 15 in. Parchment Triangles, 12 in. Disposable Decorating Bags, Cupcake Spatula, 12 in. Cake Boards, p. 161

See p. 7 for a list of Wilton essential cupcake products and other commonly used decorating items you may need.

INSTRUCTIONS

Make coral and shells. 2 days in advance, tint 2 oz. portions each of fondant pink, coral, yellow, aqua and orange. Knead ¼ teaspoon Gum-Tex into each. Reserve a ½ in. ball of pink fondant for the mermaid's top.

Press fondant in the sea life mold (p. 150) to make 24 pieces of coral and 24 shells in assorted colors. Let dry 48 hours on boards dusted with cornstarch. Reserve remaining fondant for fish.

To complete coral: Cut lollipop sticks to 3 in. long. Attach stick to back of half of the coral pieces with melted candy, leaving 2 in. extended at bottom to insert in cupcake. For larger coral pieces, attach a second piece of coral on top of main piece with melted candy. Let set.

Make fish. 1 day in advance, roll out reserved tinted fondant ¹⁄₁₆ in. thick. Cut 11 bodies using the medium round Cut-Out. Cut 11 tail fins and 11 top fins using smallest heart Cut-Out. Attach jumbo hearts sprinkles, for matching color lips to bodies with melted candy. Attach contrasting color fins. Attach candy eyeballs with melted candy. Let dry overnight on boards dusted with cornstarch. Attach fish to coral with melted candy. Let set.

Prepare cupcakes. Ice cupcake tops smooth in blue with spatula. Position on dessert stand.

Decorate mermaid. Roll out the reserved pink fondant ball ¹⁄₁₆ in. thick. Cut a strip ⅝ in. wide x 3 ½ in. long, for bikini top. Cut notches at center using the point of smallest heart Cut-Out. Attach top around doll pick with piping gel.

Make the mermaid's torso. Tint 2 oz. fondant green. Knead in ⅛ teaspoon Gum-Tex. Shape a tapered log 1 in. wide at top x 4 in. long, tapering to ½ in. wide 3¼ in. from top. Pinch area below 3¼ in. for tail. Flatten tail with fondant roller; trim and shape to 2 in. wide. Score lines in tail with veining tool. Use narrow end of tip 12 to imprint U-shaped scales over torso.

Position torso on top cupcake. Curve to the side and insert doll pick. Pinch torso around waist. Position on dessert stand.

Position remaining trims. Insert coral. Position shells. Each serves 1.

*Combine Pink with Orange for coral color shown. Combine Lemon Yellow with Golden Yellow for yellow shown. Combine Kelly Green with Sky Blue for aqua shown.

Ⓐ Princess' Party *Palace!*

Pans: Dimensions Large Cupcake, p. 159; Standard Muffin, 10 in. x 16 in. Cooling Grid, p. 158

Tips: 2, 2A, 3, 12, 14, p. 162

Colors: * Violet, Rose, Leaf Green, Brown, Black, Copper, Lemon Yellow, Golden Yellow, p. 163

Fondant: White Ready-To-Use Rolled Fondant (24 oz.), 9 in. Fondant Roller, Roll-N-Cut Mat, p.164; Fabric Fondant & Gum Paste Mold, Leaf Cut-Outs Fondant Cutters, Brush Set, p. 165

Recipes: Buttercream Icing, Thinned Fondant Adhesive, p. 143

Also: Door Pattern, Small, Medium and Large Turret Window Patterns, Side Window Patterns, p. 152; Princess Standard Baking Cups, p. 155; Crown with Hearts Royal Icing Decorations, p. 157; Cupcake Spatula, 12 in. Disposable Decorating Bags, 6 in. Cake Circles, Fanci-Foil Wrap, Plastic Dowel Rods, p. 161; Piping Gel, p. 160; 6 in. Lollipop Sticks, p. 163; sugar cones

See p. 7 for a list of Wilton essential cupcake products and other commonly used decorating items you may need.

INSTRUCTIONS

1 **Make castle turrets.** 1 day in advance, use knife to cut two dowel rods to 3¾ in. high and one each to 4½ in. high and 3 in. high.

For turret peaks, use a knife to mark sugar cones at specified heights: three at 2¾ in. from tip of cone and one at 2⅛ in. Fill glass with water and dip wide end of cones to marked heights. Remove and trim at marked heights. Let dry.

Tint 16 oz. fondant violet, 4 oz. light rose and 2 oz. dark rose. Roll out light rose 1⁄16 in. thick. Cut two strips, 2¼ in. x 3 in.; one strip, 3 in. x 3 in., and one strip, 1½ in. x 3 in. Wrap around dowel rods, securing with piping gel, leaving 1½ in. uncovered at bottom for inserting into cake.

For turret windows, roll out dark rose 1⁄16 in. thick. Use patterns and knife to cut one small, one large and two medium windows. Attach to turrets with damp brush. Press dark rose fondant into fabric mold to make one large ribbon(p. 150). Trim dotted edges off ribbons, ¼ in. wide, and cut to fit around windows, securing with damp brush.

To complete turret peaks, roll out violet fondant ⅛ in. thick. Cut strips, 3½ in. x 3 in., for each cone. Secure with piping gel, trimming to fit. Let all pieces dry 24 hours.

2 **Make fondant accents.** 1 day in advance, tint 2 oz. fondant green. Roll out ⅛ in. thick. Use small leaf Cut-Out to cut 25 to 30 leaves. Press light rose fondant in fabric mold to make seven button flowers and eight small 4-hole buttons. Cut four lollipop sticks to 3 in. Attach lollipop sticks at a 90° angle to backs of button flowers using thinned fondant adhesive. Let all dry 24 hours.

3 **Prepare 2-piece large cupcake.** Bake and cool.

4 **Decorate large cupcake bottom.** Mark side window and door areas on cake, 2 in. apart, with windows 1¼ in. from bottom of cake. Ice areas smooth in white. For door, roll out violet fondant ⅛ in. thick. Use pattern and knife to cut door. Use side window pattern and knife to cut two windows. Attach to cake with damp brush. Press violet fondant in fabric mold to make three small ribbons. Cut strips to fit around door and side windows for frames. Attach with damp brush. For door window, roll out dark rose fondant 1⁄16 in. thick. Use small window pattern and knife to cut door window; attach with damp brush.

Ⓐ

Use tip 2A to pipe vertical lines in recessed areas of cake with light rose icing. Repeat for raised areas of cake.

5 **Assemble castle.** Position large cupcake top. Cover top with tip 12 teardrop shingles in violet, starting from bottom edge. Insert turrets in cake top. Attach turret peaks to turrets with piping gel.

For bushes, roll a ball of green fondant ¾ in. dia. Position below side windows. Attach leaves and buttons with piping gel. For swags, roll out remaining violet fondant 1⁄16 in. thick. Use knife to cut seven rectangles, 4 in. x 3 in. Fold rectangles into thirds; pinch ends and shape into a curve. Use scissors to slightly trim and taper backs of swag ends. Insert button flowers on sticks, along edge of cupcake top, positioning first above door peak

and remaining 2¾ in. apart leaving ¼ in. of stick extended. Position swags, hooking over sticks.

6 **Prepare cupcakes.** Ice tops smooth with spatula in white.

7 **Decorate princesses.** Pipe tip 12 ball face, 1 in. dia., in brown or copper; smooth with finger dipped in cornstarch. Pipe tip 14 pull-out hair in brown, tip 3 outline hair in yellow or tip 3 swirl hair in black. Pipe tip 2 dot eyes and outline mouth in brown or black. Position crown icing decoration. Position cupcakes around castle. Large cupcake serves 12; each cupcake serves 1.

*Combine Violet with Rose for violet shown. Combine Lemon Yellow with Golden Yellow for yellow shown.

ⓑ Tea In China

Pans: Standard Muffin, Mini Muffin, Non-Stick Cookie Sheet, 10 in. x 16 in. Cooling Grid, p. 158

Tip: 2, p. 162

Candy: White (8 oz. makes 4 treats), Peanut Butter Candy Melts Candy (1 oz. makes 4 treats), Garden Candy Color Set (pink), Candy Dipping Set, Dessert Dome Candy Mold, p. 163

Also: Round Cut-Outs Fondant Cutters, p. 165; 15 in. Parchment Triangles, Parchment Paper, p. 161; mini pretzel twists

See p. 7 for a list of Wilton essential cupcake products and other commonly used decorating items you may need.

INSTRUCTIONS

1. **Make candy lid and saucers.** 1 day in advance, follow mold instructions to make shell in large cavity. Chill until firm. For each saucer, place largest Cut-Out on cookie sheet. Fill ⅛ in. deep with melted candy. Chill until firm.

2. **Prepare cupcakes without baking cups.** For teacups, place mini cupcakes bottom side up, on cooling grid over cookie sheet. Cover with melted white candy; tap grid lightly to release air bubbles. Chill until firm. Repeat if needed. Turn mini cupcakes bottom side down. Using melted white candy in cut parchment bag, pipe a line around top edge. Chill until firm. Pipe in top with melted peanut butter candy. Chill until firm.

   For teapot, turn cupcake bottom side up and cover top with melted candy as above. Chill until firm.

3. **Decorate teapot, cups and lid.** Tint 1 oz. white candy pink. Use tip 2 to pipe ball handle and scallops on lid, bead flowers on teapot and cups. Use melted white candy in cut bag to pipe dot flower centers. Chill until firm. Position lid on cookie sheet. Pipe a line of melted candy around base; chill until firm.

4. **Cover handles and spout with candy.** Carefully break mini pretzels in handle and spout shapes. Dip in melted candy; chill until firm. Attach to teapot and cups with melted candy; let set. Position lid on teapot and cups on saucers. Each serves 1.

ⓒ Upbeat Hearts

Pans: Dimensions Large Cupcake, p. 159; Standard Muffin, 10 in. x 16 in. Cooling Grid, p. 158

Tips: 2, 12, p. 162

Colors:* Violet, Teal, Leaf Green, Orange, Red-Red, Rose, Royal Blue, p. 163

Fondant: White Ready-To-Use Rolled Fondant (26 oz.), Gum-Tex, 20 in. Fondant Roller, Roll-N-Cut Mat, 20 in. Fondant Roller Guide Rings, Storage Board, p. 164; Hearts Cut-Outs Fondant Cutters, White Pearl Dust, Brush Set, p. 165

Recipe: Buttercream Icing, p. 143

Also: Hearts ColorCups Standard Baking Cups, p. 154; Heart Metal Cutter, p. 166; 11 in. Straight Spatula, Cake Boards, Disposable Decorating Bags, p. 161

See p. 7 for a list of Wilton essential cupcake products and other commonly used decorating items you may need.

INSTRUCTIONS

1. **Make heart toppers.** 2 days in advance, tint 2 oz. fondant each rose, orange, red, green and blue and 3 oz. violet. Knead in ¼ teaspoon Gum-Tex to 1 oz. of each color and ½ teaspoon to 2 oz. of violet. Reserve remaining fondant. Roll out colors ¹⁄₁₆ in. thick. Use medium Cut-Out to cut two or three hearts from each color. Use metal cutter to cut one violet heart. Let dry on cornstarch-dusted board.

2. **Prepare 2-piece large and 15 standard cupcakes.** Bake and cool.

3. **Create fondant overlay applique for large cupcake bottom.** Roll out reserved tinted fondant ¹⁄₁₆ in. thick. Cut eight hearts in each color using medium Cut-Out. Store hearts in storage board until needed. Make fondant overlay applique (p. 150) on white fondant strip, placing tinted hearts, ⅛ in. to ¼ in. apart. Reroll strip and position following instructions.

4. **Assemble treats.** Position top cupcake section on bottom section. Ice top fluffy in white. Ice standard cupcakes smooth with spatula and icing tinted in lighter shades of heart colors.

   Brush all hearts with white Pearl Dust. Pipe tip 2 name on large heart. Attach hearts to treats with tip 12 dots of icing. Support large heart with a 1 in. ball of fondant. Large serves 12; each cupcake serves 1.

*Combine Violet with Rose for violet shown.. Combine Orange with Red-Red for orange shown. Combine Rose with Royal Blue for dark rose shown.

Ⓐ

Ⓑ Delish *Initials*

Pans: Standard Muffin, 10 in. x 16 in. Cooling Grid, p. 158

Color: Rose, p. 163

Fondant: White Ready-To-Use Rolled Fondant (½ oz. per treat), 9 in. Fondant Roller, Roll-N-Cut Mat, p. 164; Letters/Numbers Fondant & Gum Paste Mold Set, Brush Set, p. 165

Recipe: Buttercream Icing, p. 143

Also: Zebra *Sugar Sheets!* Edible Decorating Paper (1 sheet makes 9 treats), Piping Gel, p. 160; Pink Zebra Standard Baking Cups, p. 155; Cupcake Spatula, p. 161; 101 Cookie Cutters (medium and small round), p. 167; Fine Tip Primary Colors FoodWriter Edible Color Markers (black), p. 163;

See p. 7 for a list of Wilton essential cupcake products and other commonly used decorating items you may need.

INSTRUCTIONS

1 **Prepare cupcakes.** Ice smooth with spatula in white.

2 **Make edible paper backgrounds.** Use black edible marker and medium round cutter to trace circles on shiny side of zebra edible paper. Cut out circles with scissors and position on cupcakes.

3 **Make fondant details.** Tint ½ oz. fondant light rose for each treat. Roll out ¹⁄₁₆ in. thick. Use small round cutter to cut circle. Attach to cupcake top with piping gel. Tint remaining fondant dark rose. Press into mold to make initial. Attach to fondant circle with piping gel. Each serves 1.

Fashion plates without the plates! Couture cupcakes are dressed in leopard and zebra print cups, then topped with outrageous fondant hats.

Ⓐ Greet *Sweet 16!*

Pans: Jumbo Muffin, 10 in. x 16 in. Cooling Grid, p. 158

Color: Rose, p. 163

***Sugar Sheets!* Edible Decorating Paper/Tools:** Zebra (one sheet makes 12 treats), Bright Pink (one sheet makes 30 treats), Dab-N-Hold Edible Adhesive, p. 160

Fondant: White Ready-To-Use Rolled Fondant (1 oz. per treat), 9 in. Fondant Roller, Roll-N-Cut Mat, p. 164; Brush Set, p. 165

Recipe: Buttercream Icing, p. 143

Also: 16 Pattern, p. 152; White Jumbo Baking Cups, p. 155; Round Comfort-Grip Cutter, Circle Metal Cutter, p. 166; Cupcake Spatula, p. 161; Fine Tip Neon Colors FoodWriter Edible Color Markers (pink), p. 163

See p. 7 for a list of Wilton essential cupcake products and other commonly used decorating items you may need.

INSTRUCTIONS

1 **Prepare cupcakes.** Ice smooth with spatula in white.

2 **Decorate cupcakes.** Use circle metal cutter to cut circle from zebra edible paper. Center on cupcake (some icing will show around edge).

Tint fondant rose; roll out ⅛ in. thick. Cut a circle using Comfort-Grip cutter. Beginning in center, use knife to cut assorted points, 1 in. to 1¼ in. long. Attach to zebra circle with edible adhesive. Turn back points; support with tissue until set.

Trace number pattern on bright pink edible paper. Cut out numbers with knife. Attach to zebra circle with edible adhesive. Each serves 1.

Ⓑ

The Height of *Fashion!*

Pans: Standard Muffin, 10 in. x 16 in. Cooling Grid, p. 158

Tips: 2, 5, 16, p. 162

Colors:* Copper, Brown, Red-Red, Orange, Lemon Yellow, Golden Yellow, Rose, Violet, Leaf Green, Teal, Black, p. 163

Fondant: White Ready-To-Use Rolled Fondant (24 oz. makes 24 to 26 treats), Gum-Tex, 9 in. Fondant Roller, Roll-N-Cut Mat, p. 164; Fern and Folk Fondant & Gum Paste Molds, Deep Pink Color Dust, Brush Set, p. 165

Candy: Violet, Vibrant Green, Pink, Blue Candy Melts Candy, 4 in. Lollipop Sticks, p. 163

Recipes: Buttercream Icing, Thinned Fondant Adhesive, p. 143

Also: Zebra, Leopard ColorCups Standard Baking Cups, p. 154; Leopard, Pink Zebra Standard Baking Cups, p. 155; 9 in. Angled Spatula, p. 161; Small Candy Eyeballs, p. 157; Cake Boards, p. 161

See p. 7 for a list of Wilton essential cupcake products and other commonly used decorating items you may need.

INSTRUCTIONS

1 **Make hats.** 2 days in advance, tint 2 oz. portions of fondant each dark and light rose, light and medium teal. Tint 3 oz. fondant each medium and light violet. Tint 4 oz. leaf green, 6 oz. black. Knead ⅛ tsp. Gum-Tex into each portion.

Violet hat: Press black fondant into folk mold (p. 150) to make one medium heart. Roll out light and medum violet and black fondant 1/16 in. thick. In light violet, cut one strip each ¼ in. x 3½ in., ¼ in. x 2 in. and ¼ in. x 1¾ in. long. Shape loops with 3½ in. and 1¾ in. strips; slightly twist one end of 3½ in. strip. Attach ends with adhesive. Cut a v-shape in end of 2 in. strip.

In medium violet, cut one strip each ¼ in. x 4 in., ¼ in. x 3½ in., ¼ in. x 2½ in., ¼ in. x 1½ in. and ¼ in. x 1 in. Shape loops with 4 in. and 3½ in. strips as above; slightly twist end of 3½ in. strip. Shape one 1½ in. strip into a circle; attach ends with adhesive. Cut a v-shape in end of remaining 1½ in. strip and 1 in. strip.

In black, cut one strip each ¼ in. x 2 in. and ⅛ in. x 4 in. Cut a v-shape in end of 2 in. strip. Shape the 4 in. strip into a curl, 2 in. high. Let all pieces dry 24 hours (loops on sides) on cornstarch-dusted boards.

Green hat: Press fondant in folk mold to make black bird and green broad leaf. Roll out green and black fondant 1/16 in. thick. Cut three strips in green, ¼ in. x 4½ in., ¼ in. x 4 in. and ¼ in. x 2 in.; and two strips in black, ¼ in. x 4 in. and ¼ in. x 3 in. Cut strips at angles to make one pointed end. Place strips on sides and shape into curls. Let all pieces dry 24 hours on cornstarch-dusted boards.

Teal hat: Press fondant in fern mold to make one small butterfly each in light teal and medium teal. Slightly fold light teal butterfly. Press fondant in fern mold to make one medium black scroll and one small scroll each in light teal and medium teal. Press fondant in folk mold to make two black leaves. Let all pieces dry 24 hours on cornstarch-dusted boards.

Rose hat: Press fondant in fern mold to make one small fern each in dark rose and black. Trim sides of black fern leaving three to four curls each and a 1 in. stem. Roll out light rose fondant 1/16 in. thick. Cut one strip each ⅜ in. x 3 in. and ⅜ in. x 5 in. Shape into loops as for violet hat, but do not twist. Let dry. Roll out black fondant 1/16 in. thick. Make a ribbon rose (p. 150) using a strip, ¾ in. x 5 in. Let all pieces dry 24 hours on cornstarch-dusted boards.

2 **Assemble hats.** 1 day In advance, attach fondant pieces to lollipop stick with melted candy in matching hat color (use blue for teal hat). Chill until firm.

3 **Prepare cupcakes.** Ice smooth with spatula in copper or brown icing making a mound 1 ¼ in. high. Pipe tip 16 hair in black swirls or zigzags, red swirls, yellow pull-out. Position candy eyeballs. Pipe tip 5 bead heart mouth. Insert hat in cupcake. Pipe tip 2 pull-out eyelashes. Brush cheeks with pink Color Dust. Each serves 1.

*Combine Rose with Violet for dark rose shown. Combine Lemon Yellow with Golden Yellow for yellow shown. Combine Red-Red with Orange for red hair shown.

A

B Ladybug's *Landing*

Pans: Standard, Mini Muffin, 10 in. x 16 in. Cooling Grid, p. 158

Tips: 1, 2, p. 162

Colors: Lemon Yellow, Red-Red, Black, p. 163

Recipe: Buttercream Icing, p. 143

Also: Lavender, Yellow, Pink Petal Standard Baking Cups, White Mini Baking Cups, p. 155; Cupcake Spatula, p. 161; 9 in. Fondant Roller, p. 164; black shoestring licorice, black spice drops

See p. 7 for a list of Wilton essential cupcake products and other commonly used decorating items you may need.

INSTRUCTIONS

1   **Prepare standard and mini cupcakes.** Ice smooth with spatula, standard cupcakes in yellow, mini cupcakes in red.

2   **Decorate ladybug.** For head, slightly flatten spice drop with rolling pin. Position on mini cupcake. Pipe tip 2 dot spots and eyes. Pipe tip 1 dot pupils and outline mouth. Cut licorice pieces, ¾ in. long. Insert into head for antennae. Position ladybug on standard cupcake. Each serves 1.

Kids love having their choice of colors. With these easy bee cupcakes you can give them a choice. Divide your batch and ice a rainbow!

A Lounging *Ladybugs*

Pans: Mini Muffin, 10 in. x 16 in. Cooling Grid, p. 158

Tip: 2, p. 162

Color: Leaf Green, p. 163

Fondant: White Ready-To-Use Rolled Fondant (½ oz. makes 9 treats), 9 in. Fondant Roller, Roll-N-Cut Mat, 10-Pc. Gum Paste/Fondant Tool Set, p. 164; Leaf Cut-Outs Fondant Cutters, Wave Flower Former Set, p. 165

Recipe: Buttercream Icing, p. 143

Also: Grass Mini Baking Cups, p. 154; Ladybug Icing Decorations, p. 157; Cupcake Spatula p. 161

See p. 7 for a list of Wilton essential cupcake products and other commonly used decorating items you may need.

INSTRUCTIONS

1   **Make leaves.** 1 day in advance, tint fondant green. Roll out ¹⁄₁₆ in. thick. Use medium leaf Cut-Out to cut one leaf per treat. Score vein lines with small veining tool from set. Let dry 24 hours on flower former on convex side of small section.

2   **Prepare cupcakes.** Ice tops smooth with spatula in green.

Position leaves on cupcakes. Attach ladybug decorations to leaves with a tip 2 dot of icing. Each serves 1.

B

ⓒ Beeing *Nice*

Pans: Mini Muffin, 10 in. x 16 in. Cooling Grid, p. 158

Tip: 3, p. 162

Colors: Rose, Leaf Green, Orange, Lemon Yellow, Black, p. 163

Fondant: White Ready-To-Use Rolled Fondant (½ oz. per treat), 9 in. Fondant Roller, Roll-N-Cut Mat, p. 164; Round Cut-Outs Fondant Cutters, p. 165

Recipe: Buttercream Icing, p. 143

Also: 6-Pc. Heart Nesting Plastic Cutter Set, p. 166; White Mini Baking Cups, p. 155; Cupcake Spatula, p. 161; 4 in. Lollipop Sticks, White Candy Melts Candy (½ oz. per treat), p. 163; 15 in. Parchment Triangles, p. 159; Fine Tip Primary Colors (yellow), Fine Tip Neon Colors (orange, pink, light green) FoodWriter Edible Color Markers, p. 163; 12 in. Disposable Decorating Bags, Cake Board, p. 161; black shoestring licorice

See p. 7 for a list of Wilton essential cupcake products and other commonly used decorating items you may need.

INSTRUCTIONS

1 **Make wings.** 1 day in advance, roll out fondant ⅛ in. thick. Cut two wings per treat using 2 in. heart cutter from set. Use medium round Cut-Out to cut off tip of heart, ¾ in. down from heart indent. Let dry on cornstarch-dusted board.

Draw wing details with edible marker in color to match desired cupcake color.

2 **Prepare cupcakes.** Ice tops smooth with spatula in rose, yellow, orange or green. Trim lollipop sticks to 3 in. Using a knife, make a ¼ in. cut below edge of baking cup on opposite sides. Insert lollipop stick horizontally through cupcake. Attach wings to stick and edge of baking cup using melted candy in cut disposable bag; hold until set.

3 **Decorate cupcakes.** Pipe tip 3 outline stripes and mouth, dot eyes. Cut licorice to 1½ in. long. Insert for antennae. Each serves 1.

ⓓ Flower *Flyers*

Pans: Mini Muffin, 10 in. x 16 in. Cooling Grid, p. 158

Tip: 12, p. 162

Recipe: Buttercream Icing, p. 143

Also: Yellow, Lavender, Pink Petal Mini Baking Cups, p. 154; Bumble Bee Icing Decorations, p. 157; 12 in. Disposable Decorating Bags, p. 161

See p. 7 for a list of Wilton essential cupcake products and other commonly used decorating items you may need.

INSTRUCTIONS

1 **Prepare cupcakes.** Cover tops with tip 12 swirl in white.

2 **Position bugs.** Place bee icing decoration on top of swirl. Each serves 1.

B Floral *Fiesta*

Pans: Standard Muffin, 10 in. x 16 in. Cooling Grid, p. 158

Tip: 12, p. 162

Colors:* Rose, Violet, Lemon Yellow, Golden Yellow, p. 163

Fondant: White Ready-To-Use Rolled Fondant (¾ oz. per treat), Gum-Tex, 9 in. Fondant Roller, Roll-N-Cut Mat, p. 164; Flower Cut-Outs Fondant Cutters, Brush Set, p. 165

Recipe: Buttercream Icing, p. 143

Also: Retro Floral Standard Baking Cups, p. 155; Cupcake Spatula, p. 161; Fine Tip Primary Colors (yellow), Fine Tip Neon Colors (pink, purple) FoodWriter Edible Color Markers, p. 163; Cake Boards, p. 161

See p. 7 for a list of Wilton essential cupcake products and other commonly used decorating items you may need.

INSTRUCTIONS

1 **Make flowers.** In advance, tint ½ oz. fondant violet, rose or yellow for each treat. Knead in ⅛ teaspoon Gum-Tex. Roll out ⅛ in. thick. Cut flowers using largest Cut-Out. Let dry 24 hours on cornstarch-dusted board.

Draw petal designs using matching color edible marker. For centers, roll out white fondant ¹⁄₁₆ in. thick. Cut circles using wide end of tip 12. Attach centers to flowers with damp brush.

2 **Prepare cupcakes.** Ice tops smooth with spatula in white. Pipe tip 12 dot of icing in center and position flowers on cupcakes. Each serves 1.

*Combine Violet with Rose for violet shown. Combine Lemon Yellow with Golden Yellow for yellow shown.

C Climbing *Vine*

Pans: Standard Muffin, 10 in. x 16 in. Cooling Grid, p. 158

Tip: 124, p. 162

Colors: Rose, Kelly Green, p. 163

Fondant: White Ready-To-Use Rolled Fondant (5 oz. makes 1 vine with tendrils), Gum-Tex, 9 in. Fondant Roller, Roll-N-Cut Mat, p. 164; Brush Set, p. 165

Recipe: Buttercream Icing, p. 143

Also: Rainbow Standard Baking Cups (green), p. 155; Yellow Sugar Pearls, p. 156; Cupcake Spatula, Cake Boards, p. 161

See p. 7 for a list of Wilton essential cupcake products and other commonly used decorating items you may need.

INSTRUCTIONS

1 **Make vine tendrils.** Tint 5 oz. fondant green for each vine needed. Knead in ½ teaspoon Gum-Tex. Roll out ⅛ in. thick. Cut strips: three, 1⅛ in. x 6 in.; and one, 1⅛ in. x 9 in. Curl one end and curve strip into a C-shape. Let dry on sides on cornstarch-dusted boards. Reserve remaining fondant.

2 **Prepare cupcakes.** Ice tops smooth with spatula in rose. Use stiff icing and tip 124 to pipe three rows of wild rose petals (p. 148) on each cupcake. Position three Sugar Pearls in center.

3 **Make vine.** Roll out reserved fondant ⅛ in. thick. Cut a strip, 1⅛ in. x 20 in. Curve over serving platter. Position cupcakes in curves. Position tendrils. Each serves 1.

A Garden on *Glass*

Pans: Standard Muffin, 10 in. x 16 in. Cooling Grid, p. 158

Tip: 4, p. 162

Recipe: Buttercream Icing, p. 143

Also: Bright Rainbow Standard Baking Cups (green), p. 155; Pink Posies, Leaves (each pk. makes 2 treats) Royal Icing Decorations, p. 157; Cupcake Spatula, 12 in. Disposable Decorating Bags, p. 161; champagne glasses

See p. 7 for a list of Wilton essential cupcake products and other commonly used decorating items you may need.

INSTRUCTIONS

1 **Prepare cupcakes.** Ice smooth with spatula in white. Pipe tip 4 white dots in assorted sizes; flatten slightly with fingertip.

2 **Assemble treats.** Position cupcake on overturned glass. Position large flower and small leaf on cupcake top. Attach additional flowers and leaves to glass with icing. Each serves 1.

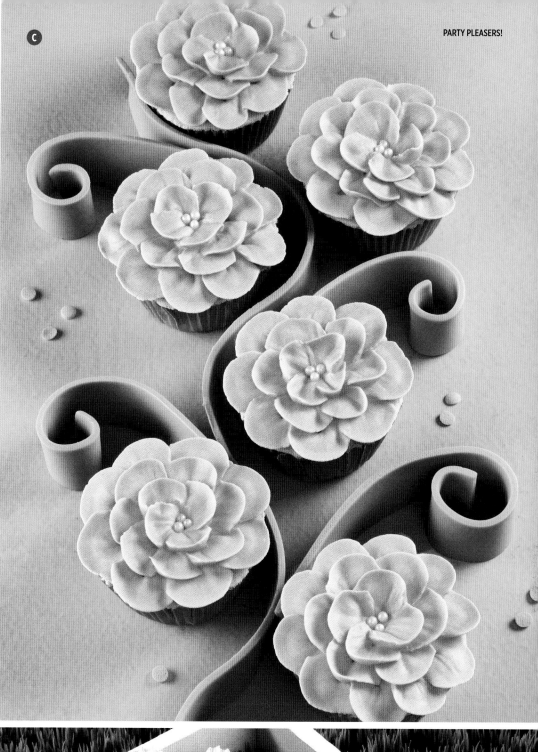

ⓓ Sunning *Butterflies*

Pans: Standard Muffin, 10 in. x 16 in. Cooling Grid, p. 158

Tips: 1A, 7, p. 162

Colors:* Rose, Violet, Sky Blue, p. 163

Recipe: Buttercream Icing, p. 143

Also: Pink, Yellow, Lavender Petal Standard Baking Cups, p. 154; White Sparkling Sugar, p. 156; Butterflies Royal Icing Decorations, p. 157

See p. 7 for a list of Wilton essential cupcake products and other commonly used decorating items you may need.

INSTRUCTIONS

1 **Prepare cupcakes.** Cover tops with tip 1A swirl in white. Sprinkle with sparkling sugar.

2 **Decorate butterflies.** Position wings on an angle. Pipe tip 4 dot head and outline body to match wing color. Each serves 1.

*Combine Violet with Rose for violet shown.

Butterfly blossoms couldn't be simpler or more captivating. Petal baking cups and butterfly icing decorations create a special effect with ease.

www.wilton.com

Ⓐ Gerbera *Garden*

Pans: Dimensions Large Cupcake, p. 159; Standard Muffin, 10 in. x 16 in. Cooling Grid, p. 158

Tip: 12, p. 162

Colors:* Leaf Green, Lemon Yellow, Violet, Rose, Golden Yellow, Orange, p. 163

Fondant/Gum Paste: White Ready-To-Use Rolled Fondant (12 oz.), Ready-To-Use Gum Paste (21 oz.), 9 in. Fondant Roller, Roll-N-Cut Mat, 10-Pc. Gum Paste/Fondant Tool Set, Shaping Foam, Storage Board Fondant Trimmer, p. 164; Gum Paste Flower Cutter Set, Flower Impression Set, Flower Forming Cups, Brush Set, p. 165

Recipes: Buttercream Icing, Gum Glue Adhesive, p. 143

Also: Green Sugar Pearls, p. 156; Piping Gel, p. 160 Zebra ColorCups Standard Baking Cups, p. 154; Zebra *Sugar Sheets!* Edible Decorating Paper (1), p. 160; 9 in. Angled, 11 in. Straight Spatula, p. 161; heavy-duty aluminum foil

See p. 7 for a list of Wilton essential cupcake products and other commonly used decorating items you may need.

INSTRUCTIONS

1 **Make flowers.** 2 days in advance, tint portions of gum paste, ½ oz. light yellow, 4 oz. each rose, violet, green, orange and yellow. Roll out all colors except light yellow ¹⁄₁₆ in. thick. Use large daisy cutter and instructions from flower cutter set to make three or four gerbera daisies in each color with light yellow centers. Use 3 in. flower forming cup to mold additional cups with 4 in. heavy-duty foil squares. Let daisies dry 48 hours in cornstarch-dusted cups.

Attach Sugar Pearls to centers with piping gel. Let dry.

2 **Prepare 2-piece large and standard cupcakes.** Bake and cool.

3 **Decorate large cupcake bottom.** Ice sides smooth with spatula in white. Roll out fondant ¹⁄₁₆ in. thick. Use fondant trimmer to cut six strips, 3½ in. x 4 in. Cut same-size strips from zebra edible paper. Attach zebra strips to fondant with piping gel. Gently press panels onto cake sides, shaping to fit indents.

4 **Assemble treats.** Position large cupcake top section on bottom section. Ice large and standard tops smooth with spatula in white.

Attach three daisies to peak of large cupcake with tip 12 dots of icing. Attach remaining daisies around edge of top section and on each standard cupcake. Large cupcake serves 12; each cupcake serves 1.

*Combine Leaf Green with Lemon Yellow for green shown. Combine Violet with Rose for violet shown. Combine Lemon Yellow with Golden Yellow for yellow shown.

Coordinate your cupcake display using the large cupcake pan. It bakes a cupcake big enough to hold a breathtaking bouquet that complements your single-size treats.

B Garden Art

Pans: Standard Muffin, Medium Non-Stick Cookie Sheet, 10 in. x 16 in. Cooling Grid, p. 158

Tip: 2, p. 162

Colors:* Leaf Green, Lemon Yellow, Rose, Orange, p. 163

Recipes: Buttercream, Royal Icings, Roll-Out Cookies, p. 143

Also: 12 in. Rolling Pin, p. 159; 4-Pc. Football Colored Metal Cutter Set (football), p. 166; Meringue Powder, p. 160; Pink, Orange Colored Sugars, Yellow Sugar Pearls, p. 156; Rainbow Pastel Baking Cups (green), p. 155; 15 in. Parchment Triangles, 9 in. Straight Spatula, p. 161

See p. 7 for a list of Wilton essential cupcake products and other commonly used decorating items you may need.

INSTRUCTIONS

1. **Make cookie petals.** 1 day in advance, prepare and roll out dough. Cut six cookies using football cutter; bake and cool.

   Outline cookies with tip 2 and full-strength royal icing, half in rose and half in orange. Pipe in with matching color thinned royal icing in cut parchment bag. Immediately cover with matching color sugar. Let dry overnight.

2. **Prepare cupcakes.** Ice smooth with spatula in buttercream, using yellow for center cupcake and green for petal cupcakes.

3. **Add trims.** Position Sugar Pearls on center cupcake. Position petal cookies on remaining cupcakes. Position around center cupcake in alternating colors. Each serves 1.

*Combine Leaf Green with Lemon Yellow for green shown.

C Growin' & Glowin'

Pans: Mini Muffin, Cookie Sheet, 10 in. x 16 in. Cooling Grid, p. 158

Tips: 2, 32, p. 162

Colors:* Lemon Yellow, Rose, Orange, Violet, p. 163

Recipes: Buttercream, Color Flow Icings, Roll-Out Cookies, p. 143

Also: 12 in. Rolling Pin, p. 159; Flower Comfort-Grip Cutter, p. 166; White Mini Baking Cups, p. 155; Color Flow Mix, p. 160; Parchment Triangles, p. 161; 6-Mix Nonpareils Sprinkle Assortment, p. 157

See p. 7 for a list of Wilton essential cupcake products and other commonly used decorating items you may need.

INSTRUCTIONS

1. **Make cookies.** In advance, prepare and roll out dough ⅛ in. thick. Cut cookies with flower cutter; bake and cool.

   Prepare one batch Color Flow icing for light colors, one for dark colors. Divide each recipe into thirds and tint light and dark violet, rose and orange.

   Use tip 2 and full-strength Color Flow in cut parchment bag to outline dark outer section of petals; let dry. Flow in with thinned dark color icing; let dry. Flow in inner section of petals with thinned light color icing. Immediately pipe tip 2 thinned dark color dots. Let dry.

2. **Prepare cupcakes.** Cover top with tip 32 swirl. Sprinkle with yellow nonpareils. Position cupcakes on cookies.

*Combine Violet with Rose for violet shades shown.

D Petal Punch

Pans: Standard Muffin, Cookie Sheet, 10 in. x 16 in. Cooling Grid, p. 158

Tip: 3, p. 162

Colors:* Teal, Kelly Green, Orange, Red-Red, Leaf Green, Lemon Yellow, Violet, Rose, p. 163

Recipes: Buttercream, Color Flow Icings, Roll-Out Cookies, p. 143

Also: Flower Cut-Outs Fondant Cutters, p. 165; Color Flow Mix, p. 160; Flowers ColorCups Standard Baking Cups, p. 154; 12 in. Disposable Decorating Bags, Cupcake Spatula, p. 161; 12 in. Rolling Pin, p. 159

See p. 7 for a list of Wilton essential cupcake products and other commonly used decorating items you may need.

INSTRUCTIONS

1. **Make cookies.** 1 day in advance, prepare and roll out dough. Cut cookies using largest flower Cut-Out. Bake and cool cookies. Prepare Color Flow recipe and reserve ½ cup white. Divide remaining icing in fourths and tint teal, green, violet and rose; reserve white. Using tip 3 and full-strength Color Flow in desired colors, outline petals. Let dry. Using thinned white Color Flow in cut disposable bag, flow in petals. Let dry 24 hours.

2. **Prepare cupcakes.** Ice smooth with spatula in orange. Position flower cookie on top. Each serves 1.

*Combine Teal with Kelly Green for teal flower shown. Combine Leaf Green with Lemon Yellow for green flower shown. Combine Violet with Rose for violet flower shown. Combine Orange with Red-Red for orange cupcakes shown.

Smiles
Every Season!

The year goes by fast, so stop and smell the cupcakes! We're filling your calendar with all kinds of timely treat ideas for holidays and every day. Melting witches and snowmen, spring chicks and stand-up bunnies, patriotic pinwheels and more. We've made it even easier to serve a timely treat with our Cupcake of the Month page—a dozen easy ideas that create a year-long cupcake celebration!

Cupcake of the *Month!*

Fill your calendar with cupcakes and celebrate every month of year! We've finished all our treats with a homemade fondant topper, cut with fondant cutters or mini cookie cutters, then added sprinkles color-matched to the season. The setup is the same for all: Make the topper 1 day in advance using white ready-to-use rolled fondant (p. 164) tinted as directed. Bake cupcakes in a standard muffin pan (p. 158) and baking cups (p. 154-155). Ice smooth in buttercream icing (p. 143). Add sprinkles and your topper (support with a tip 5 mound of icing). Each serves 1.

See p. 7 for a list of Wilton essential cupcake products and other commonly used decorating items you may need.

January

Baking Cups: Bright Rainbow (blue), p. 155

Tips: 2, 5, p. 162

Color: Royal Blue, p. 163

Recipes: Buttercream, Royal Icings, p. 143

Also: Round Cut-Outs Fondant Cutters, p. 165; White Sparkling Sugar, p. 156; Meringue Powder, p. 160

INSTRUCTIONS

For topper, roll out fondant ⅛ in. thick. Cut circle with medium Cut-Out. Use tip 2 to pipe outline main snowflake branches, ½ in. apart, in blue royal icing. Pipe tip 2 outline side branches. Let dry 24 hours on cornstarch-dusted board. Ice cupcakes smooth in blue buttercream. Sprinkle with Sparkling Sugar. Position topper.

February

Baking Cups: Pink Dots ColorCups, p. 154

Tip: 5, p. 162

Color: Rose, p. 163

Recipe: Buttercream Icing, p. 143

Also: Heart Cut-Outs Fondant Cutters, p. 165; Pink Sugar Pearls, Jumbo Hearts Sprinkles, p. 156; Piping Gel, p. 160

INSTRUCTIONS

For topper, tint ½ oz. fondant rose for each treat. Roll out fondant ⅛ in. thick. Cut heart with medium Cut-Out. Let dry 24 hours on cornstarch-dusted board. Attach two jumbo hearts to fondant heart with piping gel. Ice cupcakes smooth in white. Position Sugar Pearls and topper.

March

Baking Cups: Bright Rainbow (green), p. 155

Tip: 5, p. 162

Color: Kelly Green, p. 163

Recipe: Buttercream Icing, p. 143

Also: Heart Cut-Outs Fondant Cutters, p. 165; Light Green Colored Sugar, p. 156

INSTRUCTIONS

For topper, tint ½ oz. fondant green for each treat. Roll out fondant ⅛ in. thick. Cut three hearts with small Cut-Out. For backing piece, flatten a ball of fondant ¼ in. dia., into a circle, ½ in. dia. Attach hearts to circle in shamrock shape with damp brush. Trim circle to shape. Use knife to cut a curved stem, ⅛ in. x ⅝ in. Attach with damp brush. Let dry 24 hours on cornstarch-dusted board. Ice cupcakes smooth in white. Sprinkle with light green sugar. Position topper.

April

Baking Cups: Purple Dots, p. 155

Tips: 1, 5, p. 162

Colors:* Golden Yellow, Lemon Yellow, Kelly Green, p. 163

Recipe: Buttercream Icing, p. 143

Also: 12-Pc. Easter Mini Metal Cutter Set (egg), p. 166; Pink, Lavender, Yellow Colored Sugars, Spring Confetti Sprinkles, p. 156; Piping Gel, p. 160

INSTRUCTIONS

For topper, tint ½ oz. fondant pale yellow for each treat. Roll out ⅛ in. thick. Cut egg with mini cutter. Let dry 24 hours on cornstarch-dusted board. Use piping gel in cut parchment bag and tip 1 to pipe zigzags and dots on eggs. Sprinkle with colored sugars.

Ice cupcakes smooth in light green. Position confetti sprinkles and topper.

*Combine Golden Yellow with Lemon Yellow for yellow shown.

May

Baking Cups: Flowers ColorCups, p. 154

Tip: 12, p. 162

Colors: Orange, Teal, p. 163

Recipe: Buttercream Icing, p. 143

Also: 6-Pc. Romantic Mini Metal Cutter Set (blossom), p. 166; Flowerful Medley Sprinkles (daisies), p. 154

INSTRUCTIONS

For topper, tint ½ oz. fondant orange and ⅛ oz. teal for each treat. Roll out orange fondant ⅛ in. thick. Cut flower with mini cutter. Roll out white fondant ¹⁄₁₆ in. thick. Cut flower with mini cutter. Use scissors to cut apart six petals, trimming edges ⅛ in. smaller. Attach to flower with damp brush. Roll out teal fondant ¹⁄₁₆ in. thick. Cut flower center with narrow end of tip 12. Attach with damp brush. Let dry 24 hours on cornstarch-dusted board.

Ice cupcakes smooth in white. Position daisy sprinkles and topper.

June

Baking Cups: Color Wheel, p. 155

Tips: 1, 2, 12, p. 162

Colors:* Black, Orange, Golden Yellow, Lemon Yellow, p. 163

Recipes: Buttercream, Royal Icings, p. 143

Also: Yellow, Black Colored Sugars, p. 156; Meringue Powder, Piping Gel, p. 160

INSTRUCTIONS

For topper, tint ½ oz. fondant yellow for each treat. Roll out ⅛ in. thick. Cut circle with medium Cut-Out. Let dry 24 hours on cornstarch-dusted board. On yellow circle, use tip 2 and orange royal icing to pipe triangle sun rays, ¼ in. wide x ¼ in. deep. At center of rays, pipe tip 12 yellow dot sun. On waxed paper-covered board, use tip 2 and black royal icing to pipe sunglasses, 1 in. wide x ¼ in. deep. Let dry 24 hours. Brush sunglasses with piping gel. Sprinkle with black sugar. Attach sunglasses to sun with royal icing. Pipe tip 1 outline mouth in black.

Ice cupcakes smooth in white. Sprinkle with yellow sugar. Position topper.

*Combine Lemon Yellow with Golden Yellow for yellow shades shown.

July

Baking Cups: Celebrate Blue ColorCups, p. 154

Tips: 2, 5, p. 162

Colors: Royal Blue, Red-Red, p. 163

Recipe: Buttercream Icing, p. 143

Also: 6-Pc. Stars Nesting Plastic Cutter Set (smallest), p. 166; Jumbo Stars Sprinkles, p. 156; Red Sparkle Gel, p. 163

INSTRUCTIONS

For topper, tint ½ oz. fondant blue for each treat. Roll out ⅛ in. thick. Cut star with smallest cutter. Let dry 24 hours on cornstarch-dusted board. Outline and pipe in tip 2 center star in red. Brush center star with sparkle gel. Let dry. Ice cupcakes smooth with spatula in white. Position red and blue jumbo stars and star topper.

August

Baking Cups: Gingham, p. 155

Tip: 5, p. 162

Color: Christmas Red, p. 163

Recipe: Buttercream Icing, p. 143

Also: Dark Green, Light Green Colored Sugars, Chocolate Jimmies, p. 156; Round Cut-Outs Fondant Cutters (large), p. 165; Fine Tip Primary Colors FoodWriter Edible Color Markers (black), p. 163; Piping Gel, p. 160

INSTRUCTIONS

For topper, tint ½ oz. fondant deep pink for each treat. Roll out ⅛ in. thick. Cut a circle using largest Cut-Out. Use knife to cut a wedge shape, 1¾ in. deep with a 2 in. wide curved edge. For rind, use piping gel in cut parchment bag to pipe a line on top and side of round edge. Sprinkle with dark green sugar. Pipe a thin line along inside edge; sprinkle with light green sugar. Use black edible marker to draw seeds. Let dry 24 hours on cornstarch-dusted board.

Ice cupcakes smooth in white. Position melon topper and chocolate jimmies for ants.

September

Baking Cups: Yellow/Blue/Orange/Green Dots ColorCups, p. 154

Tip: 2, p. 162

Colors:* Lemon Yellow, Golden Yellow, Brown, Red-Red, Kelly Green, p. 163

Recipes: Buttercream, Royal Icing, p. 143

Also: 6-Pc. Harvest Mini Metal Cutter Set (apple), p. 166; Rainbow Sparkling Sugar, p. 156; Meringue Powder, p. 160; Fine Tip Primary Colors FoodWriter Edible Marker Set (black), p. 163

INSTRUCTIONS

For topper, tint ½ oz. fondant red and ⅛ oz. green for each treat. Roll out fondant ⅛ in. thick. Cut apple with metal cutter. Use tip 2 and brown royal icing to pipe pull-out worm. Cut green leaf using apple metal cutter; use knife to trim complete shape. Attach with damp brush. Let dry 24 hours on cornstarch-dusted board. Use black edible marker to draw eyes and mouth on worm and hole on apple.

Ice cupcakes smooth in light yellow buttercream. Sprinkle with sparkling sugar. Position topper.

*Combine Lemon Yellow with Golden Yellow for yellow shown.

October

Baking Cups: Jewel (purple), p. 155

Tip: 5, p. 162

Colors:* Leaf Green, Lemon Yellow, Orange, Kelly Green, p. 163

Recipe: Buttercream Icing, p. 143

Also: 6-Pc. Harvest Mini Metal Cutter Set (pumpkin), p. 166; Silver Pearlized Jimmies, p. 156; Fine Tip Primary Colors FoodWriter EdibleColor Markers (black), p. 163

INSTRUCTIONS

For topper, tint ½ oz. fondant orange, ⅛ oz. leaf green for each treat. Roll out orange fondant ⅛ in. thick. Cut pumpkin with mini cutter. Roll out green fondant ¹⁄₁₆ in. thick. Use pumpkin cutter to cut stem only. Attach stem to pumpkin with damp brush. Let dry 24 hours on cornstarch-dusted board. Use black edible marker to draw eyes, nose and mouth on pumpkin.

Ice cupcakes smooth in light green. Sprinkle with silver pearlized jimmies. Position topper.

*Combine Leaf Green with Lemon Yellow for light green buttercream shown.

November

Baking Cups: Jewel (gold), p. 155

Tip: 5, p. 162

Colors:* Orange, Lemon Yellow, Golden Yellow, p. 163

Recipe: Buttercream Icing, p. 143

Also: 6-Pc. Harvest Mini Metal Cutter Set (oak leaf), p. 166; Red Colored Sugar, Flowerful Medley Sprinkles (leaves), p. 156; Piping Gel, p. 160

INSTRUCTIONS

For topper, tint ½ oz. fondant orange for each treat. Roll out fondant ⅛ in. thick. Cut out leaf using mini cutter. Let dry 24 hours on cornstarch-dusted board. Use piping gel in cut parchment bag to pipe vein lines on leaf. Sprinkle with red sugar.

Ice cupcakes smooth in yellow. Sprinkle with leaf sprinkles. Position topper.

*Combine Lemon Yellow with Golden Yellow for yellow shown.

December

Baking Cups: Red ColorCups, p. 154

Tip: 5, p. 162

Color: Kelly Green, p. 163

Recipe: Buttercream Icing, p. 143

Also: 6-Pc. Holiday Mini Metal Cutter Set (tree), p. 166; Jumbo Nonpareils Sprinkles, Gold Pearlized Sugar, p. 156

INSTRUCTIONS

For topper, tint ½ oz. fondant green for each treat. Roll out fondant ⅛ in. thick. Cut tree using mini cutter. Let dry 24 hours on cornstarch-dusted board. Attach jumbo nonpareils to tree with piping gel in cut parchment bag.

Ice cupcakes smooth in white. Sprinkle with silver and gold pearlized sugar. Position topper.

Ⓐ Romantic *Reflections*

Pans: Standard Muffin, 10 in. x 16 in. Cookie Sheet, Cooling Grid, p. 158

Tips: 3, 4, p. 162

Colors:* Teal, Kelly Green, Rose, Orange, Red-Red, p. 163

Recipes: Buttercream, Chocolate Buttercream Icings, Roll-Out Cookies, p. 143

Also: 12 in. Rolling Pin, p. 159; Heart Cut-Outs Fondant Cutters, p. 165; Hearts ColorCups Standard Baking Cups, p. 154; 12 in. Disposable Decorating Bags, Cupcake Spatula, p. 161; Piping Gel, p. 160

See p. 7 for a list of Wilton essential cupcake products and other commonly used decorating items you may need.

INSTRUCTIONS

1 **Make heart cookies.** In advance, prepare and roll out dough. Cut cookies using medium heart Cut-Out. Bake and cool cookies.

2 **Decorate cookies.** Outline hearts with tip 3 in teal, orange or rose buttercream. Tint piping gel to match outlines. Using cut disposable bag, fill in cookies with piping gel.

3 **Prepare cupcakes.** Ice smooth with spatula in chocolate buttercream. Position cookies. Pipe tip 4 dots. Each serves 1.

*Combine Teal with Kelly Green for teal shown. Combine Orange with Red-Red for red/orange shown.

ⓑ Love's Wild *Side*

Pans: Standard Muffin, 10 in. x 16 in. Cooling Grid, p. 158

Colors:* Rose, Violet, Kelly Green, Black, p. 163

Fondant: White Ready-To-Use Rolled Fondant (1½ oz. per treat), 9 in. Fondant Roller, Roll-N-Cut Mat, p. 164; Fabric Fondant & Gum Paste Mold (bow), Brush Set, Hearts, Crinkle Cut-Outs Fondant Cutters, p. 165

Recipes: Buttercream Icing, Thinned Fondant Adhesive p. 143

Also: Zebra ColorCups Standard Baking Cups, p. 154; Zebra *Sugar Sheets!* Edible Decorating Paper (1 sheet makes 12 treats), p. 160; Pink, Green, Violet Color Mist Food Color Spray, White Candy Melts Candy, 6 in. Lollipop Sticks, p. 163; White Sparkling Sugar, p. 156; Cupcake Spatula, 15 in. Parchment Triangles, Cake Boards, p. 161; Piping Gel, p. 160

See p. 7 for a list of Wilton essential cupcake products and other commonly used decorating items you may need.

INSTRUCTIONS

1 **Make heart topper.** 1 day in advance, tint 1¼ oz. fondant per treat to match food color spray colors. Roll out ⅛ in. thick. Use large heart Cut-Out to cut base heart. Reserve remaining tinted fondant. Cut a matching size heart to cover each base from zebra edible paper. Place on cake boards and spray with food color spray in same color used for base. Let dry.

Roll out white fondant ¹⁄₁₆ in. thick. Use mini heart cutter to cut a scalloped heart for each treat. Tint 1¼ oz. white fondant black per treat. Roll out ¹⁄₁₆ in. thick. Use smallest heart Cut-Out to cut top heart.

Attach zebra heart to base with piping gel, then attach scalloped and small hearts with thinned fondant adhesive. Cut lollipop sticks in half. Attach completed heart to lollipop stick using thinned fondant adhesive, leaving 1½ in. extended at bottom to insert into cupcake.

2 **Prepare cupcakes.** Ice tops smooth with spatula in white. Sprinkle with sparkling sugar.

3 **Make bows.** Press reserved tinted fondant into fabric mold to make one bow and small ribbon for each treat. Attach ribbon around cupcake top with icing, leaving opening in the front. Attach bow over opening.

Insert heart topper. Each serves 1.

*Combine Violet with Rose for violet shown.

She lives for wild style and these are the cupcakes for her! It all coordinates—even the zebra patterned heart is in a pretty shade to match the fondant bow.

A A New Level of *Love*

Pans: Standard Muffin, 10 in. x 16 in. Cooling Grid, p. 158

Tip: 2, p. 162

Colors: Rose, Leaf Green, Creamy Peach, Orange, Violet, Sky Blue, p. 163

Fondant: White Ready-To-Use Rolled Fondant (10 oz. makes 20 treats), 9 in. Fondant Roller, Roll-N-Cut Mat, p. 164; Heart Cut-Outs Fondant Cutters, White Pearl Dust, Brush Set, p. 165

Recipes: Buttercream, Royal Icings, Thinned Fondant Adhesive, p. 143

Also: Cake Board, Cupcake Spatula, p. 161; White Standard Baking Cups, p. 155; Parchment Paper, p. 159; White Sparkling Sugar, p. 156; Meringue Powder, p. 160

See p. 7 for a list of Wilton essential cupcake products and other commonly used decorating items you may need.

INSTRUCTIONS

1   **Make hearts.** 1 day in advance, tint 2 oz. fondant each rose, peach, blue, green and violet. Roll out portions of each color ⅛ in. thick and ¼ in. thick. Using Cut-Outs, cut a large heart from ⅛ in. thick fondant and a matching color medium heart from ¼ in. thick fondant for each treat. Attach medium heart to large heart with thinned fondant adhesive. Using tip 2 and royal icing pipe dots on medium heart ¼ in. apart. Let dry. Brush medium heart with white Pearl Dust. Let dry.

2   **Prepare cupcakes.** Ice smooth with spatula in white. Sprinkle with sparkling sugar. Position hearts. Each serves 1.

*Combine Creamy Peach with Orange for peach color shown. Combine Violet with Rose for violet shown.

B Pastel *Passion*

Pans: Standard Muffin, 10 in. x 16 in. Cooling Grid, p. 158

Tip: 2, p. 162

Colors: Teal, Violet, Rose, Kelly Green, p. 163

Fondant: White Ready-To-Use Rolled Fondant (4 oz. makes 4 treats), 9 in. Fondant Roller, Roll-N-Cut Mat, p. 164; Brush Set, p. 165

Recipes: Buttercream, Royal Icings, Thinned Fondant Adhesive, p. 143

Also: 7-Pc. Hearts Metal Cutter Set, p. 166; 4 in. Lollipop Sticks, p. 163; Dotted Ring Standard Baking Cups, p. 155; Meringue Powder, p. 160; Cake Boards, Cupcake Spatula, p. 161

See p. 7 for a list of Wilton essential cupcake products and other commonly used decorating items you may need.

INSTRUCTIONS

1   **Make toppers.** 1 to 2 days in advance, for four toppers in assorted colors, tint 1 oz. fondant each teal, light violet and dark violet to match baking cup colors. Roll out ⅟₁₆ in. thick. Cut two hearts per treat using large stylized or crinkle heart cutters and small heart cutter. Attach small heart to large heart with thinned fondant adhesive. Place hearts on waxed paper-covered board. Let dry at least 24 hours.

Using tip 2 and royal icing, pipe dots on hearts, ¼ in. apart. Attach hearts to lollipop stick with thinned fondant adhesive.

2   **Prepare cupcakes.** Ice tops smooth with spatula in white. Insert topper in cupcake. Each serves 1.

*Combine Violet with Rose for light and dark violet shown. Combine teal with Kelly Green for teal shown.

Valentine's Day gets a color makeover on these fondant heart-topped treats with cool pastels replacing the traditional red and white.

Wilton

ⓓ She's Thinking *Pink*

Pans: Standard Muffin, Cookie Sheet, 10 in. x 16 in. Cooling Grid, p. 158

Tips: 2A, 3, p. 162

Color: Rose, p. 163

Fondant: White Ready-To-Use Rolled Fondant (½ oz. per treat), 9 in. Fondant Roller, Roll-N-Cut Mat, p. 164; White Pearl Dust, Brush Set, Heart, Round Cut-Outs Fondant Cutters, p. 165

Recipes: Color Flow, Buttercream Icings, Roll-Out Cookies, p. 143

Also: 12 in. Rolling Pin, p. 159; 4-Pc. Blossoms Nesting Metal Cutter Set, p. 166; Color Flow Mix, p. 160; Pink Party Standard Baking Cups, p. 155; 15 in. Parchment Triangles, Cake Board, p. 161; Pink Sugar Pearls, p. 156; 4 in. Lollipop Sticks, p. 163

See p. 7 for a list of Wilton essential cupcake products and other commonly used decorating items you may need.

INSTRUCTIONS

1 **Make fondant topper.** 1 day in advance, tint ¼ oz. fondant each light and dark rose for each treat. Roll out ⅟₁₆ in. thick. Cut light rose circle using medium round Cut-Out. Cut dark rose heart using smallest heart Cut-Out. Attach heart to circle with damp brush. Let dry on cornstarch-dusted board.

2 **Make flower cookies.** 1 day in advance, prepare and roll out dough. Cut cookies using second largest (3 ⁱ⁵⁄₁₆ in.) blossom cutter. Bake and cool cookies. Divide and tint Color Flow light and dark rose. Pipe tip 3 outline with full-strength dark rose; let set. Flow in with thinned light rose in cut parchment bag. Let dry on waxed paper-covered board.

Brush cookie and topper with white Pearl Dust. Attach lollipop stick to topper with full-strength Color Flow. Let dry.

3 **Prepare cupcakes.** Cover top with tip 2A swirl in white buttercream. Position Sugar Pearls. Insert topper. Attach cupcake to cookie with full-strength Color Flow. Each serves 1.

Instead of chocolate-covered cherries, give your Valentine homemade cupcakes crowned with a dipped truffle "cherry."

ⓒ Cheery *Cherries*

Pans: Standard Muffin, 10 in. x 16 in. Cooling Grid, p. 158

Tip: 1A (2 needed), p. 162

Color: Rose, p. 163

Recipes: Buttercream Icing, Basic Truffles, p. 143

Also: Brown Dots Standard Baking Cups, p. 155; Red, Dark Cocoa Candy Melts Candy, Brush Set, p. 165; 12 in. Disposable Decorating Bags, p. 161; Piping Gel, p. 160; Red Colored Sugar, White Sparkling Sugar, p. 156; Pearl Color Mist Food Color Spray, p. 156

See p. 7 for a list of Wilton essential cupcake products and other commonly used decorating items you may need.

INSTRUCTIONS

Make truffle cherries. In advance, prepare truffles recipe, rolling into balls, 1 in. dia. Chill until firm. Dip in melted red candy; chill until firm.

Brush truffles with piping gel and immediately roll in red sugar. Let dry on waxed paper-covered surface.

Prepare cupcakes. Tint ⅔ of icing rose; reserve remaining white icing. Edge cupcake with a tip 1A ring in rose. Pipe a second tip 1A ring in white on back edge of rose ring. Pipe tip 1A top ring in rose on back edge of white ring. Pipe tip 1A swirl in rose icing. Spray rings with pearl Color Mist food color spray. Immediately sprinkle with white sparkling sugar. Position cherry truffle. Each serves 1.

 Sweet Natured *Treats*

Pans: Standard Muffin, Cookie Sheet, 10 in. x 16 in. Cooling Grid, p. 158

Tips: 2, 3, 18, p. 162

Colors:* Leaf Green, Royal Blue, Rose, Lemon Yellow, Golden Yellow, Black, p. 163

Recipes: Buttercream, Royal Icings, Roll-Out Cookies, p. 143

Also: 12 in. Rolling Pin, p. 159; Flower Cut-Outs Fondant Cutters, p. 165; 4-Pc. Circles Nesting Metal Cutter Set, p. 166; 101 Cookie Cutters, p. 167; White Candy Melts Candy, 4 in. Lollipop Sticks, p. 163; Meringue Powder, p. 160; Pink Dots Standard Baking Cups, p. 155; 12 in. Disposable Decorating Bags, p. 161

See p. 7 for a list of Wilton essential cupcake products and other commonly used decorating items you may need.

INSTRUCTIONS

1 **Make cookies.** 1 day in advance, prepare and roll out dough. Cut bird body using smallest circle (1 ¾ in.) from 101 Cutter Set. Cut flower using medium Cut-Out. Cut base using third largest circle (3 ¼ in.) from nesting set. Bake and cool cookies. Decorate cookies with royal icing. Use tip 2 and full-strength icing to outline bird, base, flower edge and center. Let dry. Flow in areas with thinned icing. Let dry 24 hours.

2 **Prepare cupcakes.** Cover tops with tip 18 rosettes in white buttercream. Attach flower cookie to lollipop stick with melted candy, leaving 2½ in. extended at bottom; chill until firm. Insert in cupcake top.

3 **Assemble treats.** Complete decorating cookies with full-strength royal icing. For bird, pipe tip 3 bead wings and tail, pipe-in beak and dot eye. Attach cupcake to cookie base with dots of icing. Position bird against cupcake, securing with icing. Each serves 1.

*Combine Lemon Yellow with Golden Yellow for yellow shown.

Wilton

B Bevy of Bluebirds

Pans: Mini Muffin, 10 in. x 16 in. Cooling Grid, p. 158

Tips:* 2, 352, p. 162

Colors: Sky Blue, Golden Yellow, Black, p. 163

Recipe: Buttercream Icing, p. 143

Also: Pastel Mini Baking Cups (blue-green), p. 155; 12 in. Disposable Decorating Bags, 9 in. Angled Spatula, p. 161

See p. 7 for a list of Wilton essential cupcake products and other commonly used decorating items you may need.

INSTRUCTIONS

1 **Prepare mini cupcakes.** Ice smooth in mounded shape with spatula in blue.

2 **Decorate details.** Pipe tip 2 dot eyes. Pipe tip 352 pull-out beak, wings and tail. Each serves 1.

C Ready To Duck-orate?

Pans: Standard Muffin, 10 in. x 16 in. Cooling Grid, p. 158

Tips: 3, 5, 366, p. 162

Colors: Lemon Yellow, Orange, p. 163

Recipe: Buttercream Icing, p. 143

Also: Pastel Standard Baking Cups (yellow), p. 155; Cupcake Spatula, 12 in. Disposable Decorating Bags p. 161; White Ready-To-Use Rolled Fondant (1 oz. per treat), p. 164; 4 in. Lollipop Sticks, Fine Tip Primary Colors FoodWriter Edible Color Markers (black), p. 163

See p. 7 for a list of Wilton essential cupcake products and other commonly used decorating items you may need.

INSTRUCTIONS

1 **Prepare cupcakes.** Ice tops smooth with spatula in yellow.

2 **Make head.** Tint 1 oz. fondant yellow for each treat. Roll a 1¼ in. ball. Cut lollipop stick to 3 in.; insert into head, then insert head into cupcake.

3 **Decorate duck.** Pipe tip 5 pull-out feather tuft and tip 3 pull-out beak. Draw eyes with black edible marker. Pipe tip 366 pull-out wings and tail. Each serves 1.

Ⓐ Huge Holiday *Hugs*

Pans: Standard Muffin, Cookie Sheet, 10 in. x 16 in. Cooling Grid, p. 158

Tips: 2, 4, 12, p. 162

Colors: Leaf Green, Pink, Black, p. 163

Fondant: White Ready-To-Use Rolled Fondant (3 oz. per treat), 9 in. Fondant Roller, Roll-N-Cut Mat, p. 164; Brush Set, Leaf, Funny Flowers, Round Cut-Outs Fondant Cutters, p. 165

Recipes: Buttercream Icing, Roll-Out Cookies, Thinned Fondant Adhesive, p. 143

Also: Pink Dots, Teal Dots Standard Baking Cups, p. 155; 4-Pc. Circles Nesting Metal Cutter Set, p. 166; Cupcake Spatula, 12 in. Disposable Decorating Bags, Cake Boards, p. 161; 6 in. Lollipop Sticks, p. 163

See p. 7 for a list of Wilton essential cupcake products and other commonly used decorating items you may need.

INSTRUCTIONS

1 **Make cookie bases.** 1 day in advance, prepare and roll out dough. For each base, cut one circle using largest cookie cutter. Bake and cool cookies.

2 **Make fondant arms, feet and tail.** 1 day in advance, roll out white fondant ³⁄₁₆ in. thick. Cut hands using medium flower Cut-Out; cut feet using largest flower Cut-Out. Trim off one petal from each flower; pinch one end petal to shape rounded arm and heel. Let all dry overnight on cornstarch-dusted board.

3 **Make fondant ears.** 1 day in advance, tint ¼ oz. fondant pink for each bunny. Roll out white and pink ⅛ in. thick. Cut white outer ear using largest leaf Cut-Out; cut pink inner ear using smallest leaf Cut-Out. Reverse Cut-Outs for second ear. Attach pink to white with damp brush. Let dry overnight on cornstarch-dusted board.

4 **Prepare cupcakes.** Ice cookie base smooth with spatula in green. Position feet. Ice cupcake tops smooth with spatula in white. Pipe tip 2 dot eyes and outline smile, tip 4 dot nose and tip 12 dot cheeks. Position cupcake side down over feet, leaving baking cup on.

5 **Add details.** Cut lollipop sticks to 4½ in. long. For positioning arms, cut holes with knife tip on opposite sides, ¼ in. from top edge of baking cup. Slide lollipop stick through cupcake. Attach hands to ends with thinned fondant adhesive. Insert ears. Each serves 1.

Ⓑ Eclectic *Eggs*

Pans: Standard Muffin, 10 in. x 16 in. Cooling Grid, p. 158

Tips: 2, 3, 4, p. 162

Colors*: Teal, Lemon Yellow, Violet, Rose, Leaf Green, p. 163

Recipe: Buttercream Icing, p. 143

Also: Bright Rainbow Standard Baking Cups (green, yellow, pink, purple), p. 155; Cupcake Spatula, 12 in. Disposable Decorating Bags, p. 161

See p. 7 for a list of Wilton essential cupcake products and other commonly used decorating items you may need.

INSTRUCTIONS

Prepare cupcakes. Ice tops smooth with spatula in white.

Decorate designs. Use tips 3 and 4 to pipe zigzags, wavy lines and straight lines in assorted colors. Pipe tip 3 large dots and tip 2 small dots and dot flowers. Each serves 1.

*Combine Violet with Rose for violet shown. Combine Leaf Green with Lemon Yellow for green shown.

Wilton

You can pull these baskets together quick as a bunny using pretty ruffled baking cups, colorful Jordan Almond eggs, and a textured fondant handle made in our Macrame Fondant & Gum Paste Mold.

C Brimming *Baskets*

Pans: Standard Muffin, 10 in. x 16 in. Cooling Grid, p. 158

Colors:* Rose, Violet, Lemon Yellow, Golden Yellow, Kelly Green, p. 163

Fondant: White Ready-To-Use Rolled Fondant (½ oz. per treat), Gum-Tex, p. 164; Macrame Fondant & Gum Paste Mold, p. 165

Recipe: Buttercream Icing, p. 143

Also: Yellow, Pink, Lavender Ruffled Baking Cups, p. 154; Assorted Jordan Almonds, p. 157; Cake Circles, 9 in. Straight Spatula, p. 161; Parchment Paper, p. 159; shredded coconut

See p. 7 for a list of Wilton essential cupcake products and other commonly used decorating items you may need.

INSTRUCTIONS

1 **Make basket handles.** 1 day in advance, tint ½ oz. fondant for each treat in rose, violet or yellow. Knead in ⅛ teaspoon Gum-Tex for each. Press fondant into macrame mold to make rope strips; curve to form a handle measuring 3 in. wide at bottom. Let dry overnight on cornstarch-dusted board.

2 **Tint coconut.** In advance, place 2 tablespoons of coconut per treat in a zip-close plastic bag. Add a small amount of green color with toothpick. Knead until color is well-blended and to desired shade. Let dry on parchment paper.

3 **Prepare cupcakes.** Ice smooth with spatula in green. Insert almonds and handles in cupcake tops. Sprinkle coconut between almonds. Each serves 1.

*Combine Violet with Rose for violet shown. Combine Lemon Yellow with Golden Yellow for yellow shown.

D Rabbits *Run!*

Pans: Mini Muffin, 10 in. x 16 in. Cooling Grid, p. 158

Tips: 2A, 3, 4, p. 162

Colors: Sky Blue, Rose, p. 163

Fondant: White Ready-to-Use Rolled Fondant (1 oz. makes 8 treats), 9 in. Fondant Roller, Roll-N-Cut Mat, p. 164; Leaf Cut-Outs Fondant Cutters, p. 165

Recipe: Buttercream Icing, p. 143

Also: Jewel Mini Baking Cups (teal, purple), p. 155; 9 in. Angled Spatula, 12 in. Disposable Decorating Bags, p. 161

See p. 7 for a list of Wilton essential cupcake products and other commonly used decorating items you may need.

INSTRUCTIONS

1 **Make fondant ears.** A few hours in advance, roll out white fondant ⅛ in. thick. Use smallest leaf Cut-Out to cut two ears; reverse Cut-Out for second ear. Pinch vertically to shape ears. Let dry on cornstarch-dusted surface.

2 **Prepare mini cupcakes.** Cover tops with tip 2A mound of icing in white; smooth with spatula. Pipe tip 3 dot eyes in blue, tip 4 dot nose in rose.

3 **Make fondant tail.** Roll a ⅜ in. dia. ball of white fondant. Flatten slightly. Use toothpick to create fluffy texture. Attach tail to cupcake with tip 3 icing dot. Insert ears. Each serves 1.

Sparkling pinwheel pops make the 4th more festive! Round cookies-on-a-stick are covered with *Sugar Sheets!* edible decorating paper, then piped with Sparkle Gel spokes for a red, white and blue blast!

Ⓐ Firecracker *Stacker*

Pans: Mini Muffin, Non-Stick Cookie Sheet, 10 in. x 16 in. Cooling Grid, p. 158

Tip: 12, p. 162

Recipe: Buttercream Icing, p. 143

Also: Primary Mini Baking Cups (red, blue), p. 155; White, Blue Candy Melts Candy (1 oz. each for each treat), p. 163; 4-Pc. Circles Nesting Metal Cutter Set, p. 166; White Nonpareils Sprinkles, p. 156; 6 in. Cookie Treat Sticks, p. 167; Patriotic Foil Pix, p. 167; 12 in. Disposable Decorating Bags, p. 161

See p. 7 for a list of Wilton essential cupcake products and other commonly used decorating items you may need.

INSTRUCTIONS

1. **Make candy bases.** 1 day in advance, melt and mix equal amounts of blue and white candy for color shown. Place second smallest (3 ¼ in.) cookie cutter on cookie sheet. Fill ¼ in. deep; tap to settle. Cut cookie stick to 1 in. long; stand upright in center of circle. Chill until firm; unmold. Twist to remove stick. Cut cookie sticks to 4½ in. long. Dip tip in melted candy; insert upright in center hole. Let set.

2. **Prepare mini cupcakes.** Use knife tip to make center hole in cupcake bottom. Cover tops with tip 12 swirl in white; sprinkle on nonpareils. Slide four cupcakes over cookie stick, alternating cup colors. Insert pix. Each serves 1.

Wilton

B Star-Spangled Salute

Pans: Standard Muffin, Cookie Sheet, 10 in. x 16 in. Cooling Grid, p. 158

Tips: 1 (2 needed), p. 162

Recipes: Buttercream Icing, Roll-Out Cookies, p. 143

Also: White *Sugar Sheets!* Edible Decorating Paper (1 sheet makes 9 treats), p. 160; 12 in. Rolling Pin, Cupcake Spatula, 15 in. Parchment Triangles, p. 161; Round Cut-Outs Fondant Cutters, p. 165; Red, Blue Sparkle Gel, Fine Tip Primary Colors FoodWriter Edible Color Markers (black), 4 in. Lollipop Sticks, White Candy Melts Candy, p. 163; Primary Standard Baking Cups (red, blue), p. 155; Silver Stars, Gold Stars Edible Accents, p. 157

See p. 7 for a list of Wilton essential cupcake products and other commonly used decorating items you may need.

INSTRUCTIONS

1. **Make cookies.** In advance, prepare and roll out dough. Cut circles using largest round Cut-Out. Bake and cool cookies.

2. **Decorate pinwheels.** Trace largest round Cut-Out on shiny side of white edible paper with black edible marker. Cut out one circle for each treat with knife. Ice cookies smooth with spatula in white. Position circles. Squeeze sparkle gel into parchment bags fitted with tip 1. Pipe pinwheel lines on matte side of circles alternating red and blue. Let set for 30 minutes. Attach lollipop stick to back of cookie with melted candy. Chill until firm.

3. **Prepare cupcakes.** Ice smooth with spatula in white. Sprinkle with stars edible accents. Insert pinwheel cookie in cupcake. Each serves 1.

C Made In U.S.A.!

Pans: Bar, 10 in. x 16 in. Cooling Grid, p. 158

Tip: 789, p. 162

Colors:* Royal Blue, Black, p. 163

Fondant: White (12 oz.), Red (8 oz.) Ready-To-Use Rolled Fondant, 9 in. Fondant Roller, Roll-N-Cut Mat, Fondant Trimmer, p. 164; Star Cut-Outs Fondant Cutters, Brush Set, p. 165

Recipe: Buttercream Icing, p. 143

Also: White Square Baking Cups, p. 154; Piping Gel, p. 160; 12 in. Disposable Decorating Bags, Cupcake Spatula, 13 in. x 19 in. Cake Board, Fanci-Foil Wrap, p. 161

See p. 7 for a list of Wilton essential cupcake products and other commonly used decorating items you may need.

INSTRUCTIONS

1. **Prepare 24 cupcakes.** Position in four rows of six each on foil-wrapped board. Cover entire top area with tip 789 in white; smooth with spatula.

2. **Decorate flag.** Tint 4 oz. fondant blue. Roll out ⅛ in. thick. Use fondant trimmer to cut a strip, 6½ in. x 5½ in., for star background. Position on treats. Roll out white fondant ⅟₁₆ in. thick. Cut 50 stars using smallest Cut-Out. Attach stars with piping gel.

   Roll out white and red fondant ⅛ in. thick. Cut strips, ¾ in. x 15 in. (three in each color) and ¾ in. x 9 in. (three in white, four in red). Position on treats in alternating colors; trim to fit. Serves 24.

*Combine Royal Blue with Black for blue shown.

Ⓐ Eerie Eyeballs *Cupcakes*

Pans: Standard, Mini Muffin, 10 in. x 16 in. Cooling Grid, p. 158

Tip: 3, p. 162

Color: Red-Red, p. 163

Recipe: Buttercream Icing, p. 143

Also: White Standard, Mini Baking Cups, p. 154; Cupcake Spatula, p. 161; Large Candy Eyeballs, p. 157; Fine Tip Primary Colors FoodWriter Edible Color Markers (yellow), p. 163; 12 in. Disposable Decorating Bags, p. 161; spice drops, rolled fruit strips, candy-coated gum squares, paper plates

See p. 7 for a list of Wilton essential cupcake products and other commonly used decorating items you may need.

INSTRUCTIONS

1. **Prepare cupcakes.** Bake and cool one standard and one mini cupcake per treat. Ice smooth with spatula in white.

2. **Add face details.** Draw irises on candy eyeballs with yellow edible color marker; position on cupcakes. Pipe tip 3 veins with red icing. Position cupcakes on plate. Cut mouth shape from rolled fruit with scissors; position on plate. Flatten spice drop slightly for nose; position on plate. Attach gum square teeth with icing. Each face serves 1.

Ⓑ Tarantula *Terror!*

Pans: Standard Muffin, 10 in. x 16 in. Cooling Grid, p. 158

Tip: 1, p. 162

Colors:* Orange, Leaf Green, Lemon Yellow, p. 163

Candy: Black Candy Melts Candy (1 pk. makes 10 to 12 treats), Truffles Candy Mold, p. 163

Recipe: Buttercream Icing, p. 143

Also: Rainbow Standard Baking Cups (purple, green), p. 155; Cupcake Spatula, p. 161; 12 in. Disposable Decorating Bags, Parchment Paper, Cake Board, p. 161; black shoestring licorice, sour cherry candy

See p. 7 for a list of Wilton essential cupcake products and other commonly used decorating items you may need.

INSTRUCTIONS

1. **Make tarantulas.** In advance, make legs. Cut six licorice pieces for each treat, 1¼ in. long. Dip into melted candy; chill until firm on parchment paper-covered board. For heads, insert toothpick into sour cherry candy. Dip in melted candy; chill. For body, fill truffle candy mold with melted candy. Insert legs; chill until firm. Unmold body; remove toothpick from head and attach to body with melted candy. Chill until firm.

2. **Prepare cupcakes.** Ice smooth with spatula in orange. Position tarantula. Pipe tip 1 eyes and mouth. Each serves 1.

*Combine Leaf Green with Lemon Yellow for green shown.

Wilton

⊙ Glam Ghoul *Friends*

Pans: Standard Muffin, 10 in. x 16 in. Cooling Grid, p. 158

Tip: 2, p. 162

Colors:* Orange, Leaf Green, Violet, Rose, Black, p. 163

Fondant: White Ready-To-Use Rolled Fondant (2½ oz. makes 3 treats), Gum-Tex, 9 in. Fondant Roller, Roll-N-Cut Mat, p. 164; Leaf Cut-Outs Fondant Cutters, Brush Set, p. 165

Recipe: Buttercream Icing, p. 143

Also: Monochrome Standard Baking Cups (black), p. 154; Cupcake Spatula, 12 in. Disposable Decorating Bags, Cake Boards, p. 161

See p. 7 for a list of Wilton essential cupcake products and other commonly used decorating items you may need.

INSTRUCTIONS

1. **Make glasses.** 1 day in advance, tint 1 oz. fondant black, ½ oz. each violet, green and orange (for three treats). Knead ⅛ teaspoon Gum-Tex into black; roll out ⅛ in. thick. Use medium leaf Cut-Out to cut right lens; reverse to cut left lens.

    Roll out remaining colors ⅛ in. thick. Cut right and left frames as above using medium Cut-Out. Use small Cut-Out to cut open center, reversing for left frame as above. Attach frames to lenses with damp brush. Let dry on cornstarch-dusted board.

2. **Prepare cupcakes.** Ice smooth with spatula. Position sunglasses. Pipe tip 2 outline mouths. Each serves 1.

*Combine Violet with Rose for violet shown.

⊙ You and Your Big *Mouth*

Pans: Standard Muffin, 10 in. x 16 in. Cooling Grid, p. 158

Tips: 3, 5, 12, p. 162

Colors:* Violet, Rose, Leaf Green, Black, Christmas Red, Red-Red, p. 163

Recipes: Buttercream, Chocolate Buttercream Icings, p. 143

Also: Rainbow Standard Baking Cups (green, red, purple), p. 154; Cupcake Spatula, 12 in. Disposable Decorating Bags, p. 161; Large Candy Eyeballs, p. 157

See p. 7 for a list of Wilton essential cupcake products and other commonly used decorating items you may need.

INSTRUCTIONS

1. **Prepare cupcakes.** Ice tops smooth with spatula and chocolate buttercream tinted black.

2. **Decorate face.** Outline bottom edge with tip 5 for lower jaw. Outline top edge with tip 12 for upper jaw; taper ends to connect with lower jaw and pat smooth with finger dipped in cornstarch. Outline and pipe in tip 3 teeth; pat smooth. Pipe tip 5 eyebrows on candy eyeballs and attach with dots of icing. Each serves 1.

*Combine Violet with Rose for violet shown. Combine Christmas Red with Red-Red for red shown.

For cupcakes in a spookier vein, Wilton Red Decorating Gel creates a quick and creepy special effect!

 Wandering Eyes

Pans: Mini Muffin, Cookie Sheet, 10 in. x 16 in. Cooling Grid, p. 158

Tip: 4, p. 162

Colors:* Christmas Red, Red-Red, Violet, Rose, p. 163

Recipes: Buttercream Icing, Roll-Out Cookies, p. 143

Also: Jewel (purple), Primary (red) Mini Baking Cups, p. 155; Cupcake Spatula, 12 in. Disposable Decorating Bags, p. 161; Vibrant Green, Black Candy Melts Candy, p. 163; Large Candy Eyeballs, p. 157; 12 in. Rolling Pin, p. 159; 4-Pc. Circles Nesting Metal Cutter Set, p. 166; black shoestring licorice, black spice drops

See p. 7 for a list of Wilton essential cupcake products and other commonly used decorating items you may need.

INSTRUCTIONS

1   **Make cookies.** In advance, prepare and roll out dough. Cut circles using second largest cookie cutter. Bake and cool cookies. Use melted candy in cut decorating bag to outline and fill in top. Tap to settle; chill until firm.

2   **Prepare cupcakes.** Ice smooth with spatula to match baking cup color. Position candy eyeball at center. Use tip 4 to outline and pipe in eyelid; pat smooth with finger dipped in cornstarch. Postition cupcakes, side down, on cookie, securing with a tip 4 dot of icing.

3   **Make feet and legs.** For feet, trim bottom ¼ in. of black spice drops; cut each piece in half. Cut licorice to make three pairs of two-section legs. Back: 1½ in. with ⅝ in. top. Middle: ¾ in. with ½ in. top. Front: ⅝ in. with ⅜ in. top. Use melted black candy to attach angled leg sections and feet; let set. Attach legs to baking cup and cookie with melted candy. Each serves 1.

*Combine Christmas Red with Red-Red for red shown. Combine Violet with Rose and a little Red-Red for violet shown.

Wilton

B Meet Your *Creature*

Pans: Bar, 10 in. x 16 in. Cooling Grid, p. 158

Tips: 4, 8, p. 162

Colors: Leaf Green, Black, p. 163

Recipe: Buttercream Icing, p. 143

Also: White Square Baking Cups, p. 154; Cupcake Spatula, 12 in. Disposable Decorating Bags, p. 161; Large Candy Eyeballs, p. 157

See p. 7 for a list of Wilton essential cupcake products and other commonly used decorating items you may need.

INSTRUCTIONS

1 **Prepare cupcakes.** Ice smooth with spatula in green.

2 **Decorate features.** Position candy eyeballs. Pipe in tip 4 hair and outline mouth in black. Pipe tip 8 ball ears and nose in green. Each serves 1.

C Halloween's In His *Blood*

Pans: Standard Muffin, Non-Stick Cookie Sheet, 10 in. x 16 in. Cooling Grid, p. 158

Tip: 3, p. 162

Color: Black, p. 163

Fondant: Black Ready-To-Use Rolled Fondant (¼ oz. per treat), Gum-Tex, 9 in. Fondant Roller, Roll-N-Cut Mat, p. 164; Brush Set, p. 165

Candy: Red Candy Melts Candy (1½ oz. per treat), 6 in. Lollipop Sticks, p. 163

Recipe: Chocolate Buttercream Icing, p. 143

Also: Monochrome Standard Baking Cups (black), p. 154; Small Candy Eyeballs, p. 157; 7-Pc. Coffin Cutter Set (bat), p. 166; White Tube Decorating Icing, p. 163; Coupler Ring Set, p. 162; Cupcake Spatula, 15 in. Parchment Triangles, Cake Boards, p. 161

See p. 7 for a list of Wilton essential cupcake products and other commonly used decorating items you may need.

INSTRUCTIONS

1 **Make bat details.** 1 to 2 days in advance, make fondant wings and ears. For each treat, knead ⅛ teaspoon Gum-Tex into ¼ oz. black fondant. Roll out ⅛ in. thick. Cut bat using cutter from set. Remove head with a ¾ in. deep V-shaped cut; cut through middle to separate wings. For ears, cut two triangles, ½ in. x ½ in. Let all dry on cornstarch-dusted board.

2 **Make candy trims.** In advance, melt candy. Use cut parchment bag to pipe a 4 in. x 5 in. irregular puddle onto cookie sheet. Chill until firm. Pipe three or more tip 3 beads for blood drops. Chill until firm.

3 **Prepare cupcakes.** Tint chocolate icing black. Ice tops smooth with spatula. Position candy eyeballs.

Position head. Pipe tip 3 outline mouth. Use tube icing, coupler and tip 3 to outline and pipe in fangs; smooth with finger dipped in cornstarch. Position cupcake side down in puddle; secure with melted candy. Insert ears in icing. Make a ¼ in. to ½ in. cut below edge of baking cup on opposite sides. Insert lollipop stick horizontally through cupcake. Attach wings to stick using melted candy in cut parchment bag; hold until set. Attach blood drops and decorate tips of fangs with melted candy. Each serves 1.

D Hair-Raising *Zombie*

Pans: Standard Muffin, 10 in. x 16 in. Cooling Grid, p. 158

Tip: 3, p. 162

Color: Black, p. 163

Recipe: Buttercream Icing, p. 143

Also: Monochrome Standard Baking Cups (black), p. 154; Cupcake Spatula, 12 in. Disposable Decorating Bags, p. 161; Small Candy Eyeballs, p. 157, black shoestring licorice

See p. 7 for a list of Wilton essential cupcake products and other commonly used decorating items you may need.

INSTRUCTIONS

1 **Prepare cupcakes.** Ice smooth with spatula in white.

2 **Add details.** Outline and pipe in tip 3 irregular circles in black in eye areas; pat smooth with finger dipped in cornstarch. Position candy eyeballs. Pipe tip 3 outline mouth. For hair, cut licorice into 1½ in. long pieces; insert into icing. Each serves 1.

He's met his match! This fun, undead design comes to life quickly with a simple stitched mouth, candy eyeballs and licorice hair.

A

A Glittering *Graveyard*

Pans: Standard Muffin, Non-Stick Cookie Sheet, 10 in. x 16 in. Cooling Grid, p. 158

Tips: 1, 2, 2A, 4, p. 162

Color: Black, p. 163

Candy: White Candy Melts Candy (3 oz. makes 5 to 6 treats), Garden Candy Color Set (black), 4 in. Lollipop Sticks, Decorator Brush Set, p. 163

Recipes: Buttercream Icing, Roll-Out Cookies, p. 143

Also: Monochrome Standard Baking Cups (silver), p. 155; 9-Pc. Halloween Cutter Set (tombstone), p. 166; Round Cut-Outs Fondant Cutters, p. 165; Silver Color Mist Food Color Spray, p. 163; Pure Lemon Extract, p. 160; 12 in. Rolling Pin, p. 159; Cupcake Spatula, 12 in. Disposable Decorating Bags, Cak Boards, p. 161, milk

See p. 7 for a list of Wilton essential cupcake products and other commonl used decorating items you may need.

INSTRUCTIONS

1. **Make cookie tombstones.** In advance, prepare dough. Tint gray using black color; reserve a portion for piping details. Roll out and cut tombstones using cutter from set. Use knife to trim tops to vary shapes.

   Thin reserved dough with milk to piping consistency. Pipe details on tombstone edges: tip 4 bands and zigzags, tip 2 dots, tip 1 scrollwork. Bake and cool cookies.

   Spray tombstones with silver Color Mist food color spray; let dry. Tint lemon extract black, paint messages. Let dry. Attach lollipop sticks to backs with melted candy, leaving 1 in. extending at bottom to insert into cupcake. Let dry.

2. **Make candy cupcake bases.** In advance, tint melted white candy gray with black candy color. Place largest round Cut-Out on cookie sheet; fill to 1/8 in. thick with melted candy. Tap to settle; chill until firm. Make one base per treat.

3. **Prepare cupcakes.** Fill cups only 1/3 of the way with batter; bake and cool. Ic smooth with spatula in white. Press candy base on top and position cupcak candy side down. Use knife tip to make a small hole in center; insert tombstone. Each serves 1.

B Take A *Stab!*

Pans: Standard Muffin, 10 in. x 16 in. Cooling Grid, p. 158

Color: Copper (for skin tone shown), p. 163

Recipe: Buttercream Icing, p. 143

Also: Bright Rainbow Standard Baking Cups (green), p. 155; Knives Icing Decorations, p. 157; Red, Brown Color Dust, Brush Set, p. 165; Red Decorating Gel, p. 163; Cupcake Spatula, p. 161

See p. 7 for a list of Wilton essential cupcake products and other commonly used decorating items you may need.

INSTRUCTIONS

1. **Prepare cupcakes.** Ice tops smooth with spatula in copper.

2. **Make wound.** Use knife to cut a slit across top, 1/4 in. deep. Let icing set. Brush edges of wound with red and brown Color Dust. Fill wound and add drips with red decorating gel. Insert knife decoration. Each serves 1.

B

ⓒ Mad *Medusa*

Don't stare at her hair! Medusa's snakes will give some folks the shakes, but they're easy for the decorator. Just pipe them in advance using royal icing and then pop them in your iced cupcake.

Pans: Standard Muffin, 10 in. x 16 in. Cooling Grid, p. 158

Tips: 2, 3, 5, 8, p. 162

Colors: Juniper Green, Black, Red-Red, p. 163

Recipes: Buttercream, Royal Icings, p. 143

Also: Monochrome Standard Baking Cups (black), p. 155; Meringue Powder, p. 160; 12 in. Disposable Decorating Bags, 9 in. Angled Spatula, Cake Board, p. 161

See p. 7 for a list of Wilton essential cupcake products and other commonly used decorating items you may need.

INSTRUCTIONS

1 **Make snakes.** 1 day in advance, using dark green royal icing on a waxed paper-covered board, pipe tip 5 S-shaped lines in various directions, about 2 in. long. Build up end to form head; build up higher for open-mouth snakes. For mouths, dip tip of knife in cornstarch and score a notch in head. Let dry 24 hours.

2 **Add eyes and tongues to snakes.** Pipe tip 2 dot eyes. Pipe forked tongue by piping two tip 2 pull-out dots side by side.

3 **Prepare cupcakes.** Ice smooth with spatula in light green buttercream in a mounded shape, about 1¼ in. high.

4 **Add trims.** Insert snakes in cupcake. On cupcake, pipe tip 8 ball eyes with tip 3 dot pupils and outline eyebrows. Pipe tip 3 outline mouth with tip 2 pull-out fangs. Each serves 1.

Ⓐ Comfy Cat

Pans: Standard Muffin, 10 in. x 16 in. Cooling Grid, p. 158

Tips: 2, 5, 12, p. 162

Colors: Black, Orange, Lemon Yellow, p. 163

Fondant: White Ready-to-Use Rolled Fondant (½ oz. per treat), Gum-Tex, 9 in. Fondant Roller, Roll-N-Cut Mat, p. 164; Round Cut-Outs Fondant Cutters, Storage Board, p. 165

Recipe: Buttercream Icing, p. 143

Also: Tail Pattern, p. 152; Bright Rainbow Standard Baking Cups (green), p. 154; Cupcake Spatula, 12 in. Disposable Decorating Bags, p. 161

See p. 7 for a list of Wilton essential cupcake products and other commonly used decorating items you may need.

INSTRUCTIONS

1. **Make fondant head and tail.** 1 day in advance, knead ⅛ teaspoon Gum-Tex into ½ oz. fondant for each treat. Tint fondant black. Roll out ⅛ in. thick. Cut head using medium round Cut-Out. Roll a log, ¼ in. dia. x 4 in. long. Use pattern to shape tail. Let dry 24 hours.

2. **Prepare cupcakes.** Ice smooth with spatula in orange.

3. **Decorate cat.** Insert tail. Build up tip 12 body and back legs in black. Overpipe tip 12 front legs. Attach head to body. Pipe in tip 2 eyes in yellow. Pipe tip 2 dot pupils and nose, outline mouth and whiskers in black. Pipe tip 5 pull-out ears in black. Each serves 1.

Ⓑ Puddle, Puddle, Toil & Trouble!

Pans: Standard Muffin, Non-Stick Cookie Sheet, 10 in. x 16 in. Cooling Grid, p. 158

Tips: 3, 5, 44, p. 162

Colors: Leaf Green, Orange, Black, Violet, Golden Yellow, p. 163

Recipes: Buttercream Icing, Roll-Out Cookies, p. 143

Also: Black Candy Melts Candy (1 pk. makes 3 treats), p. 163; White Standard Baking Cups, p. 155; Round Cut-Outs Fondant Cutters, p. 165; 12 in. Disposable Decorating Bags, Cupcake Spatula, Cake Boards, p. 161; 9 in. Fondant Roller, Roll-N-Cut Mat, p. 164; pretzel sticks, large yellow spice drops, horn-shaped corn snacks

See p. 7 for a list of Wilton essential cupcake products and other commonly used decorating items you may need.

INSTRUCTIONS

1. **Make cookie puddle.** 1 day in advance, prepare and roll out dough ⅛ in. thick. For each treat, cut a wavy-edge oval, 7 in. x 5 in. Bake and cool cookies. Place on cooling grid over cookie sheet. Cover with melted black candy (p. 151). Tap to settle; chill until firm.

2. **Make hat.** In advance, make brim by placing largest round Cut-Out on cookie sheet. Fill ⅛ in. deep with melted black candy. Tap to settle; chill until firm.

   For top, dip corn snack in melted candy; position wide end down on waxed paper-covered board. Chill until firm. Repeat if needed. Attach top to brim using melted candy. Let set. Pipe tip 44 hat band; add tip 3 outline buckle.

3. **Make broom.** In advance, roll out spice drop between pieces of waxed paper. Use knife to cut slits ¾ in. deep on wide end for bristles; separate. Use knife tip to poke hole in top of spice drop; insert pretzel stick, securing with melted candy if needed.

4. **Prepare cupcakes.** Ice tops smooth with spatula in green for face. Pipe tip 5 pull-out nose. Pipe tip 3 outline eyes; outline and pipe in mouth (pat smooth with finger dipped in cornstarch).

5. **Assemble treats.** Position cupcake on puddle, side down, securing with melted candy. Pipe tip 5 pull-out hair. Position hat and broom. Each serves 1.

ⓒ Jumpy Jacks

Pans: Standard Muffin, 10 in. x 16 in. Cooling Grid, p. 158

Tips: 3, 8, p. 162

Colors: Orange, Black, Leaf Green, p. 163

Recipe: Buttercream Icing, p. 143

Also: Monochrome Standard Baking Cups (black), p. 155; Cupcake Spatula, Cake Boards, p. 161; Large Candy Eyeballs, p. 157

See p. 7 for a list of Wilton essential cupcake products and other commonly used decorating items you may need.

INSTRUCTIONS

1. **Prepare cupcakes.** Ice smooth with spatula in orange. Lightly run edge of spatula over icing to create section lines.

2. **Decorate faces.** Use tip 3 to pipe features, including outline and pipe-in eye areas, noses and mouths, eyebrows and teeth; smooth piped-in areas with finger dipped in cornstarch. Position candy eyeballs. Pipe tip 8 pull-out stems. Each serves 1.

SMILES EVERY SEASON!

Throw a pumpkin personalization party! Kids love making faces, and they'll have fun squeezing on the icing details and adding the candy eyeballs.

ⓐ Spinning *Pinwheels*

Pans: Mini Muffin, 10 in. x 16 in. Cooling Grid, p. 158

Colors:* Red-Red, Kelly Green, Leaf Green, Orange, Rose, Violet, Lemon Yellow, Golden Yellow, p. 163

Fondant: White Ready-To-Use Rolled Fondant (3½ oz. makes 7 treats), 9 in. Fondant Roller, Roll-N-Cut Mat, Storage Board, p. 164; Brush Set, p. 165

Recipe: Buttercream Icing, p. 143

Also: 101 Cookie Cutters (smallest round), p. 167; Silver Foil Mini Baking Cups, p. 155; Cupcake Spatula, p. 161; Pearl Color Mist Food Color Spray, p. 163

See p. 7 for a list of Wilton essential cupcake products and other commonly used decorating items you may need.

INSTRUCTIONS

1 **Prepare cupcakes.** Ice tops smooth with spatula in white.

2 **Make pinwheels.** For each treat, tint ½ oz. fondant red, kelly green, leaf green, orange, rose, violet or yellow. Roll out ⅛ in. thick. Turn smallest round cutter from set upside down on fondant; use as a guide to cut a circle for each treat with knife. Place circle under storage board until ready to cut and position.

Use knife to cut circle into six sections, ½ in. wide at bottom. Position six sections on cupcake ½ in. apart at edge of cupcake, securing with damp brush. Spray with pearl Color Mist food color spray. Each serves 1.

*Combine Violet with Rose for violet shown. Combine Lemon Yellow with Golden Yellow for yellow shown.

ⓑ Santa Makes The *Scene*

Pans: Standard Muffin, 10 in. x 16 in. Cooling Grid, p. 158

Tip: 3, p. 162

Colors:* Christmas Red, Red-Red, Black, Lemon Yellow, Golden Yellow, Copper (for skin tone shown), p. 163

Fondant: White Ready-To-Use Rolled Fondant (1⁵⁄₁₆ oz. per treat), 9 in. Fondant Roller, Roll-N-Cut Mat, p. 164; Brush Set, p. 165

Recipe: Buttercream Icing, p. 143

Also: Primary Standard Baking Cups (red), p. 155; Small Candy Eyeballs, p. 167; Cupcake Spatula, 12 in. Disposable Decorating Bags, p. 161

See p. 7 for a list of Wilton essential cupcake products and other commonly used decorating items you may need.

INSTRUCTIONS

1 **Prepare cupcakes.** Ice tops smooth with spatula in copper.

2 **Make clothes.** For each treat, tint 1 oz. fondant red, ¼ oz. black, ¹⁄₁₆ oz. yellow. Shape a high cone-shaped red hat 1 in. dia. x 1¾ in.; position on cupcake, curving end. For belt, roll out black ⅛ in. thick. Cut a strip, ¼ in. x 9 in.; attach around cupcake just above baking cup. For buckle, roll out yellow ⅛ in. thick. Cut a rectangle, ½ in. x ⅜ in.; use knife to cut out center. Attach to belt using damp brush.

3 **Decorate Santa.** Outline and pipe in mouth with tip 3 in black; pat smooth with finger dipped in cornstarch. Position eyeballs. Use tip 3 to pipe dot nose in copper, swirl pompom and zigzag brim on hat, swirl hair and beard, pull-out moustache in white. Each serves 1.

*Combine Christmas Red with Red-Red for red shown. Combine Lemon Yellow with Golden Yellow for yellow shown.

ⓒ Boys Who Make *Toys*

Pans: Standard Muffin, 10 in. x 16 in. Cooling Grid, p. 158

Tips: 2, 3, 5, p. 162

Colors:* Kelly Green, Brown, Red-Red, Black, Copper (for skin tone shown), p. 163

Fondant: White Ready-To-Use Rolled Fondant (2½ oz. per treat), 9 in. Fondant Roller, Roll-N-Cut Mat, p. 164; Brush Set, Leaf Cut-Outs Fondant Cutters, p. 165

Recipe: Buttercream Icing, p. 143

Also: Red Dots Standard Baking Cups, p. 155; Small Candy Eyeballs, p. 157; 9 in. Straight Spatula, 12 in. Disposable Decorating Bags, Cake Boards, p. 161; 4 in. Lollipop Sticks, p. 163; Piping Gel, p. 160; sugar ice cream cones

See p. 7 for a list of Wilton essential cupcake products and other commonly used decorating items you may need.

INSTRUCTIONS

1 **Make hat.** 1 day in advance, slightly dampen wide end of cones and use scissors to cut to 3½ in. high. Tint 1½ oz. fondant green per treat. Roll out ⅛ in. thick. Cut a strip, 3¼ in. x 5 in. Brush cone with piping gel; attach fondant around cone. Smooth with hands; trim away excess.

Roll out white fondant ¹⁄₁₆ in. thick. Cut a strip, ¼ in. x 18 in. Brush back with piping gel and attach around hat for stripe. For pompom, roll a ball, ¼ in. dia. Attach to tip of cone with piping gel.

2 **Make ears.** 1 day in advance, tint ¼ oz. fondant per treat copper. Roll out ¹⁄₁₆ in. thick. Cut two ears per treat using smallest leaf Cut-Out (reverse Cut-Out for second ear). Let dry on cornstarch-dusted board.

3 **Prepare cupcakes.** Ice smooth with spatula in copper, making a mounded head about 1¼ in. high. Insert lollipop stick through center. Position hat over stick, securing with extra icing, if necessary.

Insert ears. Position candy eyeballs. Pipe tip 2 outline mouth and tip 5 pull-out dot nose. Pipe tip 3 outline hair curl and dot cheeks (flatten with finger). Each serves 1.

*Combine Brown with Red-Red for brown hair shown.

Help yourself to an elf. They're what the holiday spirit is all about with impish faces, merry colors and ice cream cone caps that are twice their height.

SMILES EVERY SEASON!

Ⓐ

Pans: Mini Muffin, Cookie Sheet, 10 in. x 16 in. Cooling Grid, p. 158

Recipes: Buttercream, Color Flow Icings, Roll-Out Cookies, p. 143

Also: White Mini Baking Cups, p. 155; Small Candy Eyeballs, p. 157; Cupcake Spatula, p. 161; 9 in. Fondant Roller, p. 164; Color Flow Mix, p. 160; Parchment Paper, p. 159; large spice drops, mini candy-coated chocolate candies, pretzel sticks, black shoestring licorice

See p. 7 for a list of Wilton essential cupcake products and other commonly used decorating items you may need.

INSTRUCTIONS

Make snow melt cookies. In advance, prepare and roll out dough. For each treat, use knife to cut a wavy oval, about 4¼ in. wide x 5 in. long. Bake and cool cookies.

Prepare mini cupcakes. Ice smooth with spatula in white buttercream. Position candy eyeballs. Cut a licorice piece, ¾ in. long, for mouth; position.

Make hat and broom. For hat brim, place a black spice drop between sheets of parchment paper sprinkled with sugar. Roll to flatten into a circle, 1¾ in. dia. x ³⁄₁₆ in. thick. For hat top, trim tip off another spice drop to make a flat base; press to attach to brim, narrow end down.

For broom, flatten together two yellow spice drops, ⅛ in. thick. Use scissors to cut a rectangle, 1¼ in. x 3 in.; flatten. Cut slits ¼ in. wide; separate for bristles. Wrap around tip of pretzel stick and press to secure.

Assemble treats. Place cookies on cooling grid over parchment paper-covered cookie sheet. Pour on thinned Color Flow to cover. Tap to settle; let dry 30 minutes. Position cupcakes, side down, on cookies, securing with icing. Attach chocolate candy buttons, hat and broom with icing. Let dry. Each serves 1.

Ⓐ Global *Cooling*

Pans: Standard, Jumbo Muffin, 10 in. x 16 in. Cooling Grid, p. 158

Tips: 2, 3, 5, p. 162

Colors: Sky Blue, Kelly Green, Christmas Red, Black, p. 163

Recipe: Buttercream Icing, p. 143

Also: White Standard Baking Cups, p. 155; Green, Red Candy Melts Candy (2½ oz. for each treat), p. 163; Cupcake Spatula, 12 in. Disposable Decorating Bags, Cake Circles, p. 161

See p. 7 for a list of Wilton essential cupcake products and other commonly used decorating items you may need.

INSTRUCTIONS

1. **Make candy bases.** In advance, melt candy and pour into jumbo muffin pan cavities ½ in. thick. Tap to settle; chill until firm. Unmold.

2. **Prepare cupcakes.** Ice smooth with spatula in blue. Use tip 5 to outline and pipe in white snow area; smooth with finger dipped in cornstarch. Pipe tip 5 ball head ½ in. dia. and body ¾ in. dia.; pat smooth. Use tip 3 to outline and pipe in ½ in. high top hat; pat smooth. Pipe tip 3 outline brim. Pipe tip 2 outline scarf, dot eyes, nose and buttons, outline smile. Pipe tip 3 zigzag tree, 1 in. high. Pipe tip 3 dot snowflakes.

3. **Assemble treats.** Position cupcake sideways on candy base, securing with icing. Each serves 1.

Don't let winter get you down! When your mood is below zero, these smiling fondant snowmen will spread sunshine and help your cupcakes stand out wherever they are served.

Wilton

C Leaning Into *Winter*

Pans: Standard Muffin, 10 in. x 16 in. Cooling Grid, p. 158

Tip: 1A, p. 162

Colors: Black, Christmas Red, p. 163

Fondant: White Ready-To-Use Rolled Fondant (1½ oz. per treat), Gum-Tex, 9 in. Fondant Roller, Roll-N-Cut Mat, Brush Set, p. 164; Round Cut-Outs Fondant Cutters, p. 165

Recipes: Buttercream Icing, Thinned Fondant Adhesive, p. 143

Also: Top Hat Pattern, p. 153; Blue ColorCups Standard Baking Cups, p. 154; Bold Tip Primary Colors FoodWriter Edible Color Markers (black), 8 in. Lollipop Sticks, p. 163; Cupcake Spatula, Cake Boards, 15 in. Parchment Triangles, p. 161; 101 Cookie Cutters (smallest round used), p. 167; White Sparkling Sugar, p. 156

See p. 7 for a list of Wilton essential cupcake products and other commonly used decorating items you may need.

INSTRUCTIONS

1 **Make snowmen.** 1 day in advance, for each pair, knead ⅛ teaspoon Gum-Tex into 1½ oz. white fondant. Roll out ⅛ in. thick. Cut two each small, medium and large circles using wide end of tip 1A, smallest round from 101 Cutters Set and medium round Cut-Out. Let all pieces dry overnight on cornstarch-dusted, waxed paper-covered boards.

Use black edible marker to draw eyes and smile on small circle and buttons on medium circle. Bend lollipop stick into curve.

2 **Make top hats.** 1 day in advance, for each hat, tint ½ oz. fondant black and ¼ oz. red; knead ⅛ teaspoon Gum-Tex into black. Roll out black ⅛ in. thick. Using pattern and knife, cut hat. Cut a strip ⅛ in. x 1 in. for brim. Attach brim over narrow base of hat using damp brush. For hat band, roll out red ¹⁄₁₆ in. thick. Cut a strip, ⅛ in. x ½ in. for hat band. Attach to hat; wrap ends around sides. Let all pieces dry overnight on cornstarch-dusted, waxed paper-covered boards.

Use thinned fondant adhesive to attach snowman circles and hat to stick, leaving bottom 2 in. uncovered to insert in cupcake. Let set.

3 **Prepare cupcakes.** Ice smooth with spatula in white. Sprinkle with sparkling sugar. Insert snowman in cupcake. Each serves 1.

Ⓐ Spruce Up This *Season!*

Pans: Standard Muffin, 10 in. x 16 in. Cooling Grid, p. 158

Tip: 349, p. 162

Color: Kelly Green, p. 163

Recipe: Buttercream Icing, p. 143

Also: Tree Pattern, p. 153; Brown Dots Standard Baking Cups, p. 154; Cupcake Spatula, 15 in. Parchment Triangles, 12 in. Disposable Decorating Bags, p. 161; Light Cocoa Candy Melts

Candy (¼ oz. per treat), p. 163; Jumbo Rainbow Nonpareils, Jumbo Stars Sprinkles, p. 156

See p. 7 for a list of Wilton essential cupcake products and other commonly used decorating items you may need.

INSTRUCTIONS

1 **Make candy trees.** 1 day in advance, tape waxed paper over pattern. Using melted cocoa candy in cut decorating bag,

pipe trees. Chill until firm. Peel off trees and turn over. Overpipe back with melted candy. Chill until firm.

For trees with needles, pipe tip 349 leaves in green buttercream. Immediately attach jumbo nonpareils on branches and jumbo star sprinkle on top. Let set. For bare trees, attach jumbo nonpareils with dots of melted candy.

2 **Prepare cupcakes.** Ice smooth with spatula in white. Insert trees in cupcakes. Each serves 1.

Ⓑ Tree Of *Treats*

Pans: Standard Muffin, 10 in. x 16 in. Cookie Sheet, Cooling Grid, p. 158

Tip: 352, p. 162

Colors:* Kelly Green, Lemon Yellow, Golden Yellow, p. 163

Recipes: Buttercream Icing, Roll-Out Cookies, p. 143

Also: 12 in. Rolling Pin, p. 159; 4-Pc. Stars Nesting Metal Cutter Set, p. 166; White Sparkling Sugar, Yellow Colored Sugar, p. 156; Cupcake Spatula, 12 in. Disposable Decorating Bags, p. 161; Bright Rainbow Standard Baking Cups (green), p. 155; Jumbo Confetti, p. 166; serving plate

See p. 7 for a list of Wilton essential cupcake products and other commonly used decorating items you may need.

INSTRUCTIONS

1. **Make star cookie.** In advance, prepare and roll out dough. Cut cookie with largest star cutter. Bake and cool. Ice smooth; cover with yellow colored sugar.

2. **Prepare 15 cupcakes.** Cover tops with tip 352 leaves. Position jumbo confetti and sprinkle with white sparkling sugar. Position cupcakes in a tree shape. Position star cookie at top. Cookie and each cupcake serves 1.

*Combine Lemon Yellow with Golden Yellow for yellow shown.

Ⓐ Potted Poinsettias

Pans: Standard Muffin, 10 in. x 16 in. Cooling Grid, p. 158

Color: Moss Green, p. 163

Fondant: White (6 oz.), Red (12 oz.) Ready-To-Use Rolled Fondant, Gum-Tex, 9 in. Fondant Roller, Roll-N-Cut Mat, 10-Pc. Gum Paste/Fondant Tool Set, Shaping Foam, p. 164; Leaf Cut-Outs Fondant Cutters, Wave Flower Former Set, Brush Set, p. 165

Recipes: Buttercream Icing, Thinned Fondant Adhesive, p. 143

Also: Rainbow Standard Baking Cups (green), p. 155; White Candy Melts Candy, p. 163; Green Sugar Pearls, p. 156; 8 in. Cookie Treat Sticks, p. 167; Cake Boards, Cupcake Spatula, p. 161; 6 in. dia. clay pot, 6 in. dia. craft foam ball, green tissue paper

See p. 7 for a list of Wilton essential cupcake products and other commonly used decorating items you may need.

INSTRUCTIONS

Make poinsettia leaves. Each clay pot will hold six cupcakes, each with one poinsettia. 1 day in advance, knead ½ teaspoon Gum-Tex into 6 oz. white fondant; tint green. Knead 1 teaspoon Gum-Tex into 12 oz. red fondant. Roll out fondant ⅛ in. thick. For each poinsettia, cut five green and seven red leaves with medium Cut-Out. Cut six red leaves with small Cut-Out. Place leaves on thin foam and use narrow end of veining tool to score vein lines. Let dry on cornstarch-dusted large concave sections of wave flower former. Reserve remaining green fondant for centers.

Assemble poinsettias. Attach pieces as follows with thinned fondant adhesive on waxed paper-covered cake board. Attach five green leaves in a circle, with ends touching. Attach seven large red petals on top, between green leaf spaces. Roll seven balls from reserved green fondant, ⅛ in. dia.; attach in center. Attach six small red petals around center. Attach Sugar Pearls to center balls. Let dry.

Prepare cupcakes. Ice smooth with spatula in white. Attach poinsettia to each cupcake with icing.

Assemble bouquet. Wrap foam ball with tissue. Place in clay pot. Cut treat sticks to 4 in. long. Insert six sticks in craft ball, leaving 1 in. extended at top and leaving space between sticks for positioning cupcakes. Brush melted candy on extended portion of sticks; immediately insert cupcakes on top. Each serves 1.

B Winter *Perch*

Pans: Standard Muffin, 10 in. x 16 in. Cooling Grid, p. 158

Colors: Moss Green, Brown, p. 163

Fondant: White Ready-To-Use Rolled Fondant (3 oz. makes 3 treats), Primary Colors Fondant Multi Pack (½ oz. red makes 3 treats), Gum-Tex, 9 in. Fondant Roller, Roll-N-Cut Mat, p. 164; Brush Set, Nature Fondant & Gum Paste Mold, p. 165

Recipes: Buttercream Icing, Thinned Fondant Adhesive, p. 143

Also: Red Dots Standard Baking Cups, p. 155; 3-Pc. Trees Metal Cutter Set (triangle tree), p. 166; Cupcake Spatula, Cake Boards p. 161; 4 in. Lollipop Sticks, p. 163

See p. 7 for a list of Wilton essential cupcake products and other commonly used decorating items you may need.

INSTRUCTIONS

1 **Make fondant trees and birds.** 2 to 3 days in advance, tint 1 oz. fondant green for three trees and ½ oz. red for three birds. Knead in ⅛ teaspoon Gum-Tex. Roll out green ⅛ in. thick. Cut trees using triangle tree cutter. Press red fondant into nature mold to make one flying bird for each tree. Let dry on cornstarch-dusted boards.

2 **Make fondant trunk and branches.** 1 day in advance, tint 1½ oz. fondant brown for three trees. Press into nature mold to make one trunk, 2½ in. long, with one side branch, 1 in. long. Press trunk around lollipop stick, leaving 1½ in. extended at bottom to insert into cupcake. Mold a second side branch and attach to trunk using thinned fondant adhesive.

Attach birds to trees with thinned fondant adhesive. Let dry.

3 **Prepare cupcakes.** Ice tops fluffy with spatula in white. Insert trees in cupcakes. Each serves 1.

C Frost *Bites!*

Pans: Mini Muffin, 10 in. x 16 in. Cooling Grid, p. 158

Tip: 12, p. 162

Colors: Red-Red, Kelly Green, p. 163

Recipe: Buttercream Icing, p. 143

Also: Silver Foil Mini Baking Cups, p. 155; Pearl Color Mist Food Color Spray, p. 163; White Sparkling Sugar, p. 156

See p. 7 for a list of Wilton essential cupcake products and other commonly used decorating items you may need.

INSTRUCTIONS

1 **Prepare mini cupcakes.** Tint ¼ of icing each red and green, reserve ½ white. Pipe a tip 12 icing spiral around edge of cupcake and covering top in white or red. Pipe four smaller tip 12 spirals, in alternating white with green or red with white.

2 **Add accents.** Spray with pearl Color Mist food color spray. Sprinkle with sparkling sugar. Each serves 1.

A Rousing
Reception!

Planning a big event? Serve a little cupcake! These fun treats-for-one add a welcoming, personal touch to the day. Plus, cupcakes can be combined to create a theme design as powerful as any cake. Check out the cupcake squares woven together as a baby shower blanket, or the wedding party featuring a family of faces big and small. For any special occasion, cupcakes give you strength in numbers!

Ⓐ Petal *Pinnacle*

Pans: Dimensions Large Cupcake, Multi-Cavity Mini Cupcake, p. 159; Standard, Mini Muffin, 14.5 in. x 20 in. Cooling Grid, p. 158

Fondant: White Ready-To-Use Rolled Fondant (25 oz.), 20 in. Fondant Roller, Roll-N-Cut Mat, Fondant Smoother, p. 164; Baroque Fondant & Gum Paste Mold, Flower Forming Cups, White Pearl Dust, Brush Set, Flower Cut-Outs Fondant Cutters, p. 165

Recipe: Buttercream Icing, p. 143

Also: White Sugar Pearls, p. 156; Piping Gel, Pure Lemon Extract, p. 160; Bamboo Dowel Rods, Cake Circles, Fanci-Foil Wrap, 9 in., 11 in. Straight Spatulas, p. 161

See p. 7 for a list of Wilton essential cupcake products and other commonly used decorating items you may need.

INSTRUCTIONS

1 **Make flowers.** Roll out fondant ⅛ in. thick as needed. Use Cut-Outs to cut five large, 20 medium and 30 small flowers. For five three-layer flowers, attach large, medium and small flowers using damp brush. For 10 two-layer flowers, attach medium and small flowers using damp brush. Attach a Sugar Pearl to centers of multi-layer flowers and remaining small flowers with piping gel. Dust petals with white Pearl Dust (p. 151). Let dry in 2.5 in. Flower Forming Cups.

2 **Prepare 2-piece large cupcake and one each multi-cavity mini, standard and mini cupcakes.** Trim three largest cupcakes slightly for a flat top. Ice sides and tops smooth with spatula in white, slightly rounding tops. Prepare large cupcake for stacked construction (p. 151).

3 **Decorate cupcakes.** Press fondant into baroque mold to make 85 large pearl chains. Attach to all sides with damp brush, positioning pearls to fit into spaces of previous row. Trim as needed. Paint all with white Pearl Dust/lemon extract mixture. Let dry.

4 **Stack tiers at party.** Attach flowers and additional Sugar Pearls using icing. Large cupcake serves 12; second largest cupcake serves 3, other cupcakes serve 1.

A tower of cupcakes brings whimsy to the wedding reception. Make the tiers with a variety of Wilton cupcake pan sizes and accent with rows of fondant pearl detail.

Wilton

🅑 Bevy of Bows

Pans: Dimensions Large Cupcake, p. 159; Standard Muffin, 10 in. x 16 in. Cooling Grid, p. 158

Tips: 6, 12, p. 162

Fondant: Chocolate (37 oz.), White (1 oz.) Ready-To-Use Rolled Fondant, Gum-Tex, 9 in., 20 in. Fondant Rollers, 20 in. Fondant Roller Guide Rings, Roll-N-Cut Mat, Fondant Trimmer, p. 164; Brush Set, p. 165

Recipe: Buttercream Icing, p. 143

Also: Pink, Teal, Brown, Purple, Green, Red Dots Standard Baking Cups, p. 155; 11 in. Straight, 9 in. Angled Spatula, 10 in. x 14 in. Cake Boards, 12 in. Disposable Decorating Bags, 6 in. Cake Circle, p. 161

See p. 7 for a list of Wilton essential cupcake products and other commonly used decorating items you may need.

INSTRUCTIONS

Make large cupcake bow loops. 1 day in advance, knead 2 teaspoons Gum-Tex into 24 oz. chocolate fondant. Reserve 12 oz. for 15 standard cupcake loop bows. Roll out fondant ⅛ in. thick. Use fondant trimmer to cut six strips, 1¼ in. x 7 in., and six strips, 1¼ in. x 6 in. Fold strips over to form loops. Attach ends together with damp brush. For center loop, cut one strip, 1¼ in. x 4 in. Shape into a circle, 1½ in. dia.; attach overlapping ends with damp brush. Let all loops dry on cut sides on cornstarch-dusted board.

Make standard cupcake bow loops. 1 day in advance, roll out reserved 12 oz. chocolate fondant ⅟₁₆ in. thick. For each treat, cut six strips, ⅝ in. x 3 in. Fold strips over to form loops; attach ends with damp brush. Let dry on sides on cornstarch-dusted board.

Prepare 2-piece large and standard cupcakes. Bake and cool standard cupcakes in pink, teal, purple, red and green cups; reserve brown cups for serving.

Decorate giant cupcake. Bake and cool. Prepare bottom for rolled fondant (p. 151). Roll out 12 oz. chocolate fondant ⅛ in. thick; cover bottom with fondant. Position top section on bottom section. Ice cupcake top fluffy with spatula in white.

Roll out 1 oz. white fondant ⅟₁₆ in. thick. Use narrow end of tip 12 to cut approximately 50 dots. Attach dots to cupcake bottom with damp brush.

Assemble giant bow. Attach 7 in. loops to top section with tip 6 dots of icing. Attach 6 in. loops between 7 in. loops. Attach center loop.

Decorate standard cupcakes. Ice tops smooth with spatula in white. Position six loops on each cupcake, trimming to fit as needed. For bow centers, roll a ball of chocolate fondant, ⅜ in. dia. Attach with tip 6 dot of icing.

For serving, slightly flatten brown dots cups. Position standard cupcakes. Cake serves 12; each cupcake serves 1.

ⓐ Wedding Party *Pose*

Pans: Standard Muffin, Mini Muffin, 10 in. x 16 in. Cooling Grid, p. 158

Tips: 2, 3, 12, 16, p. 162

Colors:* Copper, Brown, Red-Red, Black, Rose, Christmas Red, Lemon Yellow, Violet, p. 163

Fondant: White Ready-To-Use Rolled Fondant (5 oz. makes 7 treats), 9 in. Fondant Roller, Roll-N-Cut Mat, p. 164; Nature Fondant & Gum Paste Mold, Brush Set, p. 165

Recipe: Buttercream Icing, p. 143

Also: Monochrome Standard Baking Cups (white, black), Purple Dots Standard and Mini Baking Cups, p. 155; Piping Gel, p. 160; 9 in. Straight Spatula, 12 in. Disposable Decorating Bags, p. 161

See p. 7 for a list of Wilton essential cupcake products and other commonly used decorating items you may need.

INSTRUCTIONS

1 **Prepare cupcakes.** Ice smooth with spatula in copper (light skin tone) or brown, mounding slightly.

Pipe tip 2 dot eyes and outline mouth. Pipe tip 3 dot cheeks; pat smooth with finger dipped in cornstarch. Pipe tip 16 outline, swirl or pull-out hair.

2 **Make blossoms.** Tint 2 oz. fondant violet. Press violet fondant in nature mold to make a large blossom for each bridesmaid. Press violet fondant in nature mold to make three small blossoms for each flower girl. Press white fondant in nature mold to make three medium blossoms for bride. Roll a small white ball for each flower center; attach with piping gel. Set blossoms aside.

3 **Make veil.** Roll out white fondant 1/16 in. thick. Cut a triangle, 8 in. wide at bottom x 6 in. high. Trim off 2½ in. from top point. Attach to bride with damp brush; trim bottom edge as needed. Attach all blossoms with piping gel.

4 **Make bow tie.** Tint ½ oz. fondant black. Roll out ⅛ in. thick. For loops, cut two triangles, ½ in. wide at bottom x ¾ in. high. Cut knot using narrow end of tip 12. Attach tie with piping gel. Each serves 1.

*Combine Brown with Red-Red and Black for brown shown. Combine Red-Red with Christmas Red for red shown.

Ask friends to be in the bridal party with a cupcake topped with a simple fondant gown topper accented with Sugar Pearls and a blossom at the sash.

www.wilton.com

B Bridal Court

Pans: Standard Muffin, 10 in. x 16 in. Cooling Grid, p. 158

Tip: 4, p. 162

Color: Rose, p. 163

Fondant: White Ready-To-Use Rolled Fondant (1¼ oz. makes 5 treats), Gum-Tex, 9 in. Fondant Roller, Roll-N-Cut Mat, p. 164; Hearts Cut-Outs Fondant Cutters, Gum Paste Flower Cutter Set, p. 165

Recipes: Buttercream Icing, Thinned Fondant Adhesive, p. 143

Also: Black Dots Standard Baking Cups, p. 155; 4 in. Lollipop Sticks, p. 163; Pink, White Sugar Pearls, p. 156; 9 in. Straight Spatula, 12 in. Disposable Decorating Bags, Cake Board, p. 161

See p. 7 for a list of Wilton essential cupcake products and other commonly used decorating items you may need.

INSTRUCTIONS

1 **Make fondant accents.** 1 day in advance, knead ⅛ teaspoon Gum-Tex into 1¼ oz. of fondant. Tint 1 oz. fondant rose. Roll out rose and ¼ oz. white fondant ⅛ in. thick. Cut four rose hearts and one white heart using medium Cut-Out. Trim angled sides ¼ in. from each edge for dress bodices. Use small blossom ejector from flower cutter set to cut a matching color flower for each treat. Let all dry 24 hours on cornstarch-dusted board.

Trim lollipop sticks to 3 in. Using thinned fondant adhesive, attach bodices to sticks, leaving 2¼ in. extended at bottom. Using adhesive attach Sugar Pearls to neckline and flower centers in matching bodice color.

2 **Prepare cupcakes.** Ice four tops in pink and one in white with spatula in a mounded shape. Insert bodice in cupcake. Pipe tip 4 outline sash. Attach flower. Each serves 1.

ⓐ A Charmed *Life*

Pans: Standard Muffin, 10 in. x 16 in. Cooling Grid, p. 158

Tip: 2, p. 162

Colors:* Violet, Rose, p. 163

Fondant/Gum Paste: Ready-To-Use Gum Paste (1 oz. per treat), 9 in. Fondant Roller, Roll-N-Cut Mat, p. 164; Silver Pearl Dust, Brush Set, p. 165

Recipes: Buttercream Icing, Gum Glue Adhesive, p. 143

Also: Zebra ColorCups Standard Baking Cups, p. 154; 6-Pc. Heart Nesting Plastic Cutter Set, p. 166; Pure Lemon Extract, p. 160; Cupcake Spatula, 12 in. Disposable Decorating Bags, Cake Boards, p. 161; 4 in. Lollipop Sticks, p. 163

See p. 7 for a list of Wilton essential cupcake products and other commonly used decorating items you may need.

INSTRUCTIONS

1. **Make curved hook.** 2 or more days in advance, roll a gum paste log, ¼ in. dia. x 10 in. long. Insert lollipop stick in bottom, leaving 1½ in. extended to insert into cupcake. Place on cornstarch-dusted board and shape into curve, 6½ in. high with a 2¼ in. wide scroll. Let dry at least 48 hours. Paint with silver Pearl Dust/lemon extract mixture (p. 151). Let dry.

2. **Make heart ornament.** 1 day in advance, for each treat, tint ¼ oz. gum paste violet. Roll out ¹⁄₁₆ in. thick. Cut two hearts using smallest cutter from set. For hanger, roll a log, ⅛ in. dia. x 3 in. long. Fold into an oval loop ½ in. wide x 1 in. long and pinch bottom ½ in. to flatten; keep loop open to slide onto post. Sandwich flattened ends between the two hearts and secure with gum glue adhesive. Let dry on cornstarch-dusted board.

   For initial, roll a violet rope, ¹⁄₁₆ in. dia., and shape desired letter. Attach with adhesive. Paint loop with silver Pearl Dust/lemon extract mixture. Let dry.

3. **Prepare cupcakes.** Ice tops smooth with spatula in white. Pipe tip 2 scrolls around edge. Slide heart onto curved hook. Insert hook into cupcake. For serving, slightly flatten a second zebra baking cup. Position cupcakes. Each serves 1.

*Combine Violet with Rose for violet shown.

ⓑ Topiary *Treat*

Pans: Standard Muffin, Cookie Sheet, 10 in. x 16 in. Cooling Grid, p. 158

Tips: 2, 12, 127D, 225, p. 162

Colors:* Violet, Rose, Moss Green, p. 163

Recipes: Buttercream, Royal Icings, Roll-Out Cookies, p. 143

Also: Jewel Standard Baking Cups (purple), p. 155; Round Cut-Outs Fondant Cutters, Brush Set, p. 165; 6 in. Lollipop Sticks, p. 163; Meringue Powder, p. 160; 12 in. Disposable Decorating Bags, 15 in. Parchment Triangles, Cake Boards, p. 161; craft foam block

See p. 7 for a list of Wilton essential cupcake products and other commonly used decorating items you may need.

INSTRUCTIONS

1. **Make flowers.** 1 to 2 days in advance, for each treat, pipe 15 tip 225 swirled drop flowers in violet royal icing on waxed paper-covered board. Pipe tip 2 dot centers in white. Let dry.

2. **Make cookies.** 1 day in advance, prepare and roll out dough. For each treat, cut top circle using wide end of tip 127D and bottom circle using medium round Cut-Out. Bake and cool cookies. Using green royal icing, cover cookies with tip 225 star drop flowers for grass. Let dry overnight. Paint lollipop sticks with thinned green royal icing, leaving bottom 1 in. unpainted; stand in craft foam block to dry.

3. **Assemble topiary.** Attach cookies, ½ in. apart, to stick with royal icing. Attach flowers to cookies. Let set.

4. **Prepare cupcakes.** Tint buttercream to match baking cups and grass. Pipe tip 12 violet outline around cupcake edge. Fill in center with tip 225 star drop flowers in green. Insert topiary. Each serves 1.

*Combine Violet with Rose for violet shown.

Treats That Tickle You!

Pans: Standard Muffin, 10 in. x 16 in. Cooling Grid, p. 158

Colors:* Teal, Violet, Rose, Leaf Green, Lemon Yellow, p. 163

Fondant: White Ready-To-Use Rolled Fondant (1½ oz. per 3 treats), Gum-Tex, 9 in. Fondant Roller, Roll-N-Cut Mat, 10-Pc. Gum Paste/Fondant Tool Set, Shaping Foam, p. 164; Leaf Cut-Outs Fondant Cutters, Sapphire Blue, White, Leaf Green, Lilac Purple Pearl Dust, Brush Set, p. 165

Recipe: Buttercream Icing, p. 143

Also: Bright Rainbow Standard Baking Cups (purple, blue, green), p. 155; 4 in. Lollipop Sticks, White Candy Melts Candy, p. 163; Pure Lemon Extract, p. 160; Cake Board, Cupcake Spatula, p. 161

See p. 7 for a list of Wilton essential cupcake products and other commonly used decorating items you may need.

INSTRUCTIONS

Make feathers. 2 days in advance, tint ½ oz. fondant per treat teal, violet or green. Knead ⅛ teaspoon Gum-Tex into each color. Roll out ⅛ in. thick. Cut feathers using largest leaf Cut-Out. Gently roll out feather from bottom to top, to 5 in. long x 1¾ in. wide at widest point.

Place feather on thin shaping foam and score lines with thin end of veining tool. Cut slits with knife. Let dry on cornstarch-dusted board.

Decorate feathers. Bend lollipop sticks slightly to follow curve of feather. Attach a stick to back of each feather with melted candy, leaving 1 in. extended at bottom to insert in cupcake. Mix colored Pearl Dust with a little white Pearl Dust, lightening to match baking cups. Paint feathers with matching Pearl Dust/lemon extract mixture (p. 151). Let dry.

Prepare cupcakes. Ice tops smooth with spatula in white. Insert feather into cupcake. Each serves 1.

Combine Violet with Rose for violet shown. Combine Leaf Green with Lemon Yellow for green shown.

They're a perfect match: the happy couple and a large cupcake with tightly packed ribbon roses on top and interlocking fondant strips on the sides.

A High Rise *Roses*

Pans: Dimensions Large Cupcake, p. 159; 10 in. x 16 in. Cooling Grid, p. 158

Colors: Pink, Black, p. 163

Fondant: White Ready-To-Use Rolled Fondant (54 oz.), 20 in. Fondant Roller, Roll-N-Cut Mat, Fondant Smoother, 10-Pc. Gum Paste/Fondant Tool Set, Fondant Shaping Foam, Fondant Ribbon Cutter, Fondant Trimmer, p. 164; Brush Set, p. 165

Recipes: Buttercream Icing, Thinned Fondant Adhesive, p. 143

Also: Piping Gel, p. 160; Pastry Brush, p. 159; 11 in. Straight Spatula, 6 in. Cake Circle, p. 161

See p. 7 for a list of Wilton essential cupcake products and other commonly used decorating items you may need.

INSTRUCTIONS

1. **Prepare 2-piece large cupcake.** Bake and cool 2-piece large cupcake. Trim off approximately 1 in. from tip on top half of cake to create rounded shape. Lightly ice both halves with spatula. Cover top with 16 oz. white fondant.

2. **Make side strips for bottom half.** Tint 4 oz. fondant each light and dark gray and light and dark pink (add a little black to pinks to soften color). You will also need 2 oz. white fondant. Roll out light and dark colors and white fondant ⅛ in. thick. Use ribbon cutter fitted with two zigzag wheels and either ¼ in. or ½ in. spacer to cut assorted 4 in. long strips. Stretch slightly so bottom is a bit narrower than top.

   Attach strips to cake sides, trimming ends as needed. Add additional strips so zigzag notches fit nicely into previous strip. Vary colors and widths as you go around cake.

3. **Position top and bottom halves.** Attach with icing to secure.

4. **Make ribbon roses.** Roll out white fondant ⅟₁₆ in. thick as needed. For white roses use fondant trimmer to cut strips, ⅜ in. wide x 24 in. long. Thin top edge of strips on shaping foam using large ball tool. Brush a small section at top center of cake with piping gel. Loosely roll up each strip to form roses on the brushed section, varying the look to create a gently rippling petal line on top. Continue to cover top cake completely with roses; you will need about 52 roses (sizes will vary to fit).

   For top ribbon rose, tint 6 oz. fondant medium pink. Roll out ⅟₁₆ in. thick. Use fondant trimmer to cut two strips each 1 in. wide x 16 in. long. Begin rolling from one end of strip, pinching bottom edge to shape. Add second strip to create large rose. Attach to top with thinned fondant adhesive. Serves 12.

B *Petals Perfected*

Pans: Jumbo Muffin, 10 in. x 16 in. Cooling Grid, p. 158

Colors:* Brown, Kelly Green, Rose, Red-Red, p. 163

Fondant: White Ready-To-Use Rolled Fondant (2 oz. per treat), 9 in. Fondant Roller, Roll-N-Cut Mat, p. 164; Fabric Fondant & Gum Paste Mold, Bronze Pearl Dust, Brush Set, Leaf Cut-Outs Fondant Cutters, p. 165

Recipes: Buttercream Icing, Thinned Fondant Adhesive, p. 143

Also: White Jumbo Baking Cups, p. 155; 9 in. Angled Spatula, p. 161; Pure Lemon Extract, p. 160

See p. 7 for a list of Wilton essential cupcake products and other commonly used decorating items you may need.

INSTRUCTIONS

Make fondant buttons. 1 day in advance, press fondant in fabric mold to make one large two-hole button per treat (¼ oz. fondant makes six buttons). Let dry overnight on cornstarch-dusted board. Paint with bronze Pearl Dust/ lemon extract mixture (p. 151). Let dry.

Make fondant petals. 1 day in advance, tint 1 oz. fondant brown and ½ oz. each green and rose for each cupcake. Roll out ⅟₁₆ in. thick as needed. Cut 10 brown base petals using largest leaf Cut-Out. Cut five rose and five green petals using medium Cut-Out; repeat using smallest Cut-Out. Place medium petals over large petals, beginning ⅜ in. down from tip; add small petals of opposite color, beginning ⅜ in. down. Roll out each petal slightly to blend layers. Fold in half and pinch ends. Petals should be ¾ in. wide at widest point.

Prepare cupcakes. Ice tops smooth with spatula in white. For each flower, position 8 to 10 petals on each cupcake, alternating colors as you go. Trim ends as needed to fit. Attach button to center with icing. Each serves 1.

*Combine Brown with Red-Red for brown shown.

ⓐ Elegant *Initials*

Pans: Standard Muffin, 10 in. x 16 in. Cooling Grid, p. 158

Color: Teal, p. 163

Fondant: White Ready-To-Use Rolled Fondant (1 oz. makes 6 to 8 letters), Gum-Tex, p. 164; Letters/Numbers Fondant & Gum Paste Mold Set, p. 165

Recipes: Buttercream Icing, Thinned Fondant Adhesive, p. 143

Also: Teal Dots Standard Baking Cups, p. 155; Cupcake Spatula, p. 161

See p. 7 for a list of Wilton essential cupcake products and other commonly used decorating items you may need.

INSTRUCTIONS

1 **Make fondant initials.** 1 day in advance, tint 1 oz. fondant teal. Knead in ⅛ teaspoon Gum-Tex. Press into mold to make desired initials. Let dry 24 hours on cornstarch-dusted surface.
   Attach toothpick to back of each initial with thinned fondant adhesive. Let dry.

2 **Prepare cupcakes.** Ice smooth with spatula in white. Insert initials in cupcakes.
   Each serves 1.

B Tie *Finish*

Pans: Standard Muffin, 10 in. x 16 in. Cooling Grid, p. 158

Fondant: Black Ready-To-Use Rolled Fondant (1½ oz. makes 3 treats), Gum-Tex, 9 in. Fondant Roller, Roll-N-Cut Mat, p. 164; Brush Set, p. 165

Sugar Sheets! **Edible Decorating Paper/Tools:** Damask (1 sheet makes 12 treats), Light Blue (1 sheet makes 24 treats), Dab-N-Hold Edible Adhesive, p. 160

Recipe: Buttercream Icing, p. 143

Also: Monochrome Standard Baking Cups (black), p. 155; Cupcake Spatula, p. 161; Circle Metal Cutter, p. 166; 101 Cookie Cutters (small circle), p. 167; Fine Tip Primary Colors FoodWriter Edible Color Markers, p. 163; Piping Gel, p. 160

See p. 7 for a list of Wilton essential cupcake products and other commonly used decorating items you may need.

INSTRUCTIONS

1. **Make bows.** 1 day in advance knead ⅛ teaspoon Gum-Tex into 1½ oz. black fondant for three treats. Roll out ¹⁄₁₆ in. thick. For bow loops, cut two strips ⅜ in. x 1½ in. Fold in half to form loops, securing ends with damp brush. Support loop openings with tissue. For knot, shape a ³⁄₁₆ in ball of fondant into a log, ⅛ in. dia. x ⅜ in. long. Attach around loops with damp brush. Let dry.

2. **Make edible paper background circle.** Use metal cutter to cut circle from damask edible paper. Using edible markers trace small circle cutter from set on light blue edible paper and cut out. Attach to damask circle with edible adhesive.

3. **Prepare cupcakes.** Ice smooth with spatula in white. Position background circle.

4. **Assemble bows.** For ribbon, cut a black fondant strip, ¼ in. x 1¾ in. Attach to blue circle with piping gel, trimming as needed. For streamers, cut two black fondant strips, ¼ in. x 1 in. Cut triangle shapes at one end. Attach to ribbon. Attach bow. Each serves 1.

C Letter-Perfect *Lambeth*

Pans: Standard Muffin, Cookie Sheet, 10 in. x 16 in. Cooling Grid, p. 158

Tips: 2, 4, 6, p. 162

Color: Royal Blue, p. 163

Recipes: Buttercream, Royal Icings, Roll-Out Cookies, p. 143

Also: Scroll Pattern, p. 153; Monochrome Standard Baking Cups, p. 155; Meringue Powder, p. 160; 12 in. Disposable Decorating Bags, Cupcake Spatula p. 161; 12 in. Rolling Pin, p. 159; Blossoms Nesting Metal Cutter Set, p. 166; Light Cocoa Candy Melts Candy (12 oz. makes 10 to 12 treats), p. 163

See p. 7 for a list of Wilton essential cupcake products and other commonly used decorating items you may need.

INSTRUCTIONS

1. **Make lambeth scrolls** (p. 149). 1 day in advance, using pattern and royal icing, make six scrolls per treat. Let dry 24 hours.

2. **Prepare cookies.** Prepare and roll out dough. Cut cookies using second largest (3 ¹⁵⁄₁₆ in.)blossom cutter. Bake and cool cookies.

   Place cookies on cooling grid over cookie sheet. Cover with melted light cocoa candy (p. 151). Let dry on waxed paper-covered surface.

3. **Prepare cupcakes.** Ice tops smooth with spatula in light blue buttercream. Position lambeth scrolls, leaving 1½ in. opening at bottom edge and attach using icing. Pipe tip 4 initial in white.

4. **Assemble treats.** Attach cupcake on its side to cookie, open area down, securing with melted candy. Each serves 1.

A ROUSING RECEPTION!

Ⓐ Brooches & Bracelets

Pans: Standard Muffin, 10 in. x 16 in. Cooling Grid, p. 158

Fondant: White Ready-To-Use Rolled Fondant (1 oz. per treat), p. 164; Jewelry, Baroque Fondant & Gum Paste Molds, Sapphire Blue, Ruby Red, Leaf Green, Silver, Gold, Orchid Pink, White Pearl Dust, Brush Set, p. 165

Recipes: Buttercream Icing, Thinned Fondant Adhesive, p. 143

Also: Pink Zebra (for brooches) Standard Baking Cups, p. 155, Leopard ColorCups (for bracelets) Standard Baking Cups, p. 154; White Sugar Pearls, p. 156; Pure Lemon Extract, p. 160; Cupcake Spatula, p. 161

See p. 7 for a list of Wilton essential cupcake products and other commonly used decorating items you may need.

Accessorize cupcakes with jewel fondant accents! They're easy to make in our jewelry and baroque molds—just add color and shine with brushstrokes of Pearl Dust.

INSTRUCTIONS

Prepare cupcakes. Ice smooth with spatula in white.

Make pearls for brooches. Press fondant into baroque mold (p. 150) to make two pearl chains for each treat. Brush all beads with white Pearl Dust. Position pearl chains in two rows on edge of cupcake top; trim to fit.

Make brooches and bracelets. Press fondant into jewelry mold to make brooches and mesh, chain link and square chain borders for bracelets. Trim bracelets to 3 in. long. Paint brooches and bracelets with silver or gold Pearl Dust/lemon extract mixture (p. 151). Let dry 10 to 15 minutes. Position on cupcakes.

Make gems. Press fondant into jewelry mold to make one round gem and one round gem back for each brooch cupcake. Press fondant into jewelry mold to make round, square or faceted gems with matching bases for bracelet cupcakes. Paint gem backs with silver or gold Pearl Dust/lemon extract mixture. Paint gems with sapphire blue, ruby red, leaf green or orchid pink Pearl Dust/lemon extract mixture. Let dry.

Assemble gems. Attach gems to backs and backs to brooches or bracelets with thinned fondant adhesive. Position Sugar Pearls on bracelet cupcakes. Each serves 1.

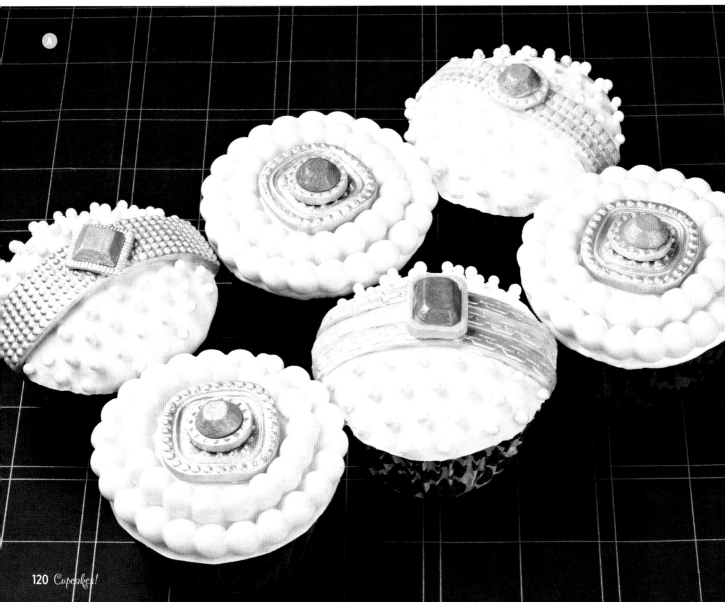

B Mini Cupcake *Necklace*

Pans: Mini Muffin, 10 in. x 16 in. Cooling Grid, p. 158

Tip: 127D, p. 162

Fondant: White Ready-To-Use Rolled Fondant (10 oz.), Gum-Tex, p. 164; Jewelry Fondant & Gum Paste Mold, Silver, Orchid Pink, Leaf Green, Lilac Purple Pearl Dust, Brush Set, p. 165

Recipes: Buttercream Icing, Thinned Fondant Adhesive, p. 143

Also: Silver Foil Mini Baking Cups, p. 155; Heart Comfort-Grip Cutter, p. 166; Cupcake Spatula, Cake Boards, p. 161; Pure Lemon Extract, p. 160

See p. 7 for a list of Wilton essential cupcake products and other commonly used decorating items you may need.

INSTRUCTIONS

1 **Make heart pendant.** 1 day in advance, knead ½ teaspoon Gum-Tex into 3 oz. white fondant. Roll out ⅛ in. thick. Use cutter to cut heart. Let dry overnight on cornstarch-dusted board. Press white fondant into jewelry mold (p. 150) to make two chain link borders. Attach around edge of heart using damp brush. Paint with silver Pearl Dust/lemon extract mixture (p. 151).

2 **Prepare 16 mini cupcakes.** Ice tops smooth with spatula in white. Reserve one cupcake to support heart.

3 **Make fondant trims.** Roll out fondant ⅛ in. thick. Cut circles using wide end of tip 127D. Attach to cupcakes using damp brush. Paint with silver Pearl Dust/lemon extract mixture.

Press white fondant into jewelry mold to make 16 brooches. Attach to cupcake tops with damp brush. Paint with silver and green or lilac Pearl Dust/lemon extract mixtures.

Press white fondant into jewlery mold to make 16 round gem backs. Place on cornstarch-dusted board; paint with silver Pearl Dust/lemon extract mixture.

Use mold to make 58 round gems. Paint with orchid pink Pearl Dust/lemon extract mixture. Attach 26 to heart, 16 to brooches and 16 to gem backs using damp brush.

4 **Assemble treats.** Position decorated mini cupcakes in an oval, ⅜ in. apart. Position plain gem backs to join cupcakes with thinned fondant adhesive. Position mini cupcakes under heart pendant. Each serves 1.

A Gilded *Lilies*

Pans: Dimensions Large Cupcake, p. 159; Standard Muffin, 10 in. x 16 in. Cooling Grid, p. 158

Tips: 1A, 8, p. 162

Color: Golden Yellow, p. 163

Fondant/Gum Paste: White Ready-To-Use Rolled Fondant (12 oz.), Ready-To-Use Gum Paste (1 pk.), 9 in. Fondant Roller, Roll-N-Cut Mat, Fondant Trimmer, Calla Lily Former Set, Storage Board, Fondant Shaping Foam, 10-Pc. Gum Paste/ Fondant Tool Set, p. 164; Gum Paste Flower Cutter Set, Flower Impression Set, White, Yellow Pearl Dust, Goldenrod Color Dust, Deluxe Brush Set, p. 165

Recipes: Buttercream Icing, Gum Glue Adhesive, p. 143

Also: 6 in. Cake Circle, Fanci-Foil Wrap, 12 in. Disposable Decorating Bags, 11 in. Straight, 9 in. Angled Spatulas, p. 161; Gold, Silver, Pearl Color Mist Food Color Spray, p. 163; Silver

Foil, Gold Foil Standard Baking Cups, p. 155; White Sugar Pearls, p. 156; corn meal (for lily centers)

See p. 7 for a list of Wilton essential cupcake products and other commonly used decorating items you may need.

INSTRUCTIONS

1. **Make calla lilies.** 2 days in advance, use calla lily cutter and instructions from flower cutter set to make 50 small gum paste calla lilies without wires. Let centers dry on waxed paper-covered board. Attach centers with a gum paste ball, ⅛ in. dia., and gum glue adhesive. Brush centers following instructions using white Pearl Dust and goldenrod Color Dust mixed with yellow Pearl Dust.

2. **Make fondant pleats.** In advance, roll out fondant ⅛ in. thick. Cut 25 strips, 1⅛ in. wide x 3½ in. long, tapering to ¾ in. wide at bottom. Gently fold strips vertically in half. Open strips and

let stand on long edges on waxed paper-covered board. Spray 12 strips with silver Color Mist food color spray and 13 strips with gold Color Mist food color spray. Let dry at least 10 minutes.

3. **Prepare 2-piece large and standard cupcakes.**

4. **Decorate large cupcake.** Position top section on bottom section. Ice top section and bottom sides smooth with spatula in white. Attach pleats to bottom sides, alternating colors and securing with tip 8 dots of icing if needed.

   Attach calla lilies to top section with tip 8 dots, starting at base and layering flowers to cover all areas.

5. **Decorate standard cupcakes.** Cover tops with tip 1A swirl in white. Immediately spray with pearl Color Mist food color spray. Position Sugar Pearls. Large cupcake serves 12; each cupcake serves 1.

Ⓑ Metallic *Magic*

Pans: Standard Muffin, 10 in. x 16 in. Cooling Grid, p. 158

Fondant: White Ready-to-Use Rolled Fondant (4 oz. makes 5 treats), Gum-Tex, 9 in. Fondant Roller, Roll-N-Cut Mat, Storage Board, p. 164; Fabric Fondant & Gum Paste Mold, Gold, Silver, White, Bronze Pearl Dust, Deluxe Brush Set, Detail Embosser, p. 165

Recipe: Buttercream Icing, p. 143

Also: Black Dots Standard Baking Cups, p. 155; 6-Pc. Star Nesting Plastic Cutter Set, p. 166; Cupcake Spatula, p. 160; Pure Lemon Extract, Piping Gel, p. 160

See p. 7 for a list of Wilton essential cupcake products and other commonly used decorating items you may need.

INSTRUCTIONS

Make fondant star stacks. 1 day in advance, knead ⅛ teaspoon Gum-Tex into 4 oz. fondant. Roll out ⅛ in. thick. Use second smallest cutter (2 ⅜ in.) to cut middle stars for each stack needed. For smooth designs shown, use smallest (1 ⅝ in.) and third smallest (3 in.) cutters to cut top and bottom stars. Set aside.

For patterned designs shown, roll out remaining fondant ⅛ in. thick. Imprint with detail embosser, using straight or bead wheels. Use smallest and third smallest cutters to cut top and bottom stars in matching designs. Paint stars with Pearl Dust/lemon extract mixtures in various colors (p. 151); let dry.

Make fondant buttons. 1 day in advance, use fabric mold and fondant to make one small four-hole button for each treat. Paint with Pearl Dust/lemon extract mixtures. Let dry.

Prepare cupcakes. Ice smooth with spatula in white.

Position stars. Stack stars largest to smallest and one button in various color combinations, securing with dots of icing. Let dry. Position stars. Each serves 1.

Ⓒ Milestone *Mums*

Pans: Standard Muffin, 10 in. x 16 in. Cooling Grid, p. 158

Tips: 2, 3, p. 162

Fondant: White Ready-To-Use Rolled Fondant (1½ oz. makes 6 assembled flowers); 9 in. Fondant Roller, Roll-N-Cut Mat, p. 164; Flower Forming Cups, Gold, Silver Pearl Dust, Brush Set, Flower Cut-Outs Fondant Cutters, p. 165

Recipes: Buttercream, Royal Icings, p. 143

Also: Gold, Silver Foil Standard Baking Cups, p. 155; 12 in. Disposable Decorating Bags, Cupcake Spatula, p. 161; Piping Gel, Meringue Powder, Pure Lemon Extract, p. 160

See p. 7 for a list of Wilton essential cupcake products and other commonly used decorating items you may need.

INSTRUCTIONS

1. **Make flowers.** 1 day in advance, roll out fondant ¹⁄₁₆ in. thick. Cut base flower using largest Cut-Out; place in 3 in. flower forming cups. Cut top flower using medium Cut-Out; place in separate flower forming cups. Brush all with gold or silver Pearl Dust (p. 151).

   Using royal icing thinned with piping gel, outline flowers with tip 2, two or three petals at a time; immediately brush icing inward for brush embroidery look (p. 151). Let dry. Attach top flowers to base flowers with tip 2 dot of icing, lining up petals. Pipe a tip 2 swirl in center. Paint brush embroidery areas with Pearl Dust/lemon extract mixture. Let dry.

2. **Prepare cupcakes.** Ice smooth with spatula in white buttercream. Position flowers. Pipe tip 3 scalloped outline following flower shape. Each serves 1.

A ROUSING RECEPTION!

Ⓓ Floating *Flowers*

Pans: Standard Muffin, 10 in. x 16 in. Cooling Grid, p. 158

Tip: 5, p. 162

Color: Black, p. 163

Fondant: White Ready-To-Use Rolled Fondant (1 oz. makes 8 to 10 treats), p. 164; Jewelry Fondant & Gum Paste Mold, Bronze Pearl Dust, Brush Set, p. 165

Recipe: Buttercream Icing, p. 143

Also: Monochrome Standard Baking Cups (silver), p. 155; Cupcake Spatula, 12 in. Disposable Decorating Bags, p. 161; White Sparkle Gel, p. 163; Pure Lemon Extract, p. 160

See p. 7 for a list of Wilton essential cupcake products and other commonly used decorating items you may need.

INSTRUCTIONS

1. **Prepare cupcakes.** Ice smooth with spatula in white.

2. **Make flower centers.** Press fondant into jewelry mold (p. 150) to make round gem and gem back. Attach gem to gem back with damp brush. Paint with bronze Pearl Dust/lemon extract mixture (p. 151). Let dry 10 minutes.

3. **Make petals.** Use tip 5 and icing to outline eight petals for each flower. Fill in with Sparkle Gel. Attach center to flower with icing. Each serves 1.

Cub On A Rug

Pans: Standard Muffin, 10 in. x 16 in. Cooling Grid, p. 158

Tip: 3, p. 162

Colors: Lemon Yellow, Leaf Green, Sky Blue, Rose, p. 163

Fondant: White Ready-To-Use Rolled Fondant (1 oz. per treat), 9 in. Fondant Roller, Roll-N-Cut Mat, p. 164; Round Cut-Outs Fondant Cutters, p. 165

Recipe: Buttercream Icing, p. 143

Also: Brown Dots Standard Baking Cups, p. 155; Cupcake Spatula, 12 in. Disposable Decorating Bags, p. 161; Bear with Gum Drop Royal Icing Decorations, p. 157

See p. 7 for a list of Wilton essential cupcake products and other commonly used decorating items you may need.

INSTRUCTIONS

1. **Prepare cupcakes.** Ice tops smooth with spatula in white.

2. **Make rugs.** Tint 1 oz. portions of fondant blue, rose, green and yellow. Roll out colors ⅟₁₆ in. thick. Cut circle using largest round Cut-Out. Position in center of cupcake.

   Pipe tip 3 pull-out fringe on edge of cupcake. Attach bear decoration with a tip 3 dot of icing. Each serves 1.

B Rainbow *Bibs*

Pans: Standard Muffin, 10 in. x 16 in. Cooling Grid, p. 158

Tip: 3, p. 162

Fondant: Pastel Colors Fondant Multi Pack (each 4.4 oz. color makes 6 treats), Gum-Tex, 9 in. Fondant Roller, Roll-N-Cut Mat, p. 164; Brush Set, Detail Embosser, Round Cut-Outs Fondant Cutters, p. 165

Recipe: Buttercream Icing, p. 143

Also: Pastel Standard Baking Cups, p. 155; Daisy Metal Cutter, p. 166; Cupcake Spatula, 12 in. Disposable Decorating Bags, Cake Boards, p. 161; Piping Gel, p. 160

See p. 7 for a list of Wilton essential cupcake products and other commonly used decorating items you may need.

INSTRUCTIONS

1. **Make bows.** 1 day in advance, knead ⅛ teaspoon Gum-Tex into 1½ oz. fondant for each color needed. Roll out fondant colors ⅟₁₆ in. thick. For bow loops, cut a strip, ¼ in. x 2½ in. Fold ends up to meet at center; secure with piping gel and pinch slightly. Support loop openings with tissue. For knot, cut a strip, ¼ in. x 1 in. Wrap around center and secure at back. For streamers, cut two strips, each ¼ in. x 1 in. Trim bottom ends at an angle. Attach behind bow. Let dry overnight on cornstarch-dusted board. Reserve remaining fondant.

2. **Prepare cupcakes.** Ice tops smooth with spatula in white.

3. **Make bibs.** Roll out reserved fondant ⅛ in. thick. Cut squares, 3 in. x 3 in. Imprint with bead wheel of detail embosser. Cut bibs using daisy cutter. Trim off top two petals. Cut neck opening using medium round Cut-Out, leaving a ⅛ in. wide top edge. Position bib on cupcake. Attach bow with icing dot. Pipe tip 3 letters. Each serves 1.

Baby Mobile
Menagerie

Pans: 6 in. x 2 in. Round, Standard Muffin, 10 in. x 16 in. Cooling Grid, p. 158

Tips: 1A, 2, 2A, 7, p. 162

Colors: * Moss Green, Ivory, Golden Yellow, Lemon Yellow, Brown, Rose, Orange, p. 163

Fondant: White Ready-To-Use Rolled Fondant (14 oz.), Gum-Tex, 9 in. Fondant Roller, Roll-N-Cut Mat, p. 164; Star, Leaf Cut-Outs Fondant Cutters, Storage Board, White Pearl Dust, Brush Set, p. 165

Recipes: Buttercream Icing, Thinned Fondant Adhesive, p. 143

Also: 13-Count Cupcakes-N-More Dessert Stand, p. 167; Green Dots Standard Baking Cups, p. 155; Cupcake Spatula, 6 in. Cake Circles, Plastic Dowel Rods, p. 161; Extra Fine Tip FoodWriter Edible Color Markers (black), p. 163; 18-gauge white florist wire (six pieces, 11 in. long), wire cutters

See p. 7 for a list of Wilton essential cupcake products and other commonly used decorating items you may need.

INSTRUCTIONS

1 **Make star mobile.** 1 day in advance, tint 3 oz. fondant light yellow. Knead ¼ teaspoon Gum-Tex into fondant. Roll out ⅛ in. thick. Use Cut-Outs to cut three each large and medium stars. Cut hanging hole in each using narrow end of tip 7. Let dry 24 hours on cornstarch-dusted boards. Reserve remaining yellow.

Cut florist wire into six pieces, 11 in. long. Use Gum-Tex container as a guide to shape curl. Curve tip around edible marker to shape hanging curl.

2 **Make animal heads.** 1 day in advance, knead ½ teaspoon Gum-Tex into 6 oz. fondant. Tint 2¼ oz. light brown, ½ oz. each light rose and orange; reserve 2½ oz. white. Roll four balls each 1 in. dia. in brown for bears, white for bunnies and reserved yellow for chicks, Reserve remaining fondant.

For bears, roll out light brown ⅛ in. thick. Use narrow end of tip 2A to cut two ears for each bear. Trim a flat edge with knife. Attach to heads using thinned fondant adhesive. Knead ¼ oz. white fondant into remaining brown. Roll out ¹⁄₁₆ in. thick. Use narrow end of tip 1A to cut muzzles. Attach to heads. Let dry.

For bunnies, roll out white ⅛ in. thick and light rose ¹⁄₁₆ in. thick. Use small leaf Cut-Out to cut two white ears for each (reverse Cut-Out for opposite ears). Let dry. Use knife to cut a small leaf shape in light rose for inner ears. Attach with thinned fondant adhesive. Use narrow end of tip 2 to cut two white cheeks (flatten) and one rose of itnose for each bunny. Attach to heads. Let dry.

For chicks, shape an orange ball, ⅜ in. dia. for bill. Flatten one side; use knife to cut a slit for opening. Attach to heads using thinned fondant adhesive. Let dry.

Draw features on all heads using black edible color marker.

3 **Prepare cake and 12 cupcakes.** Bake and cool 1-layer round cake using firm-textured batter, such as pound cake. Use knife to cut a circle from cake 3¼ in. dia.

Tint 4 oz. fondant green. Lightly ice cake smooth with spatula in white. Cover cake with green fondant (p. 151). Cut dowel rod to 3 in. long. Fill dowel rod with fondant. Insert in center of cake. Roll out remaining green fondant ⅛ in. thick. Use knife to cut a strip, 1 in. x 2¾ in. Wrap strip around extended dowel rod. Roll out white fondant ¹⁄₁₆ in. thick. Use narrow end of tip 7 to cut 40 to 45 dots. Attach to cake and dowel rod with damp brush.

Ice cupcake tops smooth with spatula in white. Position heads.

4 **Assemble treats.** Brush stars with white Pearl Dust.

Position cupcakes and cake on stand. Insert wires in dowel rod. Hang stars on wires. Cake serves 2; each cupcake serves 1.

*Combine Moss Green with Ivory for green shown. Combine Golden Yellow with Lemon Yellow for yellow shown.

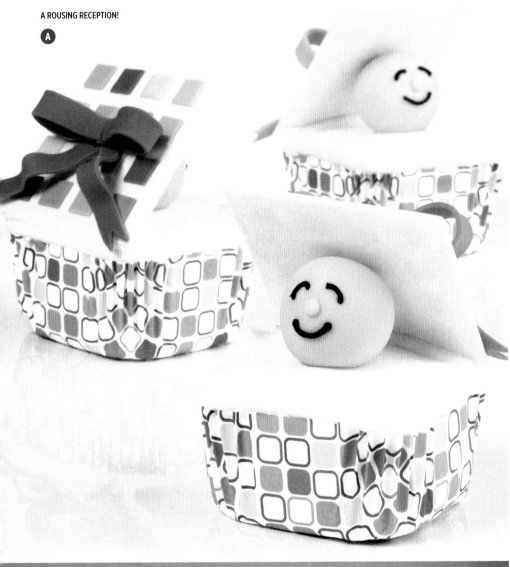

 Gifted *Children*

Pans: Bar, 10 in. x 16 in. Cooling Grid, p. 158

Tip: 3, p. 162

Colors: Violet, Orange, Leaf Green, Lemon Yellow, Sky Blue, Rose, Black, Copper (for light skin tone shown), p. 163

Fondant: White Ready-To-Use Rolled Fondant (2¾ oz. per treat), Gum-Tex, 9 in. Fondant Roller, Roll-N-Cut Mat, Fondant Trimmer, p. 164; Brush Set, p. 165

Recipes: Buttercream Icing, Thinned Fondant Adhesive, p. 143

Also: Warm Squares Square Baking Cups, p. 154; 12 in. Disposable Decorating Bags, Cupcake Spatula, p. 161

See p. 7 for a list of Wilton essential cupcake products and other commonly used decorating items you may need.

INSTRUCTIONS

1 **Make bows (p. 150).** 1 day in advance, for three treats, knead ¾ teaspoon Gum Tex into 3 oz. fondant. Tint 1 oz. portions of fondant blue, orange and violet. Roll out ⅛ in. thick. Make bows using two strips, each ⅜ in. x 4 in., for loops, two strips, each ⅜ in. x 2 in., for streamers and one strip, ⅜ in. x ¾ in., for knot. Reserve remaining fondant.

2 **Make box tops (p. 150).** 1 day in advance, cut white fondant base square and color tiles.

3 **Make heads.** 1 day in advance, for three heads, tint 1½ oz. fondant copper. Roll each ball head 1¼ in. dia. Roll a ball nose, ⅛ in. dia.; attach to head with thinned fondant adhesive.

4 **Prepare cupcakes.** Ice smooth with spatula in white.

5 **Assemble treats.** Attach bow and streamers to box top with thinned fondant adhesive. Position head in center of cupcake. Pipe tip 3 outline eyes and mouth in black. Position box top on treat, resting on head and securing with icing. Each serves 1.

 Babies on *Board!*

Pans: Standard Muffin, 10 in. x 16 in. Cooling Grid, p. 158

Tips: 2, 12, p. 162

Colors: Copper (for skin tone shown), Black, p. 163

Fondant: Pastel Colors Fondant Multi-Pack (½ oz. blue for his hat, ⅛ oz. pink for her bow), 9 in. Fondant Roller, Roll-N-Cut Mat, 10-Pc. Gum Paste/Fondant Tool Set, p. 164; Brush Set, p. 165

Recipe: Buttercream Icing, p. 143

Also: His Hat Pattern, p. 153; Rainbow Dots ColorCups Standard Baking Cups, p. 154; Cupcake Spatula, 12 in. Disposable Decorating Bags, p. 161

See p. 7 for a list of Wilton essential cupcake products and other commonly used decorating items you may need.

INSTRUCTIONS

1 **Make fondant trims.** 1 day in advance, for his hat, roll out blue fondant ¼ in. thick. Use pattern and knife to cut out hat. Use narrow veining tool from set to score seam lines. Let dry on cornstarch-dusted board.

For her bow, roll out pink fondant ⅛ in. thick. Cut bow strip, 1½ in. x ⅞ in., tapering center to ½ in. wide. For knot, cut a strip, ¼ in. x 1 in.; use damp brush to attach around center of bow. Use veining tool to score bow details. Let dry on cornstarch-dusted board.

2 **Prepare cupcakes.** Ice tops smooth with spatula in copper. Pipe tip 2 dot eyes and outline smile in black. For her, add tip 12 dot cheeks in copper; pat smooth with finger dipped in cornstarch. Attach hat or bow with tip 12 dot of icing. Each serves 1.

Wilton

C Bubbly *Babies*

Pans: Standard Muffin, Cookie Sheet, 10 in. x 16 in. Cooling Grid, p. 158

Tips: 2, 4, 7, p. 162

Colors: Copper (for skin tone shown), Black, p. 163

Recipes: Buttercream, Color Flow Icings, Roll-Out Cookies, p. 143

Also: 12 in. Rolling Pin, p. 159; Round Cut-Outs Fondant Cutters, p. 165; Color Flow Mix, Piping Gel, p. 160; 12 in. Disposable Decorating Bags, Cupcake Spatula, p. 161; Pink Dots, Teal Dots, Purple Dots Standard Baking Cups, p. 155; 6 in. Lollipop Sticks, White Candy Melts Candy, p. 163; Brush Set, p. 165; White Sugar Pearls, p. 156

See p. 7 for a list of Wilton essential cupcake products and other commonly used decorating items you may need.

INSTRUCTIONS

1 **Make cookie heads.** In advance, prepare and roll out dough. Cut one circle per treat using medium Cut-Out. Bake and cool cookies. Outline with tip 2 in full-strength copper Color Flow. Flow in with thinned Color Flow. Let dry overnight.

2 **Decorate facial features.** Use full-strength Color Flow to pipe tip 2 dot eyes and outline mouth in black, tip 4 outline ears in copper. Let dry. Cut lollipop sticks in half; attach to back of cookie using melted candy. Let set.

3 **Prepare cupcakes.** Ice tops smooth with spatula in white buttercream. Insert cookie head. Pipe various size tip 7 ball bubbles on head and top and side of cupcake. Position Sugar Pearls randomly in bubbles, securing with piping gel. Each serves 1.

D Baby Soft Colors

Pans: Bar, 10 in. x 16 in. Cooling Grid, p. 158

Colors: Rose, Teal, Lemon Yellow, Leaf Green, p. 163

Fondant: White (8 oz.), Chocolate (15 oz.) Ready-To-Use Rolled Fondant, 9 in. Fondant Roller, Roll- N-Cut Mat, Fondant Trimmer, p. 164; Letters/Numbers Gum Paste & Fondant Mold Set, p. 165

Recipe: Chocolate Buttercream Icing, p. 143

Also: Warm Squares Square Baking Cups, p. 154; Cupcake Spatula, 13 in. x 19 in. Cake Board, Fanci-Foil Wrap, p. 161

See p. 7 for a list of Wilton essential cupcake products and other commonly used decorating items you may need.

INSTRUCTIONS

Make fondant letter plaques. 1 day in advance, tint 2 oz. fondant each rose, teal, yellow and green. Roll out 1⁄16 in. thick. Use fondant trimmer to cut a square, 2¾ in. x 2¾ in. in each color. Let dry 24 hours on cornstarch-dusted board. Reserve remaining tinted fondant.

Press chocolate fondant into mold to make letters. Attach letters to plaques with damp brush.

Prepare 20 cupcakes. Lightly ice smooth with spatula in chocolate buttercream.

Assemble treats. Roll out chocolate fondant 1⁄8 in. thick. Use trimmer to cut squares, 2¼ in. x 2¼ in.; position on cupcake tops.

Roll out reserved tinted fondant 1⁄16 in. thick. Cut 10 strips in each color, 3⁄8 in. x 2½ in. Attach one strip in each color, ¼ in. apart, on 10 cupcakes using damp brush.

Position cupcakes on foil-wrapped cake board in four rows of five cupcakes. Position letter plaques. Each cupcake serves 1.

Shower guests will love these brimming bathtubs! The cupcakes are overflowing with piped icing bubbles and topped with a cute baby face cookie.

Ⓐ

Fast track treats for the grad. Roll a fondant scroll, wrap it with a bow and place atop an iced cupcake.

Ⓐ Tops of the Class!

Pans: Standard Muffin, Cookie Sheet, 10 in. x 16 in. Cooling Grid, p. 158

Tips: 6, 230, p. 162

Colors:* Royal Blue, Violet, Black, Christmas Red, Red-Red, Lemon Yellow, Golden Yellow, p. 163

Fondant: White Ready-To-Use Rolled Fondant (1 oz. makes 4 treats), Decorative Press Set, p. 164; Brush Set, p. 165

Recipes: Buttercream, Royal Icings, Roll-Out Cookies, p. 143

Also: 12 in. Rolling Pin, Parchment Paper, p. 159; Primary (red, blue), Monochrome (black) Standard Baking Cups, p. 155; 12 in. Disposable Decorating Bags, Cupcake Spatula, p. 161; Meringue Powder, p. 160; White Candy Melts candy (4 oz. makes 6 treats), p. 163

See p. 7 for a list of Wilton essential cupcake products and other commonly used decorating items you may need.

B

INSTRUCTIONS

Make mortarboard cookies. In advance, prepare and roll out dough ⅛ in. thick. Use knife to cut cookies, 3¾ in. square. Bake and cool. Place cookies on cooling grid over parchment paper-lined cookie sheet. Tint royal icing to match baking cups. Cover cookies with thinned royal icing; tap grid lightly to release air bubbles. Let dry. Reserve some of each color full-strength icing for decorating.

Prepare cupcakes. Fill blue, red and black cups halfway with batter so that tops will be flat; bake and cool. Trim crowns flat if needed. Use tip 230 to fill cupcakes with buttercream (p. 10).

Attach cookies. Ice cupcake tops with melted candy. Chill until firm. Turn cupcakes bottom side up. Attach cookie with melted candy; let set.

Make tassel. Tint ¼ oz. fondant yellow for each treat. Use decorative press with 3-hole insert to press strands, 9 in. long. Cut six pieces, 1½ in. long; reserve remainder. Press six pieces together at top to form tassel. From reserved portion, cut a single strand, 1¾ in. long, for cord. Attach cord to top of cookie and tassel to cord with full-strength royal icing. Wrap a 1½ in. length around the top of tassel for knot, securing with damp brush. Use reserved icing to pipe tip 6 button over cord. Pat smooth with finger dipped in cornstarch. Each serves 1.

*Combine Royal Blue with Violet and Black for navy blue shown. Combine Lemon Yellow with Golden Yellow for yellow shown. Combine Christmas Red with Red-Red for red shown.

C CAPital Letters

Pans: Standard Muffin, Cookie Sheet, 10 in. x 16 in. Cooling Grid, p. 158

Tip: 3, p. 162

Colors: Orange, Teal, Golden Yellow, Black, p. 163

Fondant: White Ready-To-Use Rolled Fondant (2 oz. makes 3 treats), 9 in. Fondant Roller, Roll-N-Cut Mat, p. 164

Recipes: Buttercream, Color Flow Icings, Roll-Out Cookies, Thinned Fondant Adhesive, p. 143

Also: 12 in. Rolling Pin, p. 159; 101 Cookie Cutters (letters), p. 167; Color Flow Mix, p. 160; 15 in. Parchment Triangles, Cupcake Spatula, Cake Boards, p. 161; White Candy Melts Candy, 4 in. Lollipop Sticks, p. 163; Yellow, Blue, Orange, Green Dots ColorCups Standard Baking Cups, p. 154; Silver Stars Edible Accents, p. 157

See p. 7 for a list of Wilton essential cupcake products and other commonly used decorating items you may need.

INSTRUCTIONS

1 **Make letter cookies.** 1 day in advance, prepare and roll out dough. Cut letters using cookie cutters. Bake and cool cookies.

Tint portions of Color Flow icing orange, yellow and teal. Outline cookies with tip 3 and full-strength Color Flow. Flow in with thinned Color Flow. Let dry 24 hours.

Trim lollipop sticks to 3 in. Attach to backs of cookies with melted candy, leaving 1½ in. extended from bottom for inserting in cupcake. Chill until firm.

2 **Make graduation caps.** 1 day in advance, tint 1½ oz. fondant black and ½ oz. yellow for three treats. Roll out black 1/16 in. thick. Cut a square, 1 in. x 1 in., for mortarboard. Let dry overnight.

For cap, roll ¾ in. ball of black fondant; cut in half. Attach half, flat side down, to mortarboard with fondant adhesive. For tassel, roll out yellow fondant 1/16 in. thick. Cut a strip, ¾ in. x 1 in. Cut slits, 1/16 in wide and ½ in. deep. Roll and taper uncut end to form tassel. Attach to mortarboard with damp brush. For top button, roll a ball of black fondant, ⅛ in. dia.; attach with damp brush. Let dry.

3 **Prepare cupcakes.** Ice tops smooth with spatula in white; immediately sprinkle with edible accents. Insert cookies. Attach caps with melted candy; hold until set. Each serves 1.

It's elementary that grade-school grads will love colorful cookies with their cupcakes. The A-B-C's are capped off with a fun fondant mortarboard.

B A Senior's Sendoff!

Pans: Standard Muffin, 10 in. x 16 in. Cooling Grid, p. 158

Colors: Sky Blue, Red-Red, p. 163

Fondant: White Ready-To-Use Rolled Fondant (1½ oz. per treat), Gum-Tex, 9 in. Fondant Roller, Roll-N-Cut Mat, p. 164; Brush Set, p. 165

Recipe: Buttercream Icing, p. 143

Also: Celebrate Blue ColorCups Standard Baking Cups, p. 154; Cupcake Spatula, 12 in. Disposable Decorating Bags, Cake Board, p. 161; Piping Gel, p. 160

See p. 7 for a list of Wilton essential cupcake products and other commonly used decorating items you may need.

INSTRUCTIONS

1 **Make diplomas.** 1 day in advance, roll out white fondant 1/16 in. thick. Cut a rectangle, 2½ in. x 3 in. Roll up loosely for scroll; secure with piping gel.

2 **Make bows.** 1 day in advance, knead ⅛ teaspoon Gum-Tex into 1½ oz. fondant fot 3 treats. Tint red. Roll out 1/16 in. thick. For loops, cut a strip, ¼ in. x 2½ in. Fold ends up to meet at center; secure with piping gel and pinch slightly. Support loop openings with tissue. For knot, cut a strip, ¼ in. x 1 in. Wrap around center and secure at back. For tails, cut two strips, ¼ in. x 1 in. Trim bottom ends at an angle. Attach behind bow at an angle. Cut a red strip, ¼ in. x 2½ in. Wrap around diploma and secure ends in back; trim as needed. Attach bow with piping gel. Let dry overnight on cornstarch-dusted board.

3 **Prepare cupcakes.** Ice tops smooth with spatula in blue. Position diplomas. Each serves 1.

C

Must-Try
Recipes

Our cupcakes definitely look amazing, but they also taste fantastic! Find a wide range of flavors—some traditional and some truly unexpected—in this recipe section. Looking for something light and sweet... try the Lemon Drop or Fruit Tart Cupcakes. If decadence is what you're leaning toward, you'll love Salted Caramel or Banana Walnut Cupcakes. Or, try something totally new, like the Earl Grey or Ants on A Log Cupcakes.

Piña Colada Cupcakes

A Piña Colada *Cupcakes*

Pack your bags and grab your shades because this cupcake will take you on a vacation! The pineapple and coconut add great texture and subtle sweetness.

FOR CUPCAKES:

2½ cups all-purpose flour

2 teaspoons baking soda

½ teaspoon salt

1 cup buttermilk

¾ cup vegetable oil

3 eggs

1 teaspoon coconut extract

1½ cups granulated sugar

2 cups sweetened shredded coconut

FOR ICING:

1 can (20 oz.) pineapple slices in natural juice, drained and divided

½ cup solid vegetable shortening

½ cup (1 stick) butter, softened

1 teaspoon Wilton Imitation Clear Vanilla Extract

4 cups sifted confectioners' sugar (about 1 lb.)

1½ tablespoons Wilton Light Green Colored Sugar

Toasted shredded coconut for garnish

INSTRUCTIONS:

Cupcakes: Preheat oven to 325°F. Line muffin pan with baking cups.

In medium bowl, stir together flour, baking soda and salt.

In large bowl, whisk together buttermilk, oil, eggs and coconut extract. Stir in sugar and coconut. Add flour mixture; mix well. Fill baking cups ⅔ full.

Bake 18-22 minutes or until Cake Tester or toothpick inserted in center of cupcake comes out clean. Remove from oven. Cool cupcakes in pan on cooling grid 5 minutes. Remove from pan; cool completely.

Icing: Finely chop 3 slices pineapple. Quarter remaining slices; reserve.

In large bowl, beat shortening and butter with electric mixer until creamy. Add vanilla. Gradually add sugar, one cup at a time, beating well on medium speed. Scrape sides and bottom of bowl often. Add finely chopped pineapple and beat until well combined.

To Assemble: Ice cupcakes. Dip edges of cupcake in green sugar. Garnish with toasted coconut and reserved quartered pineapple slices.

Makes about 24 cupcakes.

Serve the unique taste of Piña Colada Cupcakes with a twist. Pour colored sugar in a cocktail glass and top with your cupcake.

B Fruit Tart *Cupcakes*

These light and sweet cupcakes are sure to be a crowd pleaser! Add blackberries, raspberries or peaches for more flavor and sweet fun!

FOR CUPCAKES:

1 box (16-18.25 oz.) white cake mix

Eggs, water, vegetable oil to prepare mix

Fresh strawberries, sliced

2 kiwi, peeled and sliced

1 pint blueberries

FOR PASTRY CREAM:

6 tablespoons granulated sugar

¼ cup all-purpose flour

½ teaspoon salt

1 cup milk

4 egg yolks

1 teaspoon Wilton Pure Vanilla Extract

2 tablespoons unsalted butter

INSTRUCTIONS:

Cupcakes: Preheat oven to 350°F. Line muffin pan with baking cups.

In large bowl, beat cake mix, eggs, water and oil with electric mixer at low speed 30 seconds. Scrape bottom and sides of bowl; beat at medium speed 2 minutes. Fill baking cups ⅔ full with batter.

Bake 18-20 minutes or until Cake Tester or toothpick inserted in center of cupcake comes out clean. Cool cupcakes in pan on cooling grid 5 minutes. Remove from pan; cool completely.

In small saucepan, combine sugar, flour and salt. Whisk in milk and egg yolks until combined. Cook over medium heat, stirring constantly with a spoon, until mixture is thickened, 5-8 minutes. Remove from heat; stir in vanilla and butter.

Fill large bowl with ice. Pour mixture into small bowl and place inside large bowl to cool quickly. To prevent skin from forming, place plastic wrap directly on surface of cream mixture. Chill until ready to use.

To Assemble: Cut a hole approximately 1 in. wide x 1 in. deep with paring knife in the top of each cupcake. Spoon about 2 tablespoons pastry cream into cupcake and spread to edges so top is covered. Arrange strawberries, kiwi and blueberries on top.

Makes about 24 cupcakes.

Fruit Tart
Cupcakes

C Peaches & Cream *Cupcakes*

Enjoy the taste of peach cobbler in a cup! Adding fruit to the batter makes these cupcakes moist and flavorful, while the velvety smooth icing helps them melt in your mouth.

2 cans (15 oz. ea.) sliced peaches, drained and divided

1 package (16.5 oz.) yellow cake mix

3 eggs

⅓ cup vegetable oil

1 package (10 oz.) Wilton Whipped Icing Mix

INSTRUCTIONS:

Cupcakes: Preheat oven to 350°F. Line muffin pan with baking cups.

Reserve 6 peach slices for garnish. In bowl of food processor, pulse remaining peach slices until pureed. Measure 1 cup; reserve remaining puree.

In large bowl, mix 1 cup peach puree, cake mix, eggs and oil with electric mixer at low speed 30 seconds. Scrape bottom and sides of bowl; beat at medium speed 2 minutes. Fill baking cups ⅔ full with batter.

Bake 18-20 minutes or until Cake Tester or toothpick inserted in center of cupcake comes out clean. Cool cupcakes in pan on cooling grid 5 minutes. Remove from pan; cool completely.

Dip tops of cupcakes in remaining peach puree, shaking off excess.

Prepare whipped icing mix following package instructions. Ice cupcakes with icing; add reserved peaches.

Makes about 24 cupcakes.

Peaches & Cream Cupcakes

Fresh summer flavor and aroma delight the senses in our Peaches & Cream Cupcakes. With a dollop of whipped icing and bits of peach on top, it's pure sunshine for your celebration.

Turtle Cupcakes

Ⓐ Turtle Cupcakes

The classic candy combination—gooey caramel, crunchy pecans and intense chocolate—makes these cupcakes irresistible! It's a rich, decadent dessert that works for birthdays or banquets.

FOR CUPCAKES:

2½ cups all-purpose flour

1 teaspoon baking soda

½ teaspoon salt

6 ounces semi-sweet chocolate

¾ cup (1½ sticks) unsalted butter

1½ cups granulated sugar

3 eggs

2 teaspoons Wilton Pure Vanilla Extract

1½ cups milk

Chocolate Buttercream Icing
   (see p. 143)

FOR FILLING:

1 cup caramel ice cream topping, divided

1 cup chopped pecans, divided

1 cup hot fudge ice cream topping

INSTRUCTIONS:

Cupcakes: Preheat oven to 350°F. Line muffin pan with baking cups.

In medium bowl, stir together flour, baking soda and salt.

In large bowl, melt chocolate and butter on 50% power in microwave for 1 minute.

Stir and continue to melt at 50% power until smooth. (Mixture can also be melted on top of stove in heavy saucepan over low heat. Transfer to large bowl.) Add sugar to chocolate mixture and beat with electric mixer until well blended. Add eggs, one at a time, and vanilla; mix well. Add flour mixture alternately with milk; beat until well combined. Fill baking cups ⅔ full with batter.

Bake 18-20 minutes or until Cake Tester or toothpick inserted in center of cupcake comes out clean. Cool cupcakes in pan on cooling grid 5 minutes. Remove from pan; cool completely.

Filling: In small bowl, combine ¾ cup caramel topping and ¾ cup pecans; mix well. Reserve remaining caramel topping and pecans for garnish.

To Assemble: Cut a hole approximately 1 in. wide x 1 in. deep with paring knife in the top of each cupcake; spoon 1 tablespoon filling into each. Ice cupcakes with Chocolate Buttercream Icing, if desired, decorate wth tip 21 swirls. Drizzle with fudge and reserved caramel topping; sprinkle with remaining pecans.

Makes about 24 cupcakes.

Ⓑ Creamy Chocolate Hazelnut Cupcakes

Ground hazelnuts in the batter and sprinkled on top add a mellow flavor which contrasts with the rich devil's food cake.

FOR CUPCAKES:

1 box (16.5 oz) devil's food cake mix

1¼ cups milk

3 eggs

1 jar (26.5 oz.) hazelnut chocolate spread, divided

⅓ cup finely ground hazelnuts, plus additional for garnish

FOR ICING:

½ cup (1 stick) butter, softened

½ cup solid vegetable shortening

2 cups sifted confectioners' sugar (about ½ lb.)

Reserved chocolate hazelnut spread

2 tablespoons milk

INSTRUCTIONS:

Preheat oven to 350°F. Line muffin pan with baking cups.

In medium bowl, beat cake mix, milk, eggs, ½ cup hazelnut chocolate spread and ⅓ cup ground hazelnuts with electric mixer on low speed for 30 seconds. Stop mixer, scrape bottom and sides of bowl, and beat 2 minutes on medium speed. Fill baking cups ⅔ full.

Bake 17-19 minutes or until Cake Tester or toothpick inserted in center of cupcakes comes out clean. Cool cupcakes in pan on cooling grid 5 minutes. Remove from pan; cool completely.

Icing: In medium bowl, beat butter and shortening with electric mixer until creamy. Gradually add sugar, one cup at a time, beating well on medium speed. Add remaining chocolate hazelnut spread and mix until well combined. Scrape sides and bottom of bowl often. Add milk and beat at medium speed until light and fluffy.

To Assemble: Cut a hole approximately 1 in. wide x 1 in. deep with paring knife, in the top of each cupcake. Fill with 1½ teaspoons hazelnut chocolate spread. Ice filled cupcakes with Chocolate Hazelnut Buttercream Icing; if desired, decorate with tip 2A swirls. Sprinkle with additional ground hazelnuts, if desired.

Makes about 24 cupcakes.

A sinful surprise waits inside Creamy Chocolate Hazelnut Cupcakes. They're filled with smooth hazelnut chocolate spread, adding an intense flavor finish.

Creamy Chocolate Hazelnut Cupcakes

Wilton

Salted Caramel Cupcakes

C Salted Caramel *Cupcakes*

This sweet and savory dessert will surprise your palate. Pair this cupcake with vanilla ice cream or caramel latte for extra flavor.

FOR CUPCAKES:

3 cups cake flour, sifted

2½ teaspoons baking powder

½ teaspoon salt

⅔ cup butter, softened

1¾ cups granulated sugar

2 eggs

1½ teaspoons Wilton Pure Vanilla Extract

1¼ cups milk

1 jar (12-14 oz.) caramel ice cream topping, divided

FOR ICING:

½ cup solid vegetable shortening

½ cup (1 stick) butter, softened

⅔ cup caramel ice cream topping

1 teaspoon Wilton Pure Vanilla Extract

4 cups sifted confectioners' sugar (about 1 lb.)

Sea salt

INSTRUCTIONS:

Cupcakes: Preheat oven to 350°F. Line muffin pan with baking cups.

In large bowl, stir together flour, baking powder and salt.

In large bowl, beat butter and sugar with electric mixer until light and fluffy. Add eggs, one at a time, mixing well after each. Add vanilla. Alternately add dry ingredients with milk, scraping bottom and sides of bowl often. Fill baking cups ⅔ full with batter.

Bake 18-20 minutes or until Cake Tester or toothpick inserted in center of cupcake comes out clean. Remove from oven and place on cooling grid. Immediately poke cupcakes with fork; spoon 1 teaspoon caramel topping onto each cupcake. Reserve remaining topping. Cool 5-8 minutes. Remove from pan; cool completely.

Icing: In large bowl, beat shortening and butter with electric mixer until creamy. Add caramel topping and vanilla. Gradually add sugar, one cup at a time; beat until light and fluffy.

To Assemble: Ice cupcakes with Caramel Buttercream Icing; if desired, decorate with tip 2A swirls. Drizzle with remaining caramel topping; sprinkle with sea salt.

Makes about 24 cupcakes.

D Black Eye *Cupcakes*

you love coffee and a caffeine buzz, these are the cupcakes for you! These cupcakes are named after the popular offee house drink, the Black Eye, made by pouring two shots of espresso into a cup of drip-brewed java. The drink as named for the way the espresso ring looked while being poured into the coffee. Delicious and fragrant, these upcakes are for true coffee lovers!

OR CUPCAKES:

¼ cups milk

cup instant espresso powder

cups sifted cake flour

teaspoon baking powder

teaspoon baking soda

teaspoon salt

0 tablespoons (1¼ sticks) butter, softened

½ cups granulated sugar

eggs

teaspoon Wilton Pure Vanilla Extract

OR FILLING:

cup granulated sugar

½ tablespoons instant espresso powder

¼ teaspoons cornstarch

inch salt

cup milk

tablespoons heavy whipping cream

egg yolks

OR ICING:

tablespoons instant espresso powder

cup milk

cup solid vegetable shortening

cup (1 stick) butter, softened

cups sifted confectioners' sugar (about 1 lb.)

INSTRUCTIONS:

Cupcakes: Preheat oven to 350°F. Line muffin pan with baking cups.

In small bowl, heat milk in the microwave until steaming. Whisk in espresso powder until dissolved. Cool.

In medium bowl, sift together flour, baking powder, baking soda and salt.

In medium bowl, beat butter and sugar with electric mixer until light and fluffy. Add eggs and vanilla; mix well. Add flour mixture alternately with espresso mixture, beating well after each addition. Continue beating one minute. Fill baking cups ⅔ full with batter.

Bake 18-20 minutes or until Cake Tester or toothpick inserted in cupcake comes out clean. Cool cupcakes in pan on cooling grid 5 minutes. Remove from pan; cool completely.

Filling: Set a fine mesh strainer inside a small bowl.

In small saucepan, stir together sugar, espresso powder, cornstarch and salt. In medium bowl, whisk together milk, cream and egg yolks. Stir into saucepan. Cook over medium heat, stirring constantly, until mixture thickens and boils. Push through strainer. Cover top of filling directly with plastic wrap. Chill completely.

Icing: In small bowl, whisk together espresso powder and milk.

In large bowl, beat shortening and butter with electric mixer until light and fluffy. Alternately add confectioners'sugar, one cup at a time, with milk mixture, scraping sides and bottom of bowl often. Beat until fluffy.

To Assemble: Using tip 22, pipe a ring of espresso icing around the outer edge of the cupcake. Using Bismarck tip #230, fill cupcakes with espresso filling, letting it mound up and fill in the center of the icing ring.

Makes about 24 cupcakes.

Black Eye Cupcakes

D

Cupcakes! **135**

Ⓐ Ants On A Log *Cupcakes*

Carrot cake is commonplace, but have you ever thought about adding other veggies to your treats? Inspired by the classic children's snack, Ants On A Log Cupcakes feature crunchy bits of celery in the cake. Topped with creamy peanut butter icing and chewy raisins, they'll take you back to childhood!

2½ cups all-purpose flour

1¾ cups granulated sugar

2 teaspoons baking powder

½ teaspoon celery seed

½ teaspoon salt

4 eggs

¾ cup vegetable oil

¼ cup water

1 cup finely diced celery (about 3 medium stalks) plus additional for garnish

½ cup raisins, plus additional for garnish

Peanut Butter Buttercream Icing

INSTRUCTIONS:

Preheat oven to 350°F. Line muffin pan with baking cups.

In medium bowl, stir together flour, sugar, baking powder, celery seed and salt.

In large bowl, beat eggs with electric mixer until foamy. Add oil and water in a thin stream; beat well. Add flour mixture to egg mixture; mix until just combined. Stir in 1 cup celery and ½ cup raisins. Fill baking cups ½ full with batter.

Bake 20-23 minutes or until Cake Tester or toothpick inserted in center of cupcake comes out clean. Cool cupcakes in pan on cooling grid 5 minutes. Remove from pan; cool completely.

To Assemble: Ice cupcakes with Peanut Butter Buttercream Icing; if desired, decorate with a tip 21 swirl. Garnish with additional celery and raisins.

Makes about 24 cupcakes.

Peanut Butter Buttercream *Icing*

If you want an icing that will work for just about any chocolate or fruit-flavored cupcake, go for this nutty, creamy delight.

⅓ cup solid vegetable shortening

⅓ cup butter, softened

¾ cup peanut butter

1 teaspoon Wilton Clear Vanilla Extract

4 cups sifted confectioners' sugar (about 1 lb.)

¼ cup milk

INSTRUCTIONS:

In large bowl, beat shortening and butter with electric mixer until creamy. Add peanut butter, and vanilla. Gradually add sugar, one cup at a time, beating well at medium speed. Scrape sides and bottom of bowl often. When all sugar has been mixed in, icing will appear dry. Add milk, a tablespoon at a time, and beat at medium speed until light and fluffy.

Makes about 3 cups icing.

Ⓐ

Ants On a Log Cupcakes with
Peanut Butter Buttercream Icing

B

ⓑ Peanut Butter & Jelly Cupcakes

PB&J sandwiches are every child's favorite lunchtime choice. This nostalgic sweet treat will definitely steal the spotlight at your next party. Pair cupcakes with a cold glass of milk and enjoy!

1 box (16.5 oz.) yellow cake mix

3 eggs

1 cup water

⅓ cup creamy peanut butter

¾ cup grape jelly, divided

Peanut Butter Buttercream Icing

⅓ cup finely chopped peanuts

INSTRUCTIONS:

Preheat oven to 350°F. Line muffin pan with baking cups.

In large bowl, beat yellow cake mix, eggs, water and peanut butter with electric mixer at low speed 30 seconds. Beat at medium speed 2 minutes. Fill baking cups ⅔ full with batter. Spoon 1 teaspoon jelly on top of batter in the center of each cup. Reserve remaining jelly for garnish.

Bake 18-20 minutes or until Cake Tester or toothpick inserted in center of cupcake comes out clean. Cool cupcakes in pan on cooling grid 5 minutes. Remove from pan; cool completely.

To Assemble: Ice cupcakes with Peanut Butter Buttercream Icing; if desired, decorate with tip 21 swirls. In microwave-safe bowl, microwave remaining jelly on High 10-15 seconds; stir until smooth. Drizzle over cupcakes and sprinkle with peanuts.

Makes about 24 cupcakes.

www.wilton.com

Think outside the lunchbox! Our Peanut Butter & Jelly Cupcakes posess the ideal flavor combo to please young and old.

Tart lemon is always a palate pleaser. With citrus-laced cake and icing plus colorful lemon zest on top, Lemon Drop Cupcakes are a refreshing choice.

Earl Grey Cupcakes

Lemon Drop Cupcakes

Ⓐ Lemon Drop *Cupcakes*

Zesty flavor and color make this the perfect all-occasion cupcake. Combine your favorite lemon cake mix with Wilton Pure Lemon Extract for a mildly tart taste with great appeal!

FOR CUPCAKES:

1 box (18.25 oz.) lemon flavored cake mix

3 eggs

1⅓ cups milk

6 tablespoons (¾ stick) butter, melted

2 teaspoons Wilton Pure Lemon Extract

FOR ICING:

4 egg whites

1 cup granulated sugar

Pinch of salt

1½ cups (3 sticks) butter, softened and cut into chunks

2 teaspoons grated lemon zest

1 teaspoon Wilton Pure Lemon Extract

Additional lemon zest (optional)

INSTRUCTIONS:

Cupcakes: Preheat oven to 350°F. Line muffin pan with baking cups.

In large bowl, beat cake mix, eggs, milk, butter and lemon extract with electric mixer 30 seconds at low speed. Scrape bottom and sides of bowl well. Increase speed to medium and beat 2 minutes. Fill baking cups ⅔ full with batter.

Bake 18-20 minutes or until Cake Tester or toothpick inserted in center of cupcake comes out clean. Cool cupcakes in pan on cooling grid 5 minutes. Remove from pan; cool completely.

Icing: In double boiler, combine egg whites, granulated sugar and salt. Whisk constantly over low heat until mixture reaches 140°F on a thermometer. Transfer to large bowl; whip at high speed with electric mixer until mixture cools to room temperature. Switch to paddle attachment on mixer. While beating at medium speed, add butter, one chunk at a time, scraping bottom and sides of bowl as necessary. Add lemon zest and lemon extract; beat until well combined.

To Assemble: Ice cupcakes with Lemon Drop Buttercream Icing. If desired, decorate with tip 1M swirl and garnish with lemon zest.

Makes about 24 cupcakes.

Wilton

ⓑ Earl Grey *Cupcakes*

It's tea time! You'll love the soothing qualities of Earl Grey that's steeped in the batter, but feel free to substitute your favorite tea bags to bake up the brew that's right for you.

FOR CUPCAKES:

1⅓ cups milk

6 Earl Grey tea bags

2¼ cups cake flour

1 tablespoon baking powder

½ cup (1 stick) unsalted butter, softened

1 cup + 2 tablespoons granulated sugar

½ teaspoon Wilton Pure Vanilla Extract

6 egg whites

FOR GLAZE:

2 teaspoons grated orange zest

3 tablespoons orange juice

1½ cups confectioners' sugar

Mint leaves

INSTRUCTIONS:

Cupcakes: Preheat oven to 350°F. Line jumbo muffin pan with standard baking cups.

In small saucepan, heat milk just until boiling; turn off heat. Add tea bags. Steep 40 minutes or until milk is at room temperature. Remove tea bags.

In large bowl, sift together flour and baking powder.

In large bowl, beat butter and sugar with electric mixer until light and fluffy. Add vanilla and egg whites, one at a time, scraping bottom and sides of bowl. Alternately add flour mixture with milk, scraping bottom and sides of bowl often. Mix until thoroughly combined. Fill baking cups ⅔ full with batter.

Bake 15-18 minutes or until Cake Tester or toothpick inserted in center of cupcake comes out clean. Cool cupcakes in pan on cooling grid 5 minutes. Remove from pan; cool completely.

Glaze: In medium bowl, stir together orange zest, orange juice and confectioners' sugar.

To Assemble: Spread Orange Glaze onto cupcakes. Garnish with orange slice, mint leaf and a twist of orange peel, if desired.

Makes about 24 cupcakes.

ⓒ Banana Walnut French Toast *Cupcakes*

Wake up your taste buds with a breakfast-inspired flavor combo that's welcome all day long. Hearty maple syrup, sweet bananas and crunchy candied walnuts combine with rich cream cheese icing for the cupcake of your dreams.

FOR CUPCAKES:

1 cup chopped walnuts

2 tablespoons maple syrup

2¾ cups all-purpose flour

1½ teaspoons baking soda

¼ teaspoon salt

1 cup (2 sticks) butter, softened

1 cup granulated sugar

¾ cup firmly-packed brown sugar

3 eggs

3 ripe bananas, mashed (about 1¼ cups)

1½ teaspoons Wilton Pure Vanilla Extract

¾ cup sour cream

FOR MAPLE CREAM CHEESE ICING:

2 packages (8 oz. ea.) cream cheese, softened

½ cup (1 stick) butter, softened

¼ teaspoon maple extract

3 cups confectioners' sugar, sifted

INSTRUCTIONS:

Cupcakes: Preheat oven to 350°F. Line muffin pan with paper baking cups.

In non-stick skillet, toast walnuts over low heat, stirring occasionally until fragrant, about 5 minutes. Add maple syrup; stir to coat nuts. Continue cooking and stirring until bottom of pan is nearly dry, about 2 minutes. Remove nuts from pan; cool completely.

In medium bowl, combine flour, baking soda and salt; set aside. In large bowl, beat butter and sugars with electric mixer until light and fluffy. Add eggs, mashed banana and vanilla; mix well. Add flour mixture alternately with sour cream; blend thoroughly. Mix in ¾ cup candied walnuts. Fill baking cups ⅔ full.

Bake 20-25 minutes or until Cake Tester or toothpick inserted in center of cupcake comes out clean. Cool cupcakes in pan on cooling grid 5 minutes. Remove from pan; cool completely.

Icing: In large bowl, beat cream cheese and butter until creamy. Add maple extract and confectioners' sugar, 1 cup at a time, scraping down bottom and sides of bowl as necessary. Beat in maple extract.

To Assemble: Ice cupcakes with Maple Cream Cheese Icing; if desired, decorate with tip 21 zigzags. Top with remaining candied walnuts.

Makes about 24 cupcakes.

Banana Walnut French Toast Cupcakes

Red Velvet
Cheesecake
Cupcakes

A Red Velvet Cheesecake Cupcakes

The rich gets richer! Creamy cheesecake and moist red velvet cake come together in one amazing cupcake. Set off sparks at patriotic parties by adding blue icing color to the cream cheese filling for a red, white and blue finale.

FOR GRAHAM CRACKER CRUST:

1 cup graham cracker crumbs

3 tablespoons butter, melted

3 tablespoons granulated sugar

FOR FILLING:

2½ packages (20 oz.) cream cheese, softened

¾ cup granulated sugar

2½ teaspoons Wilton Imitation Clear Vanilla Extract

2 eggs

1 tablespoon all-purpose flour

¼ cup sour cream

FOR CAKE:

1 box (18.25 oz.) red velvet cake mix

Eggs, water and vegetable oil to prepare mix

FOR CREAM CHEESE ICING:

1½ packages (12 oz.) cream cheese, softened

2 teaspoons Wilton Imitation Clear Vanilla Extract

1 cup (2 sticks) butter, softened

4 cups sifted confectioners' sugar (about 1 lb.)

Pecan halves (optional)

INSTRUCTIONS:

Crust: Line muffin pan with baking cups.

In small bowl, stir together graham cracker crumbs, butter and sugar. Press ½ tablespoon of mixture in each baking cup; press down with back of spoon.

Filling: Preheat oven to 350°F.

In large bowl, beat cream cheese with electric mixer until smooth. Add sugar and vanilla; mix until thoroughly combined. Beat in eggs, flour and sour cream; mix until smooth. Spoon about 2 tablespoons mixture over crust in baking cups.

Bake 10-12 minutes or until cheesecake is just set. Remove from oven, place on cooling grid and cool 5 minutes.

Cake: In large bowl, beat cake mix, eggs, water and oil with electric mixer at low speed 30 seconds. Scrape bottom and sides of bowl; beat at medium speed 2 minutes. Spoon batter over baked cheesecake mixture, filling baking cups ¾ full.

Bake 10-12 minutes or until Cake Tester or toothpick inserted in center of cupcake comes out clean. Cool cupcakes in pan on cooling grid 5 minutes. Remove from pan; cool completely.

Icing: In large bowl, beat cream cheese and butter with electric mixer until light and fluffy. Add vanilla. Gradually add confectioners' sugar and beat until smooth.

To Assemble: Ice cupcakes with Cream Cheese Icing. Top with pecans if desired.

Makes about 36 cupcakes.

Candied Yam
Cupcakes

B

Wilton

Taffy Apple Cupcakes

When it comes to true fruit flavor, our Taffy Apple Cupcakes don't fall far from the tree. Finely chopped apples are in the batter and rich caramel and peanuts enrobe the top.

Ⓑ Candied Yam *Cupcakes*

If you only get candied yams at Thanksgiving, bake up a batch of these treats anytime! All the hearty spiced goodness is here with sweet potatoes, nutmeg, pecans and marshmallow crème blending for a memorable taste sensation.

FOR CUPCAKES:

2¾ cups all-purpose flour

1 tablespoon baking powder

1½ teaspoons ground cinnamon

½ teaspoon ground nutmeg

½ teaspoon salt

½ cup (1 stick) butter, softened

1¼ cups firmly-packed brown sugar

2 eggs

1 can (15 oz.) sweet potatoes, drained and pureed (about 1 cup)

1 teaspoon Wilton Pure Vanilla Extract

1 teaspoon maple extract

½ cup milk

¾ cup chopped pecans, toasted

FOR TOPPING:

1 jar (about 7½ oz.) marshmallow crème

INSTRUCTIONS:

Preheat oven to 350°F. Line muffin pan with baking cups.

In medium bowl, stir together flour, baking powder, cinnamon, nutmeg and salt.

In large bowl, beat butter and sugar with electric mixer until light and fluffy. Add eggs, one at a time, scraping bottom and sides of bowl. Add pureed sweet potatoes, vanilla and maple extracts; beat until well combined. Alternately add flour mixture with milk, scraping bottom and sides of bowl often. Stir in pecans. Fill baking cups ½ full.

Bake 20-23 minutes or until Cake Tester or toothpick inserted in center of cupcake comes out clean. Adjust oven to broil and position oven rack 8-10 inches from top. Cover each cupcake with a heaping tablespoon of marshmallow crème; if desired, decorate with a tip 1M swirl. Broil 30-45 seconds or until marshmallow is toasted. Remove from oven. Cool cupcakes in pan on cooling grid 5 minutes. Remove from pan; cool completely.

Makes about 24 cupcakes.

Ⓒ Taffy Apple *Cupcakes*

Taffy apples are a favorite treat, so why not add the ingredients to a cupcake?! The diced apples and caramel candy in the cake give this treat good texture and a fall flavor.

FOR CUPCAKES:

2¼ cups all-purpose flour

2½ teaspoons baking powder

½ teaspoon ground cinnamon

¼ teaspoon salt

½ cup (1 stick) butter, softened

1¼ cups granulated sugar

3 eggs

1½ teaspoons Wilton Pure Vanilla Extract

¾ cup milk

1¾ cups finely chopped apples (about 2 large)

FOR TOPPING:

1 package (14 oz.) caramel candy pieces

2 tablespoons water

¾ cup chopped peanuts

6 in. Cookie Treat Sticks

INSTRUCTIONS:

Cupcakes: Preheat oven to 350°F. Line muffin pan with baking cups.

In medium bowl, combine flour, baking powder, cinnamon and salt; set aside.

In large bowl, beat butter and sugar with electric mixer until light and fluffy. Add eggs, one at a time, mixing well after each; add vanilla. Alternately add dry ingredients with milk, scraping bottom and sides of bowl often. Fold in apples. Fill baking cups ⅔ full with batter.

Bake 18-20 minutes or until Cake Tester or toothpick inserted in center of cupcake comes out clean. Cool cupcakes in pan on cooling grid 5 minutes. Remove from pan; cool completely.

Topping: In small bowl, microwave caramel candy and water on 50% power 2-3 minutes; stir at 1 minute intervals until fully melted and smooth.

To Assemble: Dip tops of cupcakes in topping. Sprinkle peanuts around rim of each cupcake and insert cookie stick through middle. Let stand at least 5 minutes for the caramel to set.

Makes about 24 cupcakes.

A Pistachio Raspberry Cupcakes

The delicious nutty flavor of pistachio partners with lush, ripe raspberries for one unforgettable cupcake. What could be better? Ice these treats with delectable White Chocolate Buttercream Icing!

FOR CUPCAKES:
2¼ cups all-purpose flour
⅔ cup finely ground toasted pistachios
2 teaspoons baking powder
1 teaspoon baking soda
½ teaspoon salt
½ cup (1 stick) butter, softened
1½ cups granulated sugar
3 eggs
2 teaspoons Wilton Pure Vanilla Extract
¼ teaspoon Wilton Imitation
  Almond Extract
Wilton Leaf Green Icing Color (optional)
1 cup milk
½ cup seedless raspberry jam

FOR ICING:
½ cup solid vegetable shortening
½ cup (1 stick) butter
3 cups sifted confectioners' sugar
4 ounces white chocolate, melted
1-2 tablespoons milk
Fresh raspberries (optional)
Chopped pistachios (optional)

INSTRUCTIONS:

Cupcakes: Preheat oven to 375°F. Line muffin pan with baking cups.

In large bowl, stir together flour, ground pistachios, baking powder, baking soda and salt.

In large bowl, beat butter and sugar with electric mixer until light and fluffy. Add eggs one at a time, scraping down sides and bottom of bowl as necessary. Add vanilla and almond extracts and icing color, if desired. Alternately add flour mixture with milk; beat until just combined. Fill baking cups ⅔ full with batter.

Bake 15-17 minutes (7-8 minutes for mini cupcakes) or until Cake Tester or toothpick inserted in center of cupcakes comes out clean. Cool cupcakes in pan on cooling grid for 5 minutes. Remove from pan; cool completely.

In small bowl, microwave jam for 30-45 seconds. Stir until smooth. Dip tops of cooled cupcakes in jam, shaking off excess.

Icing: In large bowl, beat shortening and butter with electric mixer. Gradually add sugar, one cup at a time, beating well on medium speed. Scrape sides and bottom of bowl often. Add melted white chocolate and beat at medium speed until well combined. Icing will appear dry. Add 1 tablespoon milk and beat at medium speed. If icing is still dry, add additional tablespoon milk.

To Assemble: Ice cupcakes with White Chocolate Buttercream Icing; if desired, decorate with tip 1M star. Garnish with fresh raspberries and chopped pistachios.

Makes about 24 standard cupcakes or 48 mini cupcakes.

Pistachio Raspberry Cupcakes

B Cherries Jubilee Cupcakes

A classic dessert made cupcake size! Luscious cherry pie filling with a touch of brandy adds to the flavor of your favorite yellow cake mix. Top it off with a scoop of vanilla ice cream and more cherry pie filling.

FOR CUPCAKES:
1 box (15-18.25 oz.) yellow cake mix
Eggs, water, vegetable oil to prepare mix
1 tablespoon grated orange zest
1 can (21 oz.) cherry pie filling
3 tablespoons brandy (optional)

FOR TOPPING:
1 quart vanilla ice cream
Mint leaves (optional)

INSTRUCTIONS:

Preheat oven to 350°F. Line muffin pan with baking cups.

In large bowl, beat cake mix, eggs, water, oil and orange zest with electric mixer at low speed 30 seconds. Scrape bottom and sides of bowl; beat on medium speed 2 minutes. Fill baking cups ⅔ full with batter.

Bake 18-20 minutes or until Cake Tester or toothpick inserted in center of cupcake comes out clean. Cool cupcakes in pan on cooling grid 5 minutes. Remove from pan; cool completely.

In skillet, heat cherry pie filling and brandy over medium-high heat, stirring occasionally, until boiling. Continue cooking 1 minute. Remove from heat; cool completely.

To Assemble: Cut a hole approximately 1 in. wide x 1 in. deep with paring knife in the top of each cupcake. Spoon cherries onto cupcake. Top with a scoop of vanilla ice cream and additional cherry filling. If desired garnish with mint leaves.

Variations: Omit brandy from recipe. Do not cook cherry pie filling before filling cupcakes. Or, top cupcakes with Wilton Whipped Icing Mix in place of vanilla ice cream.

Makes about 24 cupcakes.

Cherries Jubilee Cupcakes

Additional Cupcake Recipes

CHOCOLATE CUPCAKES

1 package (16.5 oz.) chocolate cake mix
⅓ cup unsweetened cocoa powder
3 eggs
1⅓ cups water
1 cup mayonnaise

INSTRUCTIONS:

Preheat oven to 350°F. Line muffin pan with baking cups.

In large bowl, combine cake mix, cocoa, eggs, water and mayonnaise. Beat with electric mixer on low speed 30 seconds, scraping bowl frequently. Beat on medium speed 2 minutes. Fill baking cups ⅔ full with batter.

Bake 18-20 minutes or until Cake Tester or toothpick inserted in center of cupcake comes out clean. Cool cupcakes in pan on cooling grid 5 minutes. Remove from pan; cool completely.

Makes about 24 cupcakes.

YELLOW CUPCAKES

3 cups sifted cake flour
2½ teaspoons baking powder
½ teaspoon salt
⅔ cup butter or margarine, softened
1¾ cups granulated sugar
2 eggs
1½ teaspoons Wilton Pure Vanilla Extract
1¼ cups milk

INSTRUCTIONS:

Preheat oven to 350°F. Line muffin pan with baking cups.

In large bowl, combine flour, baking powder and salt; set aside.

In second large bowl, beat butter and sugar with electric mixer until light and fluffy. Add eggs and vanilla; mix well. Add flour mixture alternately with milk, beating well after each addition. Continue beating 1 minute. Fill baking cups ⅔ full.

Bake 18-20 minutes or until Cake Tester or toothpick inserted in center of cupcake comes out clean. Cool cupcakes in pan on cooling grid 5 minutes. Remove from pan; cool completely.

Makes about 24 cupcakes.

WHITE CUPCAKES

3 cups sifted cake flour
1 tablespoon baking powder
½ cup (1 stick) butter or margarine, softened
1½ cups granulated sugar
½ teaspoon Wilton Imitation Clear Vanilla Extract
¾ cup milk
5 egg whites

INSTRUCTIONS:

Preheat oven to 350°F. Line muffin pan with baking cups.

In large bowl, sift together flour and baking powder.

In large bowl, beat butter and sugar with electric mixer until light and fluffy. Add vanilla; mix well. Add flour mixture alternately with milk; mix well. In separate clean bowl, beat egg whites until stiff but not dry; fold into batter. Fill baking cups ⅔ full.

Bake 17-19 minutes or until Cake Tester or toothpick inserted into center of cupcake comes out clean. Cool cupcakes in pan on cooling grid 5 minutes. Remove from pan; cool completely.

Makes about 24 cupcakes.

Icing Recipes

These fantastic recipes are perfect for either spreading on cupcakes or creating incredible icing accents.

BUTTERCREAM ICING

Our Buttercream Icing recipe is perfect for spreading or decorating. Follow our instructions to make it the ideal consistency you need. (Medium Consistency)

½ cup solid vegetable shortening
½ cup (1 stick) butter or margarine, softened
1 teaspoon Wilton Imitation Clear Vanilla Extract
4 cups sifted confectioners' sugar (about 1 lb.)
2 tablespoons milk

INSTRUCTIONS:

In large bowl, beat shortening and butter with electric mixer. Add vanilla. Gradually add sugar, one cup at a time, beating well on medium speed. Scrape sides and bottom of bowl often. When all sugar has been mixed in, icing will appear dry. Add milk and beat at medium speed until light and fluffy. Keep bowl covered with a damp cloth until ready to use. For best results, keep icing bowl in refrigerator when not in use. Refrigerated in an airtight container, this icing can be stored 2 weeks. Rewhip before using. Makes about 3 cups.

For thin (spreading) consistency icing, add 2 tablespoons light corn syrup, water or milk.

PURE WHITE ICING

INSTRUCTIONS:

(Stiff Consistency) Omit butter; substitute an additional ½ cup vegetable shortening for butter and ½ teaspoon Wilton Imitation Clear Butter Flavor. Add up to 4 tablespoons light corn syrup, water or milk to thin for icing cakes.

CHOCOLATE BUTTERCREAM ICING

INSTRUCTIONS:

Add ¾ cup cocoa powder (or three 1 oz. squares unsweetened chocolate, melted) and an additional 1-2 tablespoons milk to buttercream icing. Mix until well blended.

DARK CHOCOLATE BUTTERCREAM ICING

INSTRUCTIONS:

Add an additional ¼ cup cocoa powder (or 1 additional 1 oz. square unsweetened chocolate, melted) and 1 additional tablespoon milk to chocolate buttercream icing.

ROYAL ICING

This smooth, hard-drying icing is perfect for making decorations that last. It is also useful as a "cement" to fasten decorations together.

3 tablespoons Wilton Meringue Powder
4 cups sifted confectioners' sugar (about 1 lb.)
6 tablespoons water

INSTRUCTIONS:

Beat all ingredients at low speed 7-10 minutes (10-12 minutes at high speed for portable mixer) until icing forms peaks. Makes about 3 cups.

Thinned Royal Icing: To thin for pouring, add 1 teaspoon water per cup of royal icing. Use grease-free spoon or spatula to stir slowly. Add ½ teaspoon water at a time until you reach proper consistency.

COLOR FLOW ICING

Color Flow is used to make detailed icing decorations you let dry and harden before positioning on your cupcakes. You can "draw" almost any design using this special icing, and with care, your projects can be saved.

Full-strength for outlining:

¼ cup + 1 teaspoon water
4 cups sifted confectioners' sugar (about 1 lb.)
2 tablespoons Wilton Color Flow Mix

INSTRUCTIONS:

With electric mixer, using grease-free utensils, blend all ingredients on low speed 5 minutes. If using hand mixer, use high speed. Color Flow icing "crusts" quickly, so keep bowl covered with a damp cloth while using. Stir in desired icing color. Makes about 2 cups.

Thinned for filling in areas: To fill in an outlined area, the recipe above must be thinned with ½ teaspoon of water per ¼ cup of icing (just a few drops at a time as you near proper consistency). Use grease-free spoon or spatula to stir slowly. Color Flow is ready for filling in outlines when a small amount dropped into the mixture takes a count of ten to disappear.

NOTE: Color Flow designs take a long time to dry, so plan to do your Color Flow piece at least 2 or 3 days in advance.

Cookie Recipes

Cookies are great toppers, bases, or accents for cupcakes. Try these tasty recipes that are right for any cupcake.

ROLL-OUT COOKIES

A delicious sugar cookie that melts in your mouth, this recipe is perfect to use with all our cookie cutters.

1 cup (2 sticks) unsalted butter, softened
1½ cups granulated sugar
1 egg
1½ teaspoons Wilton Imitation Clear Vanilla Extract
½ teaspoon Wilton Imitation Almond Extract
2¾ cups all-purpose flour
1 teaspoon baking powder
1 teaspoon salt

INSTRUCTIONS:

Preheat oven to 350°F. In large bowl, beat butter and sugar with electric mixer until light and fluffy. Beat in egg and extracts. Combine flour, baking powder and salt; add to butter mixture 1 cup at a time, mixing after each addition. Do not chill dough. Divide dough into 2 balls. On a floured surface, roll each ball into a circle approximately 12 in. wide and ⅛ in. thick. Dip cookie cutter in flour before each use. Bake cookies on ungreased cookie sheet 8-11 minutes or until cookies are lightly browned. Makes about 3 dozen 3 in. cookies. Recipe may be doubled.

GINGERBREAD COOKIES

Just like Grandma used to make, it's a quick and easy recipe to create delicious spiced cookies.

5½ - 6 cups all-purpose flour
1 teaspoon baking soda
1 teaspoon salt
2 teaspoons ground cinnamon
2 teaspoons powdered ginger
1 teaspoon ground nutmeg
1 teaspoon ground cloves
1 cup solid vegetable shortening
1 cup granulated sugar
1¼ cups molasses
2 eggs, beaten

INSTRUCTIONS:

Preheat oven to 375°F. Thoroughly mix flour, baking soda, salt and spices. In large saucepan, melt shortening. Cool slightly. Add sugar, molasses and eggs to saucepan; mix well. Add 4 cups dry ingredients and mix well.

Turn mixture onto lightly floured surface. Knead in remaining dry ingredients by hand. Add a little more flour, if necessary, to make firm dough.

On floured surface, roll out ⅛ in. to ¼ in. thick for cut-out cookies. Bake on ungreased cookie sheet, small and medium-sized cookies 6-10 minutes, large cookies 10-15 minutes. Makes 40 medium sized cookies.

NOTE: If you're not going to use your gingerbread dough right away, wrap in plastic wrap and refrigerate. Refrigerated dough will keep for a week. Substitute 1¼ cups light corn syrup for molasses to make Blonde Gingerbread.

Specialty Recipes

Kitchen-tested, these specialty recipes will help you achieve several of the projects in this publication.

THINNED FONDANT ADHESIVE

Use this mixture when attaching dried fondant to other fondant decorations or for attaching freshly cut fondant pieces to lollipop sticks or florist wire.

1 oz. Wilton Ready-To-Use Rolled Fondant (p. 164) (1½ in. ball)
¼ teaspoon water

INSTRUCTIONS:

Knead water into fondant until it becomes soft and sticky. To attach a fondant decoration, place mixture in decorating bag fitted with a small round tip, or brush on back of decoration. Recipe may be doubled.

GUM GLUE ADHESIVE

This easy-to-make mixture is used to attach gum paste decorations to each other.

¼ teaspoon Wilton Ready To-Use Gum Paste
1 tablespoon water

INSTRUCTIONS:

Break gum paste into very small pieces. Dissolve pieces in 1 tablespoon water. Let rest about 1 hour. Mixture will be ready to use even if some pieces have not dissolved. Brush it on to your decorations. Store unused portions covered in the refrigerator for up to 1 week.

CREAMY GELATIN

A delicious and easy treat, it is perfect to serve all year round.

1 package (3 oz.) favorite flavor gelatin mix
1 cup hot water
½ cup cold water
½ cup frozen non-dairy whipped topping, thawed

INSTRUCTIONS:

In large bowl, prepare gelatin mixture following package directions, using 1 cup hot water and ½ cup cold water. Chill until slightly thickened.

Gently fold whipped topping into gelatin until combined. Pipe or spoon mixture into serving glasses following project directions. Chill at least 3 hours.

MERINGUE TOPPING

1 tablespoon Wilton Meringue Powder
¼ cup cold water
⅓ cup granulated sugar, divided

INSTRUCTIONS:

In large bowl, combine meringue powder, water and half the sugar. Whip at high speed 5 minutes. Gradually add remaining sugar and continue whipping at high speed 5 minutes until meringue is stiff and dry. Makes about 3 cups.

BASIC TRUFFLES

1 package (12 oz.) Candy Melts Candy (p. 163)
⅓ cup heavy whipping cream
1 tablespoon liqueur (optional)

INSTRUCTIONS:

Chop candy (you can use a food processor). Heat whipping cream in saucepan just to boiling point. Do not boil. Remove from heat and add chopped candy. Stir until smooth and creamy. Refrigerate until firm.

Roll into 1 in. dia. balls. Can be used as center for dipped candies, served plain or rolled in nuts, coconut or cocoa powder. Store truffles in refrigerator up to 3 weeks. Makes about 2 dozen (1 in.) balls.

Cupcake *Techniques*

Set your cupcakes apart by decorating them with exciting accents, flowers and borders! You will find that the cupcakes in this book are easy to decorate when you follow the step-by-step instructions in this section. Your cupcake creations will be the highlight of any celebration!

Your cupcakes will be sensational after you practice these easy techniques. Whether you are adding a pretty star border or spectacular icing flowers, just follow the step-by-step instructions and you will be amazed at what you can do.

Coloring Icing

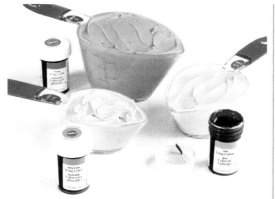

With Wilton Icing Colors (p. 163), it's easy to tint buttercream, royal icing or Color Flow to the perfect shade. Remember, our concentrated color goes a long way, so add small amounts at a time until you reach the desired color.

Dip a toothpick into the color, then swirl it into the icing.

Add color a little at a time until you achieve the shade you desire.

Always use a new toothpick each time you add color. Avoid getting icing in your jar of color. Blend icing well with a spatula.

Decorating With a Bag and Tip

Preparing the Bag
Decorating bags hold the icing and decorating tip so you can create a variety of decorations.

90° Angle   **45° Angle**

Correct Bag Position
The way your decorations curl, point and lie depends not only on icing consistency but also on the way you hold the bag and the way you move it. Bag positions are described in terms of both angle and direction.

Angle
Refers to the position of the bag relative to the work surface. There are two basic angles.

90° angle is straight up, perpendicular to the work surface. It is used when making stars or drop flowers.

45° angle is halfway between vertical and horizontal. It is used for writing, borders and many flowers.

Bag Direction
The angle of the bag to the work surface, when holding it at 45°, is only half the story of bag position. The other half is the direction in which the back of the bag is pointed.

Correct bag position is easiest to learn when you think of the back of the bag as the hour hand of a clock. When you hold the bag with the tip in the center of the clock, you can sweep out a circle with the back end of the bag. Pretend the circle you formed in the air is a clock face. The hours on the clock face correspond to the direction you point the back end of the bag.

Technique instructions in this section will list the correct direction for holding the bag; when the bag direction differs for left-handed decorators, that direction will be listed in parentheses. (Example: When right-handers hold bag at 3:00, left-handers hold bag at 9:00.)

Right-handed decorators always decorate from left to right. Left-handed decorators always decorate from right to left, except for writing.

Right-Handed

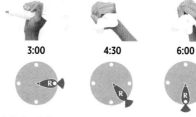

3:00   **4:30**   **6:00**

Left-Handed

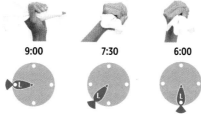

9:00   **7:30**   **6:00**

Most decorating tip openings are the same shape all the way around—so there is no right side or wrong side up when squeezing the bag. For tips such as petal, ruffle, basketweave and leaf, which have irregularly shaped openings, you must watch tip position as well as bag position. Instructions will state correct tip position if needed.

Pressure Control
The size and uniformity of your decorations depends on the amount of pressure you apply to the bag and the steadiness of the pressure. Learn to apply pressure so that you can move the bag in a free and easy glide while just the right amount of icing flows through the tip.

Heavy Pressure   **Medium Pressure**   **Light Pressure**

Icing Techniques

DOT

Hint: When making large dots, lift the tip as you squeeze to allow icing to fill out completely.

Decorate with: Round tip 3 and medium consistency icing. Hold bag at 90° straight up, with tip slightly above surface.

1. Squeeze bag and keep point of tip buried in icing until the dot is the size you want.
2. Stop pressure, pull tip up and to the side to help prevent points in dots.

BALL

Hint: Vary the basic look by adding stars, dots or spirals on the ball shapes.

Decorate with: Round tip 8 and medium consistency icing. Hold bag at 90° straight up with tip slightly above surface.

1. Squeeze the bag, applying a steady, even pressure. As the icing begins to build up, raise the tip with it, but keep the tip buried in the icing.
2. Stop squeezing as you bring the end of the tip to the surface. Lift the tip up and pull away from your piped ball. Use the edge of the tip to shave off any point so that your ball is nicely rounded.

BEAD

Hint: If you can pipe a shell, (p. 146) you can pipe a bead. The movements are similar.

Decorate with: Round tip 5 and medium consistency icing. Hold bag at 45° at 3:00 (9:00), with tip slightly above surface.

1. Squeeze as you lift tip slightly so that icing fans out.
2. Relax pressure as you draw the tip down and bring the bead to a point. Stop squeezing and pull tip away.
3. To make a bead border, start the next bead a little behind the previous one so that the fanned out end covers the tail of the preceding bead to form an even chain.

Icing Techniques Cont.

OUTLINE

Hint: Can be done with round or star tips, depending on whether perfectly round or ridged outlines are desired.

Decorate with: Round tip 3 and thin consistency icing. Hold bag at 45° at 3:00 (9:00), with tip slightly above surface.

1. Touch tip to surface. Lift tip slightly; squeeze and guide tip along surface.

2. Stop squeezing. Touch tip to surface. Pull away.

PRINTING

HAPPY BIR

Hint: Adding piping gel to thinned icing will help your lines flow without breaking. Add ½ teaspoon piping gel per cup.

Decorate with: Round tip 3 and thin consistency icing. Right-handers hold bag at 45° at 6:00 for vertical lines, 45° at 3:00 for horizontal and curving lines. Left-handers hold bag at 45° at 6:00 for vertical lines, 45° at 9:00 for horizontal and curving lines. Hold tip lightly touching surface.

1. Letters can be piped freehand, or marked with a toothpick.

2. Raise tip slightly and with steady pressure, squeeze out a straight line, lifting the tip off the surface to let the icing string drop.

3. Stop squeezing, touch tip to surface, and pull tip away. Be sure that the end of the tip is clean before you go on to another line.

STAR

Hint: After squeezing out a star, be sure to stop pressure completely before you pull your tip away. This will give you a perfectly formed star shape, without peaks.

Decorate with: Star tip 16 and medium consistency icing. Hold bag at 90° straight up, with tip about ⅛ in. above the surface.

1. Squeeze the bag to form a star. Increase or decrease pressure to change star size.

2. Stop pressure completely. Pull tip straight up and away.

   For pull-out stars: gradually decrease pressure as you pull away. Stop pressure and pull tip away. Work from the bottom to the top of the area to be covered with pull-out stars.

ZIGZAG

Hint: When piping zigzags, think about two motions simultaneously. The movement of your arm determines the height of the waves and the distance between them. The pressure on your bag determines the thickness of the line. Strive for uniform thickness and even spacing as you go.

Decorate with: Star tip 16 and medium consistency icing. Hold bag at 45° at 3:00 (9:00) with tip lightly touching surface.

1. Steadily squeeze and glide tip along the surface in an up and down motion.

2. Continue piping up and down with steady pressure. To end, stop pressure and pull tip away. For more elongated zigzags, move your hand to the desired height while maintaining a steady pressure. For a more relaxed look, increase the width as you move the bag along.

SHELL

Hint: Lift the tip only slightly when piping, to avoid a bumpy look.

Decorate with: Star tip 21 and medium consistency icing. Hold bag at 45° at 6:00, with tip slightly above the surface.

1. Squeeze hard, letting icing fan out generously as it forces the tip up.

2. Gradually relax pressure as you lower tip. Pull the bag toward you until tip reaches the surface. Relax pressure and pull tip along the surface to form a point.

3. To make a shell border, start your next shell so that the fanned end just covers the tail of the preceding shell to form a chain.

REVERSE SHELL

Hint: Use the cupcake nail from the Decorating Nail Set (p. 162). This nail works like a turntable in your hand, allowing you to pipe a border while rotating the cupcake.

Decorate with: Star tip 21 and medium consistency icing. Hold bag at 45° at 6:00, with tip slightly above surface.

1. Squeeze bag to form a shell. As you begin to form a shell, squeeze hard, letting the icing fan out. To form curve, lift tip up and over the shell as you move tip from 9:00 (right- or left-handed) to 12:00 to 6:00. Relax pressure, lower tip. Pull tip straight toward yourself at 6:00 to form tail. Relax pressure, lower tip. Pull tip straight toward yourself at 6:00 to form tail.

2. Repeat with another shell, curving from 3:00 (right- or left-handed) to 12:00 to 6:00. To continue the reverse shell border, pipe a chain of swirling reverse shells, with the fan end of each new shell covering the tail of the previous shell. If you are making the border on a round cake, turn the cake as you go so that the back of the bag is at 6:00 and you are working toward yourself.

ROSETTE

Hint: Rosettes can be used in place of piped roses on the side of your cupcake—for the effect of a rose without the work. Try finishing rosettes with a center star or dot.

Decorate with: Star tip 16 and medium consistency icing. Hold bag at 90° straight up with tip slightly above surface.

1. Squeeze out icing to form a star. Without releasing pressure, raise tip slightly as you drop a line of icing on top of the star in a tight, complete rotation.

   Begin at 9:00 (3:00), move to 12:00, then 3:00 (9:00) and continue to 6:00.

2. Stop pressure at 6:00 but continue to move the tip back to the starting point to make a complete rotation.

3. Pull tip away, continuing the circular motion so that the tail maintains the circular shape of the rosette. For a rosette border, pipe a line of uniform rosettes, touching one another.

RUFFLE

Hint: Moving your hand quickly up and down will give you a tight ruffle. For a looser look, move more slowly across the surface. Practice different looks to perfect your pressure control.

Decorate with: Petal tip 104 and medium consistency icing. Hold bag at 45° at 3:00 (9:00) with wide end of tip lightly touching surface and narrow end facing away from surface.

1. As you keep the wide end against the cupcake, move wrist up to pull up icing.

2. Move wrist down to complete one curl of the ruffle.

3. Repeat up and down motion.

4. Raise and lower the narrow end as you move around the cupcake. Repeat this motion for the entire ruffle.

DROP FLOWER

Hint: The swirled look of the petals happens when you twist your wrist the proper way. Practice your wrist movement, keeping your knuckles in the position described below. You can also create a star flower by not moving your wrist and letting icing build up as you squeeze.

Decorate with: Drop flower tip 2D for petals and round tip 3 for center; medium consistency buttercream (or royal icing for flowers made in advance). Hold bag at 90° straight up with tip lightly touching the surface.

1. Before piping, turn your hand ¼ turn so the back of your hand is away from you and your knuckles are at 9:00 (3:00). Lightly touch the surface with tip 2D.

2. As you squeeze out icing, slowly turn your hand until the back of your hand returns to its natural position, with knuckles at 12:00.

3. For flower center, hold the bag straight up and squeeze out a tip 3 dot of icing. Keep the tip buried as you squeeze. Stop squeezing, Pull tip up and off to the side, shaving off the point on the dot.

SWEET PEA

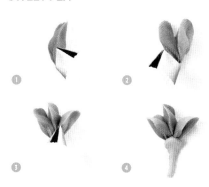

Hint: These quick and easy flowers can be made right on top of your cupcake in buttercream. It's a good idea to practice squeezing and slightly lifting the tip to form petals before piping on cupcakes.

Decorate with: Tip 104 and stiff consistency buttercream icing in desired color for flower. Prepare a second bag with tip 3 and green thin consistency icing for calyx. Hold decorating bag at 45° at 6:00 for center petal and calyx, 45° at 4:30 for left petal, 45° at 7:30 for right petal.

1   Wide end of tip should touch surface, keep narrow end straight up. Squeeze the bag and lift the tip slightly off the surface (about ¼ in.) as the icing curls.

2   Continue to squeeze without changing position. Relax pressure, and return the tip to the surface. Stop squeezing, pull tip away.

3   Position your bag slightly to the left of the center petal. Follow the same procedure as you did for the center petal: squeeze, and while the petal curls, lift the tip, relaxing your pressure and lowering the tip back to the surface before pulling away. Repeat for the right side petal, holding the tip to the right of the center petal.

4   Make the calyx with tip 3. Squeeze, letting the icing build up. Slowly draw the tip toward you, relaxing the pressure as you move away from the flower. Stop and pull out and away.

MUM

Hint: This fall classic is easier to pipe than you might think. The secret to success—the curved opening of tip 81, piped with a simple petal-making motion.

Decorate with: Tip 5 for center mound, tip 81 for petals and stiff consistency icing royal icing. Use flower nail no. 7 with rose template from flower nail templates set covered with icing flower square. Hold bag at 90° angle to flower nail for center, 45° for petals.

1   Attach icing flower square over template on flower nail with a dot of icing. Hold bag at 90° angle to flower nail. Pipe a tip 5 mound of orange royal icing on center circle of template.

2   Insert tip 81 into mound (postioning half moon curve down), squeeze firmly and pull out to the second circle on the template (approx. ¼ in. long). Lift up and away slightly at a 45° angle as you release pressure for each petal. Repeat as needed to form first row of petals. Petals should extend only to second circle of template.

3   Repeat, piping the next row of petals slightly shorter, positioning them between petals in first row. Pipe additional rows of petals a little shorter and remember to pull tips up slightly.

DAISY

Hint: Big and bold flowers can be made just the right size to cover your cupcake top. You can make daisies in advance using royal icing or directly on your cupcake top in buttercream. For larger daisies on cupcakes use a tip 125.

Decorate with: Petal tip 104 for petals, round tip 5 for center and medium consistency royal icing or buttercream icing. For royal icing flowers, use flower nail no. 7 with daffodil template flower square. Hold tip 104 at a 45° angle to surface 3:00 (9:00), with wide end lightly touching surface ¼ in. away from center of nail, narrow end pointing out to outer edge.

1   Dot the center of surface with icing as a guide for your flower center. Starting at any point near the outer edge, squeeze and move tip toward center icing dot. Stop pressure, pull tip away.

2   Repeat for a total of 12 or more petals, piping two petals in each section of template. Hold round tip 5 at a 90° angle to surface. Pipe tip 5 dot flower center. Press to flatten.

PANSY

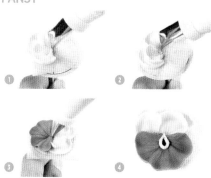

Hint: The pansy features petals in complementary colors and a distinctive loop center. Choose colors to complement your baking cups. You can do one-color flowers in yellow or dark blue, or mix white, yellow or purple petals with yellow centers.

Decorate with: Petal tip 104 and medium consistency royal icing. Use flower nail no. 7 with violet template from flower nail templates set. Hold bag at 45° at 3:00 (9:00) with wide end of tip lightly touching flower nail center, narrow end pointing out and raised ¼ in. above nail surface.

1   Pipe two back petals, squeezing and moving tip out to edge of nail. Turn nail slowly while squeezing, relax pressure as you return to nail center. Repeat to form second back petal.

2   Use the same sequence to add two shorter petals atop the first two.

3   Squeeze out a base petal that equals the width of the back petals, using a back and forth hand motion for a ruffled effect.

4   Add tip 1 string loop centers.

CARNATION

Hint: Make the petals of this richly textured flower using a tight up-and-down motion. Piping on the apple blossom/primrose template from our flower nail templates set will help guide you to proper petal position.

Decorate with: Petal tip 104 and stiff consistency royal icing. Use flower nail no. 7 with apple blossom/primrose template covered with icing flower square. Hold bag at 45° angle with wide end of tip lightly touching nail surface, narrow end pointing out and raised ⅛ in. above nail surface.

1   Begin the first row of five petals. Pipe first petal moving tip 104 in a jiggling up-and-down motion.

2   Continue with four more petals, slightly overlapping the previous petal.

3   Pipe the second row of four petals, then the third row of three petals.

4   Angle tip up slightly. Finish with one or two center petals at top. Let dry.

BACHELOR BUTTON

Hint: This simple version of a bachelor button can be piped in buttercream icing, directly on a cupcake or made ahead of time in royal icing.

Decorate with: Tip 12 for center mound, tip 16 for center pull out stars, tip 18 for pull out star petals and medium consistency icing. Use flower nail no. 7 with rose template covered with icing flower square. For center, hold bag at 90° angle to flower nail, slightly touching surface. Hold tip slightly above center of flower nail. For petals, hold bag at 45° angle with tip just above mound.

1   With heavy pressure, pipe tip 12 mound, approximately ¾ in. dia. Stop squeezing, lift tip just above icing and shave off any point with the end of tip.

2   For center, pipe pull-out stars using tip 16. Hold tip so it is slightly touching center of mound; squeeze, lifting tip up approximately ³⁄₁₆ in. high. Release pressure and pull tip away.

3   Holding bag at 45° angle, cover mound with tip 18 stars. Position tip just above mound, squeeze until star shape is formed. Release pressure and pull away. Start at base and work upward toward center.

Icing Techniques Cont.

VIOLET

Hint: These petite flowers are great for cupcakes. Gather them on an icing mound to create a center bouquet with all the elegance you could want.

Decorate with: Tip 59s (right-hand) or tip 101s (left-hand) for petals, tip 1 for center dots and medium consistency royal icing. Use flower nail no. 7 and violet template from flower nail templates set covered with pre-cut icing flower square. Hold bag at a 45° angle with tip lightly touching surface.

1. Squeeze with light pressure, move tip out slightly as you spin the nail to form first bottom petal. Relax pressure as you move tip back to starting point. Stop, lift away.

2. Repeat to make two more bottom petals.

3. Make one shorter rounded top petal. Repeat to make the second top petal. Add two center dots.

ROSEBUD WITH SIDE PETALS

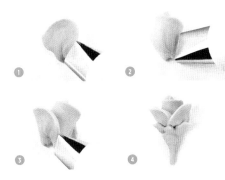

Hint: This flower can be piped directly on the cupcake in your favorite colors. The outer petals give it a more dimensional look, but rosebuds can be made without them if you want a smaller flower.

Decorate with: Tip 104 for petals, round tip 3 for sepals and calyx. Use buttercream—stiff consistency for petals, thin consistency for sepals and calyx. For petals, hold bag at 45° at 4:30 (7:30); for sepals and calyx, hold bag at 45° at 6:00.

1. Using tip 104, make the base petal. Keep the narrow end of the tip raised up and slightly to the right (left for lefties). While squeezing, move the tip along the surface away from you in a straight line about ¼ in. long. Pause, then continue squeezing as the icing fans out. Returning the tip to the original position and halfway back, start to release pressure, move tip to starting point, stop pressure and pull tip away.

2. Using tip 104, make the overlapping petal. Touch the wide end of the tip to the outside edge of completed petal. The bag is positioned as for the base petal, at 4:30 (7:30); hold it steady in this position until the second petal is completed. As you continue squeezing, the icing will catch the edge of the base petal and roll over it naturally. When the second petal looks complete, stop pressure completely, touch the tip back down to the surface and pull tip away. For a rosebud without side petals, move to step 4.

3. Using tip 104, make the right and left side petals. Touch the wide end of the tip to the left side of rosebud. Raise the tip,

then pull back down for a stand-up look. Repeat for right side petal.

4. Using tip 3, make the sepals and calyx. Form the middle sepal first by squeezing and letting icing build up. Lift the bag up and away from the flower. Stop pressure as you pull away to form the point of the sepal. Repeat, making a sepal on the left and right sides. For the calyx, insert tip into the base of the center sepal. Squeeze, letting the icing build up. Slowly draw the tip toward you, relaxing pressure as you move away from the flower. Stop pressure, pull away. You may want to blend the calyx into the stem using a damp brush.

RIBBON ROSE

Hint: These ribbon roses are straight-up spirals which show off deep ridged petal edges. You can create a taller ribbon rose by piping a heavy base of icing, then proceeding with the steps below.

Decorate with: Tip 104 using stiff consistency royal icing. Use flower nail no. 7 covered with pre-cut icing flower square. Hold bag at a 45° angle with wide end of tip lightly touching surface.

1. Position bag so wide end of tip is down, narrow end slightly tilted in. Squeeze the bag as you rotate flower nail to create a tight center bud.

2. Move narrow end straight up. Continue squeezing and turning nail.

3. When rose is the size you want, stop pressure and lift tip away.

PRIMROSE

Hint: The primrose is a flat flower with textured petals. Key to the heart-shaped petals is perfecting a "curve-dip-curve" motion as you spin the flower nail.

Decorate with: Tip 104 for petals, tip 14 for star center, tip 1 for dot and medium consistency royal icing. Use flower nail no. 7 and apple blossom/primrose template from flower nail templates set covered with pre-cut icing flower square. For petals hold bag at 45° at 3:00 (9:00); for center and dots, hold bag at 90° straight up.

1. Use tip 104. Wide end is slightly touching the center of the nail, narrow end is pointing out and angled ¼ in. above the nail surface.

2. Use medium pressure, move tip out ¼ in. along the dotted line of the template. Use a curve-dip-curve motion as you turn the nail, letting the spin of nail form the petal. Relax pressure as you move back to the starting point to form the first petal.

3. Repeat to form the remaining four petals. flower will be the size of the entire flower nail. For center, add tip 14 yellow star center. Add tip 1 dot to star.

TRI-LEVEL ROSEBUD

Hint: This fantasy flower covers your cupcakes with amazing texture. Build petals in groups of three vertical petals to create an elongated multi-layered blossom.

Decorate with: Tip 150 and stiff consistency buttercream icing. Hold bag at 90° angle at 6:00.

1. Starting at edge of cupcake and working toward center, use tip 150 to pipe a left-cupped petal, then a right-cupped petal.

2. Move tip down about halfway on first petals. Squeeze to pipe a right-cupped petal.

3. Continue squeezing, moving tip halfway down on previous petal to pipe another right cupped petal, then pull down toward center of cupcake.

4. Repeat sequence to cover cupcake, turning cupcake as needed.

WILD ROSE

Hint: The wild rose is a pretty year-round flower piped about the size of the head of flower nail no. 7. For a more cupped shape, increase the angle you hold the tip.

Decorate with: Tip 104 for petals; tip 3 for center and medium consistency royal icing. Use flower nail no. 7 with apple blossom/primrose template from flower nail templates set covered with icing flower square. Hold bag at 45° angle at 3:00 (9:00).

1. Use tip 104 and hold bag at a 45° angle at 3:00 (9:00). Touch center of nail with wide end of tip; narrow end should be just slightly above nail surface. Begin at center of nail and squeeze out first petal, turning nail ⅕ turn as you move tip out toward edge of nail. Relax pressure as you return to center of nail, curving tip slightly upward to create a cupped shape. Stop squeezing as wide end touches center of nail and lift up.

2. Repeat to form the remaining four petals.

3. Pipe dot stamens with tip 3.

Icing Techniques Cont.

THE WILTON ROSE

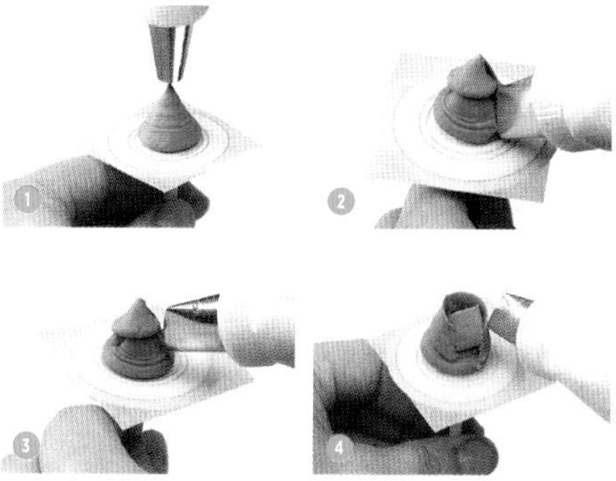

Hint: If you are going to be placing roses on your cupcake immediately, it's not necessary to place a pre-cut icing flower square on the flower nail. Just slide the flower from the nail onto your cupcake using a spatula.

Decorate with: Use flower nail no. 7 for larger roses. For base, pipe with round tip 12; for petals, pipe with petal tip 104. Use stiff consistency royal or buttercream icing. For base, hold bag at 90° straight up, with tip slightly above flower nail. For petals, hold bag at 45° at 4:30 (7:30), wide end of tip touching base.

1 **Rose Base:** Use tip 12 and heavy pressure to build up a base. Remember to keep tip buried as you squeeze. Start to lift the tip higher, gradually raise the tip and decrease the pressure.

Stop pressure, pull up and lift away. The base should be 1½ times as high as the opening of your petal tip.

2 **Center Bud:** Use tip 104. Hold nail containing base in your left (right) hand and bag in right (left) hand. Wide end of tip 104 should touch the base at or slightly below the midpoint. Narrow end of tip should point up and be angled in over top of base.

Now, do three things at the same time: Squeeze the bag, move the tip and rotate the nail. As you squeeze the bag, move the tip up from the base, forming a ribbon of icing. Slowly turn the nail counterclockwise (clockwise for lefties) to bring the ribbon of icing around to overlap at the top of the mound, then back down to starting point. Move tip straight up and down only; do not loop it around the base.

3 **Top Row of Three Petals:** Touch the wide end of tip 104 to the midpoint of bud base, narrow end straight up.

4 Turn nail, keeping wide end of tip on base so that petal will attach. Move tip up and back down to the midpoint of mound, forming the first petal.

Start again, slightly behind end of first petal and squeeze out second petal. Repeat for the third petal, ending by overlapping the starting point of the first petal. Rotate the nail ⅓ turn for each petal.

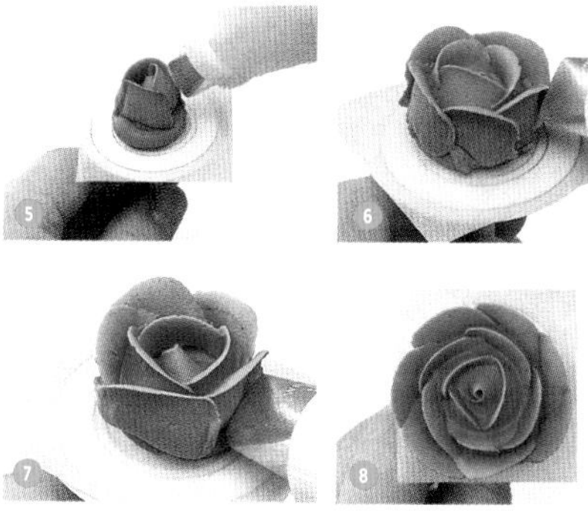

5 **Middle Row of Five Petals:** Touch the wide end of tip 104 slightly below the center of a petal in the top row. Angle the narrow end of tip out slightly more than you did for the top row of petals.

6 Squeeze bag and turn nail, moving tip up, then down to form first petal. Repeat for a row of five petals, rotating the nail ⅕ turn for each petal. The last petal end should overlap the first's starting point.

7 **Bottom Row of Seven Petals:** Touch the wide end of tip below the center of a middle row petal, again angling the narrow end of tip out a little more.

8 Squeeze bag and turn nail, moving tip up, then down to form first petal. Repeat for a total of seven petals, rotating the nail 1/7 turn for each petal. The last petal end should overlap the first's starting point.

PIPING A FLOWER ON A CUPCAKE

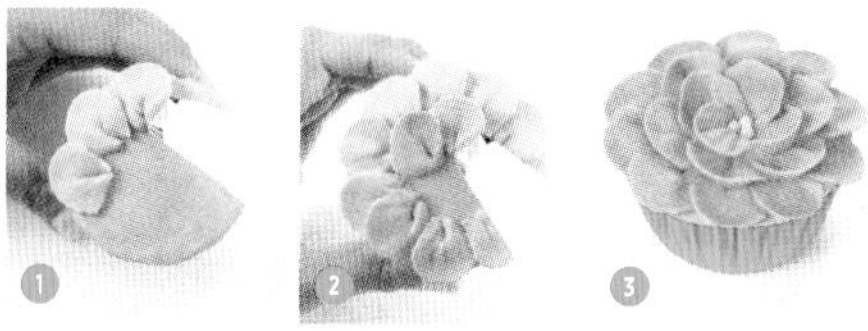

A cupcake top is the perfect spot to plant a flower! Think of the circular surface as a flower nail on which you can pipe petals for a larger-than-life blossom. This technique will work for larger petal tips, such as tip 125 used here. Try your favorite petal shapes to create your own fantasy flower.

1 Hold the cupcake in one hand as you pipe petals with your other hand. Use tip 125 and medium consistency buttercream, holding bag at 45° angle. Touch cupcake with wide end of tip, keeping narrow end slightly above surface. Turn cupcake slightly counterclockwise as you move tip out toward edge. Relax pressure as you return to base of petal, curving tip slightly upward to create a curved shape. Continue piping an outer row of petals on edge of cupcake. Angle the cupcake as needed.

2 Repeat with a second row of petals, slightly inside the first row.

3 Add a third row of petals slightly inside second row. Pipe tip 3 dot center or add, yellow Sugar Pearls for center.

LEAVES

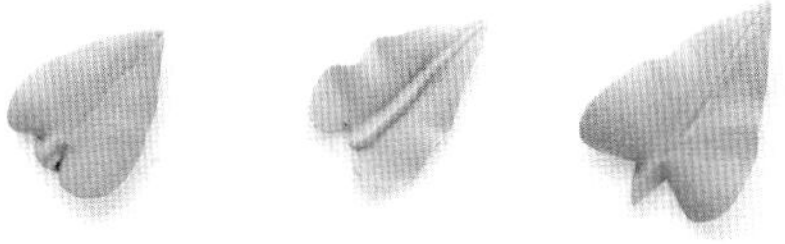

Basic Leaf Tip 352 | **Veined Leaf Tip 67** | **Large Leaf Tip 366**

Hint: Add piping gel to your icing to keep your leaves from breaking.

Decorate with: Tips 352, 67 or 366. Use thin consistency buttercream icing. Hold bag at 45° at 6:00, with tip lightly touching surface.

1 Squeeze hard to build up the base and at the same time, lift the tip slightly.

2 Relax pressure as you pull the tip toward you, drawing the leaf to a point.

3 Stop squeezing and lift away.

PUDDLE DOTS

Thin royal icing (or Color Flow), adding ½ teaspoon water per ¼ cup of icing. Icing is ready for flowing when a small amount dripped back into mixture takes a count of 10 to disappear. On waxed paper-covered boards, pipe a ball, ¼ in. to 1¼ in. dia., depending on project instructions, using thinned icing in a cut parchment bag or bag and tip. Let dry 48 hours. Decorate following project instructions.

LAMBETH SCROLL

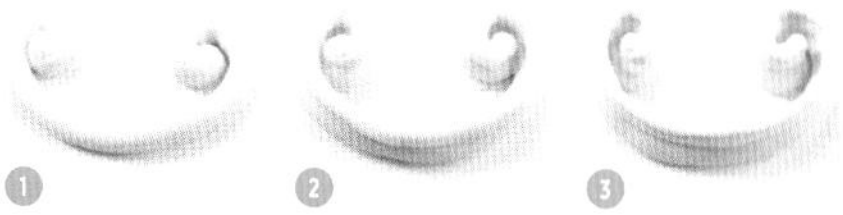

(see Letter-Perfect Lambeth, p. 119)

Lambeth adds a new dimension to your cupcake! This traditional method involves overpiping the same shape using gradually smaller tips to create a layer-upon-layer look. Here, we've used a pattern to make the shape easy.

1 Tape pattern to board. Cover with waxed paper. Pipe tip 6 scroll.

2 Overpipe the scroll with tip 4.

3 Use tip 2 to overpipe scroll again. Let dry.

COLOR FLOW ON A COOKIE

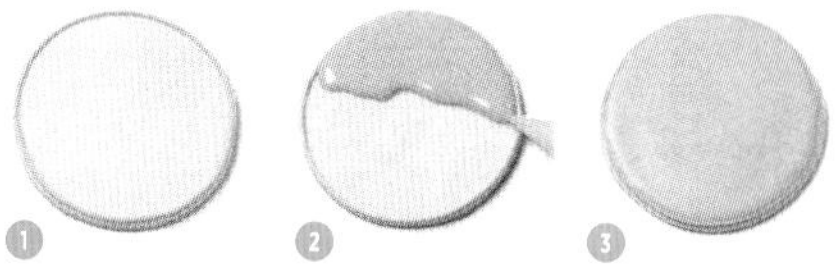

Smooth and shiny decorations are the hallmark of Color Flow icing. To make a Color Flow shape, use full-strength Color Flow to outline, let dry, then pipe in the area with thinned Color Flow. Creating a Color Flow cookie is a fun way to top a cupcake! Find the Color Flow icing recipe on p. 143

1 Outline shape with tip 3 and parchment bag half-filled with full-strength Color Flow. Squeeze, pull and drop icing string following shape. Stop, touch tip to surface and pull away. If you will be using the same color to fill in, let outline dry a few minutes until it "crusts."

2 Thin Color Flow mixture with water following recipe directions. Cut opening in parchment bag to the size of tip 2. Fill in design with thinned Color Flow.

3 Let cookies air dry thoroughly, at least 24 hours.

Coloring Fondant

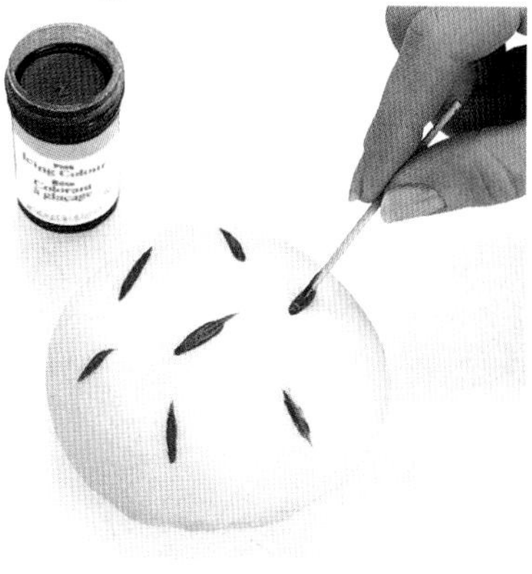

Hint: Another way to color fondant is by blending portions of pre-tinted fondant from our multi-packs.

Cut off the desired amount of white fondant or gum paste and roll into a ball, kneading until soft and pliable.

Using a toothpick, add dots of icing color in several spots.

Knead color into your fondant or gum paste ball, stretching and folding until color is evenly blended.

Fondant Techniques

Add dimension and detailed accents on cupcakes with these fondant techniques.

CURLICUES

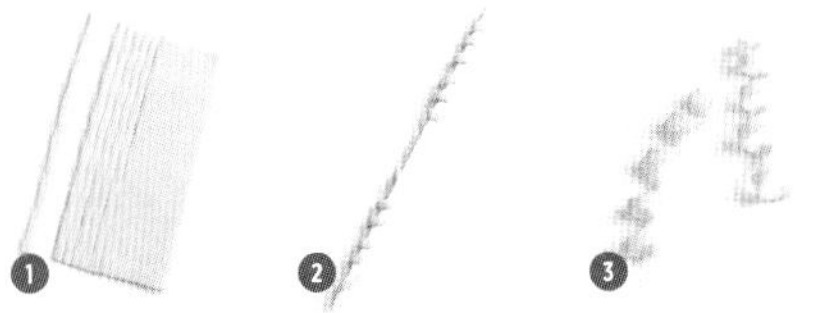

Toothpicks, lollipop sticks, cookie sticks or dowel rods may be used for various sizes.

1. Roll out fondant 1/16 in. thick on Roll-N-Cut Mat lightly dusted with cornstarch. Cut into thin strips.
2. Loosely wrap strips around a lollipop stick several times to form curls. Let set 5 to 10 minutes.
3. Slide curl off lollipop stick and let dry.

MULTI-COLOR ROPES

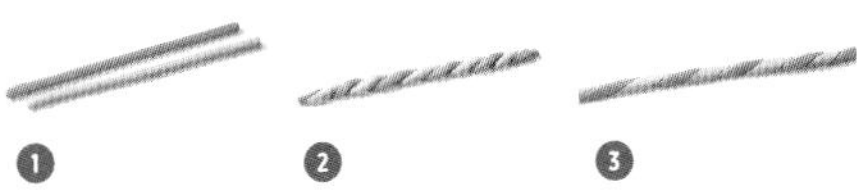

1. Make fondant logs following project instructions for color and size. Follow project instructions for tinting and rolling logs.
2. Gently press two or three logs together at one end to join. Holding the joined end in a stationary position, loosely twist the other end two to three complete turns (twisting loosely creates wider space between colors).
3. After twisting, roll back and forth using palms of hands to create a smooth rope.

MOLDING WITH FONDANT & GUM PASTE MOLDS

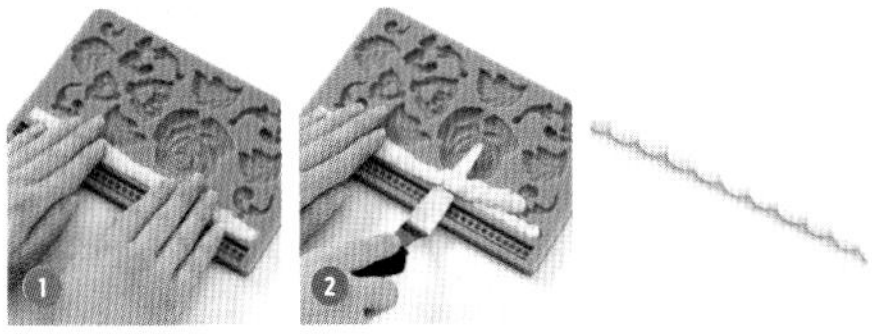

It's easy to create detailed shapes in exciting designs that are ready to place on your cake.

1. Lightly dust mold cavities with cornstarch. Fill cavity with fondant or gum paste. Press down on fondant or gum paste with fingers to cover all areas of the cavity. To evenly distribute the material, you can also press with Shaping Foam.
2. Trim excess fondant or gum paste using spatula or palette knife from 10-Pc. Gum Paste Tool Set. Turn mold over and flex to release shapes. Follow project instructions for placing design on your cupcake. Or, let dry as needed.

FONDANT BOW

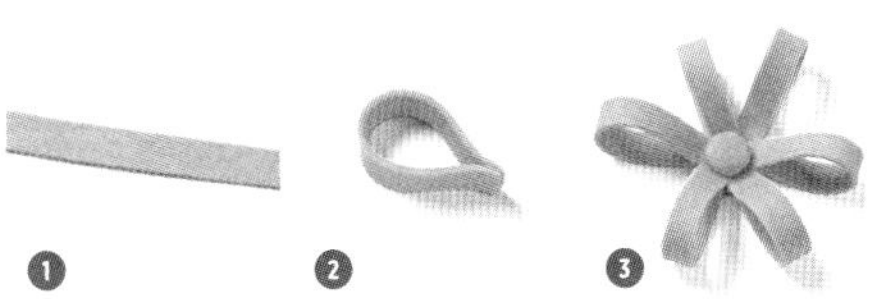

1. Roll out fondant and cut strips for loops, knot and streamers (if needed) following dimensions listed in project. Your bow may use more loops than shown here, or it may omit the center knot.
2. Fold strips over to form loops. Brush ends lightly with damp brush. Align ends and pinch slightly to secure. Support loops with crushed facial tissue and let dry.
3. Assemble bow on cupcake following project instructions.

COVERING LARGE CUPCAKES WITH ROLLED FONDANT

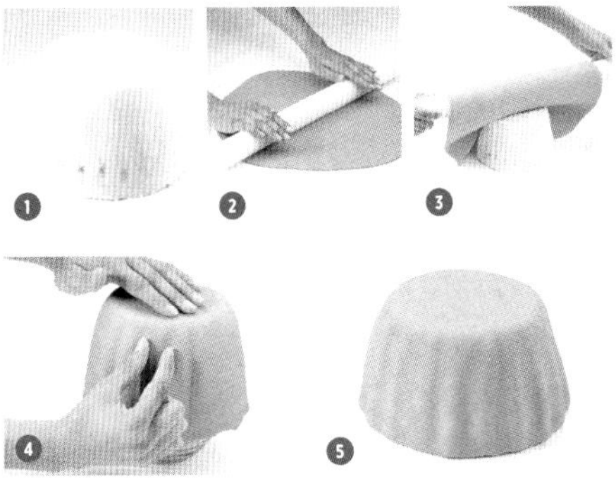

1. Bake and cool top and bottom halves in Dimensions Large Cupcake Pan. Turn cupcake bottom narrow end up. Prepare for rolled fondant by lightly icing with buttercream.
2. Roll out fondant ⅛ in. thick using 20 in. Fondant Roller to create a circle about 14 in. dia.
3. Lift fondant onto fondant roller and move onto cupcake bottom.
4. Use hands to smooth fondant on top and around sides, pressing into indented areas of cake.
5. Turn cake upright; trim excess from top edge. Follow project directions for positioning cupcake top and completing cake.

To cover round and square cakes with fondant, the basic process is the same as for covering the large cupcake. However, with straight sides and no angles, there is no need to turn the cake over or press fondant into indented areas. We recommend using the Fondant Smoother (p. 164) to smooth and shape fondant and remove air bubbles. If an air bubble appears, insert a pin on an angle, release air and smooth the area again. Use the straight edge of the fondant smoother to mark fondant at the base of the cake. Trim off excess fondant using the fondant cutter, a spatula or sharp knife.

FONDANT OVERLAY APPLIQUES

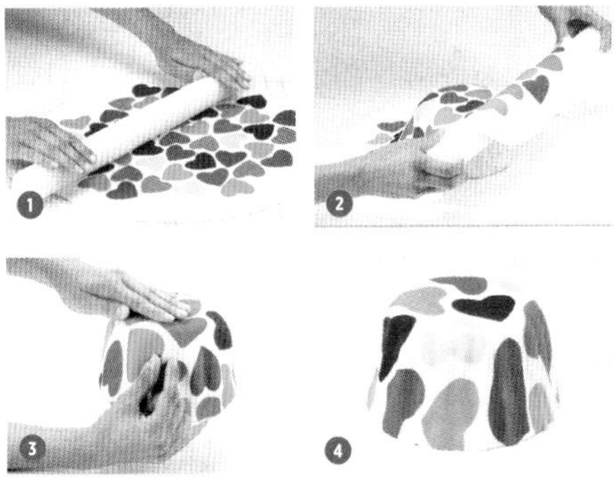

(see Upbeat Hearts, p. 69, Painter's Party, p. 45)

1. Follow steps 1 and 2 for Covering Large Cupcakes with Rolled Fondant. Prepare tinted fondant shapes following project directions. Place tinted shapes on white fondant in a random pattern. Re-roll fondant to ⅛ in. thick.
2. Lift fondant onto Fondant Roller and move onto cupcake bottom.
3. Use hands to smooth fondant on top and around sides, pressing into indented areas of cake.
4. Turn cake upright; trim excess from top edge. Follow project directions for positioning cupcake top and completing cake.

FONDANT RIBBON ROSE

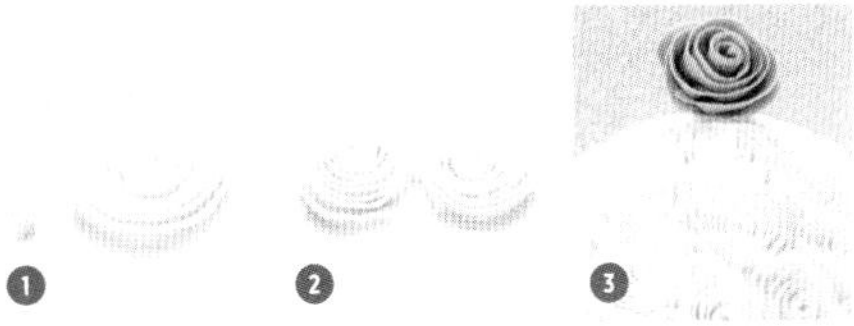

Loosely wrapped roses are shaped directly on the large cupcake top to create a great packed-in look.

1. Roll out fondant 1/16 in. thick. Cut strips following dimensions listed in project. Thin top edge of strips on shaping foam using large ball tool.
2. Brush a small section at top center of cupcake top with piping gel. Loosely roll up each strip to form roses on the brushed section, varying the look to create a gently rippling petal line on top.
3. Continue to cover the cupcake top completely with roses. You will need about 52 roses (sizes will vary to fit).

FONDANT FAIRY

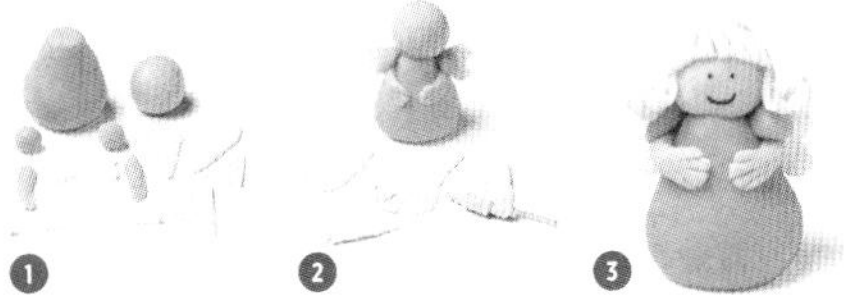

(See Garden Party Guests, p. 66)

1. Make fairies 1 to 2 days in advance. For each, tint 1 oz. dress color, ¼ oz. skin tone, ⅛ oz. hair color. For dress, reserve two balls ¼ in. dia. for sleeves. Roll remainder into a cone 1¼ in. high with flat top, ½ in. dia. and a flat bottom, 1¼ in. dia. Using skin tone, roll a ⅝ in. ball for head. Attach to dress using damp brush.

   For arms, roll logs, 3/16 in. dia. x ¾ in. long. Flatten one end for hand; cut slits ¼ in. deep for thumb and fingers. Attach in position. Shape sleeves by cupping reserved balls. Attach. Roll out white fondant 1/16 in. thick. Cut two wings using smallest heart Cut-Out. Attach to back.
2. Make hair, roll out fondant 1/16 in. thick. For each treat, cut three hearts using medium Cut-Out; cut two hearts in half vertically. Place three heart halves on cornstarch-dusted mat, points facing up. Cut slits on wide end, ¾ in. deep x 1/16 in. wide. Wrap ends around toothpick to form flip. Attach halves over back and sides of head, positioning pointed ends at top.

   For bangs, cut ½ in. off bottom point of whole heart. Cut slits on wide end of cut point, ⅜ in. deep x 1/16 in. wide. Attach bangs, point up.
3. Fold one glitter stamen into a "V" shape; insert for antennae. Use edible marker to draw dot eyes and outline smile. Let dry overnight on cornstarch dusted board.
4. Fairies are ready for your cupcakes!

BOX TOPS

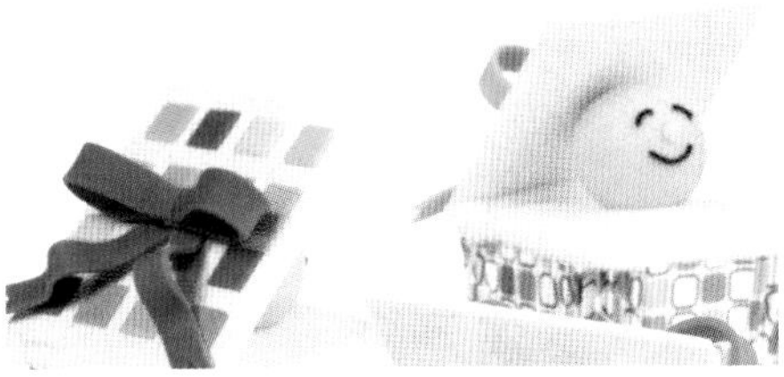

(see Gifted Children, p. 124)

Knead 1 teaspoon Gum-Tex into 3 oz. white fondant for three tops. Roll out 1/16 in. thick. Use fondant trimmer to cut into squares, 2½ in. x 2½ in. Let dry on cornstarch-dusted surface.

For color tiles, tint ¼ oz. portions of fondant, leaf green, lemon yellow and rose to make three treats. Roll out colors and reserved colors 1/16 in. thick. Use trimmer to cut squares, ⅜ in. x ⅜ in., two or three in each color per treat. Attach 16 various color squares to each box top, 3/16 in. apart, with damp brush. Let dry.

Candy Techniques

CANDY SHELLS IN BAKING CUPS

Mold a sweet pleated holder for candies, ice cream or a cereal treat cupcake top! Use Wilton Candy Melts candy and any Wilton standard baking cup in our standard muffin pan to create the perfect shape.

1. Spoon or pipe 1 to 2 tablespoons of melted candy into the bottom of a standard baking cup. Brush candy up sides, to desired height, forming an even edge.

2. Chill 5 to 8 minutes. Repeat process if a thicker shell is needed. Chill until firm.

3. Carefully peel baking cup off candy shell. Fill shell following project instructions.

COVERING TREATS WITH CANDY MELTS CANDY

Give cupcakes or cookies a dazzling finish—coat them in easy-melting Wilton Candy Melts candy. Candy Melts candy is perfect for kids' treats because it's shiny, colorful, easy to handle and eat.

1. Melt Candy Melts candy following package directions. Place cooled treat on cooling grid positioned over cookie sheet or pan. To cover completely, ice top with melted candy; let set. Treats which will be covered completely should be turned bottom side up.

2. Pipe candy on center of treat using a cut decorating bag or spoon. Cover the treat completely.

3. Let set.

CANDY CANDELABRA BASE

(See Candy Candelabras!, p. 109)

Hint: To trim candy, place tip in hot water to warm. Dry and immediately use.

1. 1 day in advance, use black candy and dessert accents mold to make six scrolls for each treat. Chill until firm. Place two scrolls side by side on waxed paper, one flat side down with curved edge to right, one flat side up with curved edge to left. Attach together at small round end using melted candy. Chill until firm.

2. Use narrow end of a warm tip 12 to cut a notch into each small, round end. Stand up first two scrolls. Attach next two scrolls at an angle with melted candy. Hold in position until set.

3. Attach last two scrolls at an angle with melted candy. Hold in position until set.

Other Decorating Techniques

TOPSY TURVY CUPCAKES

(see Cockeyed Cupcakes, p. 31)

1. Trim large cupcake halves. Position top half of large cupcake on bottom half. Imprint circle metal cutter from tip of top half, angling down right side. Gently push in cutter to create a circle, ½ in. deep at tip and ⅛ in. deep at right edge. Lift away cutter and use knife to cut out cake from circle.

2. Stack jumbo and standard cupcakes. Remove baking cups. Position jumbo cupcake in large cupcake opening; support with icing if needed. On jumbo cupcake, build up icing 1¼ in. from left edge with tip 12 to create a wedge shape ½ in. high. Position standard cupcake. Insert dowel rod through all three cupcakes for support.

STACKED CONSTRUCTION

Stacking is the most architectural method of tiered cake construction. Tiers are placed directly on top of one another and pillars are not used. Cupcakes are supported and stabilized by dowel rods and cake boards.

1. Dowel rod all tiers except smallest cupcake.

2. Position the jumbo and standard cupcakes on the large cupcake, centering exactly.

3. Repeat with the top cupcake.

4. To stabilize cupcakes further, sharpen one end of a long dowel rod and push it through all cupcakes and cake boards to the base of the bottom cupcake. To decorate, start at the top and work down.

PEARL DUST & COLOR DUST COLOR EFFECTS

Pearl Dust and Color Dust are used to brush color on gum paste or fondant designs. You can use a brush to paint wet or apply dry. For fine detail, a small round head brush works best. For larger areas, use a wider, flatter brush.

Brushing dry onto your flowers or details creates a softer look. Painting with a mixture of Pearl Dust or Color Dust and Pure Lemon Extract (p. 160) creates a more vivid look.

To make a "paint": In a small bowl, mix equal parts Pearl or Color Dust and lemon extract. Dissolve the dust completely into extract before painting. Since the extract can evaporate quickly, mix small amounts of paint at a time and use immediately.

Some projects may take more than one coat of "paint" for even coverage. Let each coat dry completely before starting a new one.

BRUSH EMBROIDERY

Decorate flowers and leaves with the soft look of lace using this easy icing technique. Works best with the square tip brush from the Wilton Brush Set (p. 165).

1. Thin royal or buttercream icing with piping gel. Using tip 2, outline two or three small sections of flower petal sections at one time. Before outline can dry, using narrow edge of square tip bur+h, immediately brush out lines toward the center of area with damp brush. Work in quick, short strokes.

2. Clean brush with water after brushing each section to create distinct lines of icing. Repeat to complete design.

3. Add smaller brush embroidery flower for more dimension, pipe tip 2 dot center.

Cupcake Patterns

Use these patterns to cut precisely! Multiple patterns used for the same project are shaded in the same color. For left-side and right-side decorations, like hands, reverse the pattern if only one appears. Patterns may be copied to reproduce desired designs.

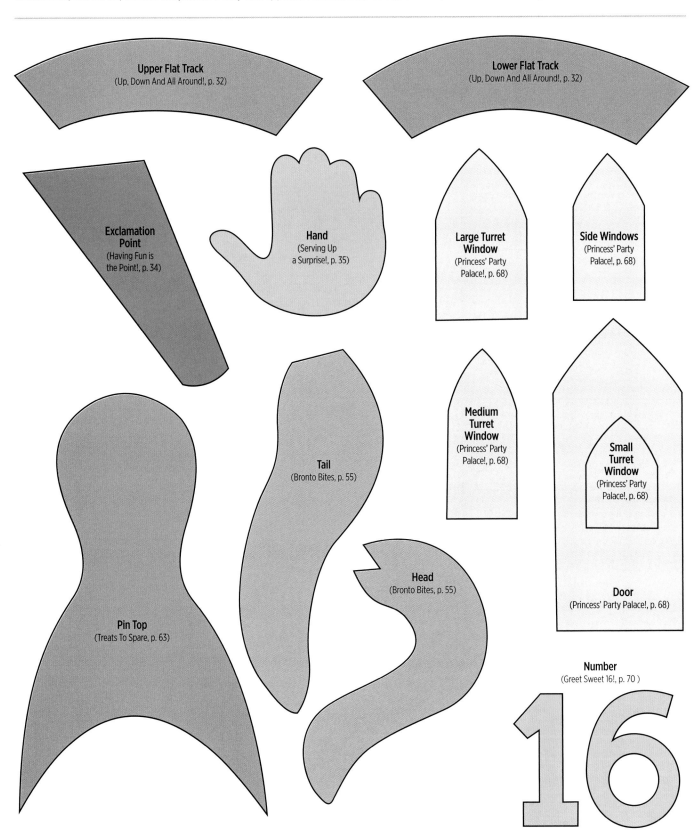

Upper Flat Track
(Up, Down And All Around!, p. 32)

Lower Flat Track
(Up, Down And All Around!, p. 32)

Exclamation Point
(Having Fun is the Point!, p. 34)

Hand
(Serving Up a Surprise!, p. 35)

Large Turret Window
(Princess' Party Palace!, p. 68)

Side Windows
(Princess' Party Palace!, p. 68)

Tail
(Bronto Bites, p. 55)

Medium Turret Window
(Princess' Party Palace!, p. 68)

Small Turret Window
(Princess' Party Palace!, p. 68)

Head
(Bronto Bites, p. 55)

Door
(Princess' Party Palace!, p. 68)

Pin Top
(Treats To Spare, p. 63)

Number
(Greet Sweet 16!, p. 70)

16

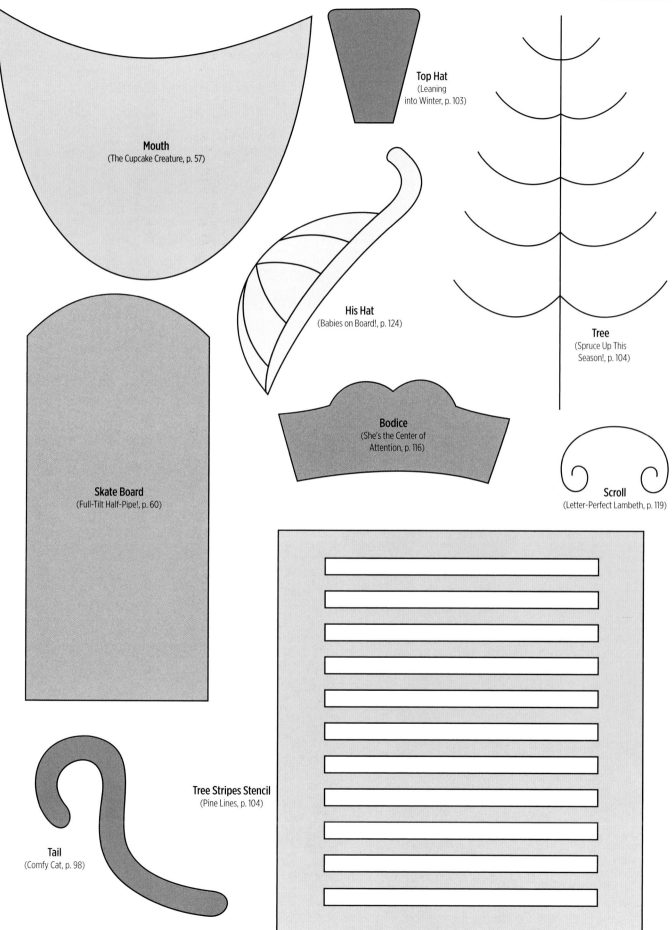

Mouth
(The Cupcake Creature, p. 57)

Top Hat
(Leaning
into Winter, p. 103)

His Hat
(Babies on Board!, p. 124)

Tree
(Spruce Up This
Season!, p. 104)

Skate Board
(Full-Tilt Half-Pipe!, p. 60)

Bodice
(She's the Center of
Attention, p. 116)

Scroll
(Letter-Perfect Lambeth, p. 119)

Tree Stripes Stencil
(Pine Lines, p. 104)

Tail
(Comfy Cat, p. 98)

Cupcake *Products*

It's the great cupcake makeover! With Wilton products, you have endless options for baking, serving and decorating. Discover exciting new shapes, dazzling cup designs, tasty toppers and more. Our product selection changes constantly and some products in this book may no longer be available. For the latest selection, see your Wilton retailer or visit www.wilton.com.

Specialty Baking Cups

Make everyday cupcakes extraordinary with wild prints, colors and shapes.

ColorCups
Always bright, colorful and fun!

Let your celebration colors stay true! Baking cups are foil-lined to keep colors on the outside bright and fun for every celebration. Place on a cookie sheet or bake in a standard-sized muffin pan. Standard size, 2 in. dia. Pk./36.

Flowers
415-0500

Pink Dots
415-0486

Yellow Dots
415-0487

Black Dots
415-0488

Red Dots
415-0490

Hearts
415-0499

Chevron
415-0636

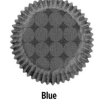
Pink/Purple/ Orange Dots
415-0483

Yellow/Blue/ Orange/Green Dots
415-0485

Zebra
415-0516

Leopard
415-0517

Rainbow Dots
415-0627

Pink/Purple/ Orange Stripes
415-0492

Rainbow Paint
415-0625

Blue
415-0480

Red
415-0481

Celebrate Blue
415-0496

RUFFLED

Gently flared edges and a softly rippled texture make these a great alternative to crisply pleated cups. Pk./24.

Rose
415-1391

Pink
415-1396

PETAL

A pretty pastel flower in full bloom! Perfect for shower, Mother's Day and birthday cupcakes. Standard size, Pk./24.; Mini size, Pk./48.

Red
Standard 415-1380
Mini 415-0466

Pink
Standard 415-1375
Mini 415-95046

Peach
Standard 415-1376
Mini 415-0467

Lavender
Standard 415-1442
Mini 415-95045

Yellow
415-1393

Teal
415-1390

Yellow
Standard 415-1443
Mini 415-0465

White
Standard 415-1379
Mini 415-0468

White Rose
Standard 415-1439

Grass
Standard 415-7051
Mini 415-0469

Lavender
415-1395

White
415-1389

SQUARE

Go cubical with your cupcakes! Use these paper cups with the Bar Pan (p. 158) for fun-to-eat party treats. Pk./24.

White
Standard
415-0666

Warm Squares
Standard
415-0668

UNBLEACHED

Let your decorated cupcake be the center of attention in these unbleached paper cups.

Standard
Pk./75.
415-1864

Mini
Pk./100.
415-1865

PATTERNED BAKING CUPS

With colorful Wilton designs, your cupcakes become part of the party! There's a baking cup pattern or color to suit every celebration! Standard size, 2 in. dia., Pk./75; Mini size, 1.25 in. dia., Pk./100, unless otherwise indicated.

Retro Dots
Standard 415-1878

Color Wheel
Standard 415-1868

Pink Zebra
Standard 415-0524

Leopard
Standard 415-1627

Dotted Ring
Standard 415-1870

Brown Dots
Standard 415-0152

Green Dots
Standard 415-0154

Teal Dots
Standard 415-0156

Pink Dots
Standard 415-0158

Red Dots
Standard 415-0148

Black Dots
Standard 415-7068

Purple Dots
Standard 415-0162

Light Pink Dots
Standard 415-0150

Gingham
Standard 415-0377

Retro Floral
Standard 415-1876

Silver Celebrate
Standard 415-1544

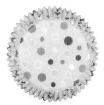
Sweet Dots
Standard 415-1052
Mini 415-1183

Modern Garden Party
Standard 415-0170
Mini 415-0171

Pink Party
Standard 415-0166
Mini 415-0167

Princess
Standard 415-1142
Mini 415-1145

MULTI-COLORED ASSORTMENTS

Always have colorful baking cups on hand for any celebration or simply "just because."

Rainbow
Yellow, blue, red, white, green, purple. Pk./150.
Standard 415-1623

Bright Rainbow
Yellow, blue, pink, white, green, purple. Pk./150.
Standard 415-1624

Jewel
Gold, purple, teal.
Standard Pk./75.
415-1078
Mini Pk./100. 415-1111

Primary
Red, yellow, blue.
Standard Pk./75.
415-987
Mini Pk./100.
415-1110

Pastel
Pink, yellow, blue-green.
Standard Pk./75. 415-394
Mini Pk./100. 415-2123

Monochrome
White, black, silver. Pk./75.
Standard
415-0374

BASIC

Classic colors that are right for any occasion or celebration.

White
Jumbo Pk./50.
415-2503
Standard Pk./75.
415-2505
Mini Pk./100.
415-2507

Silver Foil
Wax-laminated paper on foil.
Standard Pk./24.
415-207
Mini Pk./36.
415-1414

Gold Foil
Wax-laminated paper on foil.
Standard Pk./24.
415-206
Mini Pk./36.
415-1413

CUPCAKE COMBO

Quick and colorful way to serve cupcakes that set the tone for your celebration. Contains 24 each 2 in. dia. baking cups and 3 in. high paper party picks. Pk./24.

Princess
Standard 415-1313

Cupcakes! **155**

Cupcake Accents

You've never had more exciting ways to accent your cupcakes! Wilton makes decorating quick, easy and colorful with a great variety of toppings to give your iced cakes, cupcakes and cookies the perfect finishing touch.

PEARLIZED SPRINKLES

Add the soft, shimmering look of Sugar Pearls in six glistening shades. Or, shake on the sparkle with dazzling pearlized sugars and jimmies! Certified Kosher, except for Silver Pearlized Jimmies.

Silver Pearlized Jimmies
4.23 oz. 710-1127

White Pearlized Jimmies
4 oz. 710-0222

Black Sugar Pearls
4.8 oz. 710-1129

Green Sugar Pearls
5 oz. 710-1130

Yellow Sugar Pearls
5 oz. 710-1131

Pink Sugar Pearls
5 oz. 710-1132

Blue Sugar Pearls
5 oz. 710-1133

White Sugar Pearls
5 oz. 710-044

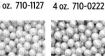

Ruby Pearlized Sugar
5.25 oz. 710-046

Gold Pearlized Sugar
5.25 oz. 710-041

Silver Pearlized Sugar
5.25 oz. 710-042

Sapphire Pearlized Sugar
5.25 oz. 710-047

Emerald Pearlized Sugar
5.25 oz. 710-048

CAKE SPARKLES

Brilliant edible sparkles in a variety of colors. Great for stencilling, snow scenes and highlighting messages. 0.25 oz. Certified Kosher.

Orange
703-1308

Pink
703-1260

Red
703-1284

Purple
703-1266

Blue
703-1314

Green
703-1278

Silver
703-1285

White
703-1290

Black
703-1302

Yellow
703-1272

SPARKLING SUGARS

Easy-pour sugars have a coarse texture and a brilliant sparkle that makes cupcakes, cookies and cakes really shine. Certified Kosher.

Blue
5.25 oz. 710-039

Yellow
5.25 oz. 710-036

Pink
5.25 oz. 710-038

Rainbow
8 oz. 710-991

White
8 oz. 710-992

EDIBLE ACCENTS

Adds glimmering touches to treats. Perfect for use on iced cupcakes, cakes and cookies—or sprinkle on drinks for twinkling toasts! Thousands of pieces in every jar! Certified Kosher.

 Pink Hearts
0.06 oz. 703-205

Silver Stars
0.04 oz. 703-201

Silver Hearts
0.06 oz. 703-204

Gold Stars
0.04 oz. 703-200

Gold Hearts
0.06 oz. 703-203

JUMBO SPRINKLES

These big and bold decorations are perfect for cupcakes, mini cakes, jumbo and king-sized cupcakes, brownies and cookies. Certified Kosher.

Jumbo Daisies
3.25 oz. 710-028

Jumbo Confetti
3.25 oz. 710-029

Jumbo Hearts
3.25 oz. 710-032

Jumbo Stars
3.25 oz. 710-026

Jumbo Nonpareils
4.8 oz. 710-033

SUGAR GEMS

Colorful, chunky sugars add a sparkling crystal-look finish to cupcakes and other treats. 4.25 oz. Certified Kosher.

Red
710-1140

Blue
710-1141

Green
710-1142

Pink
710-1143

SPRINKLES

Great shapes and colors add a dash of excitement to cupcakes, cakes, ice cream and more. Certified Kosher.

Spring Confetti
3 oz. 710-970

Chocolate Flavored Jimmies
2.5 oz. 710-774
6.25 oz. 710-168

Rainbow Jimmies
2.5 oz. 710-776
6.25 oz. 710-994

Rainbow Nonpareils
3 oz. 710-772

White Nonpareils
3 oz. 710-773

Cinnamon Drops
3 oz. 710-769

CRUNCHES

Add delicious flavor and a colossal crunch! Sprinkle over iced cupcakes or brownies. Certified Kosher.

 Cookies 'N Cream
5 oz. 710-9702

Turtle
5 oz. 710-9703

Rainbow Chips
Certified Kosher Dairy.
5.25 oz.
710-9704

 **Jordan Almonds**
Certified Kosher.
16 oz. bag. Assorted.
1006-779

6-MIX ASSORTMENTS
Assorted fun shapes in an easy-pour flip-top bottle. Certified Kosher.

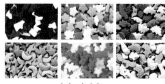

Flowerful Medley
Contains confetti, colorful leaves, daisies, pastel hearts, wild flowers, butterflies. 2.54 oz. total.
710-4122

Animals & Stars
Contains cows, stars, dinosaurs, stars and moons, bears, dolphins. 2.4 oz. total.
710-4123

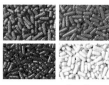

Nonpareils
Contains pink, orange, green, red, yellow, purple. 3 oz. total.
710-4125

Jimmies
Contains pink, orange, green, red, yellow, blue. 3.18 oz. total.
710-4127

SPRINKLE SETS
Create hair, noses, ears and more to bring your cupcakes to life. Convenient, individual flip-top containers. 3.74 oz. total weight.

People Faces
Contains diamonds, jimmies, circles.
710-056

Animal Faces
Contains triangles, jimmies, ovals.
710-055

COLORED SUGARS
Fill in brightly colored designs on cupcakes, cakes and cookies. 3.25 oz. bottle. Certified Kosher.

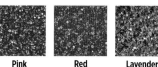

Pink 710-756 | **Red** 710-766 | **Lavender** 710-758
Orange 710-759 | **Light Green** 710-752 | **Dark Green** 710-764
Yellow 710-754 | **Blue** 710-750 | **Black** 710-762

DIMENSIONAL ICING DECORATIONS
Create impressive decorated cupcakes easily with our icing decorations. Perfect way to dress up brownies, cakes and other treats, too.

Multi Flower
Four large, 1.5 in.; six small, 0.875 in. Assorted color combinations. Pk./10.
710-8888

Purple Posies
Four large, 1.25 in.; six small, 1 in. Pk./10.
710-1101

Daisies
Four large, 1.25 in.; six small, 0.875 in. Pk./10.
710-7157

Pink Posies
Four large, 1.25 in.; six small, 0.875 in. Pk./10.
710-7158

Leaves
Four large, 1.25 in.; six small, 0.875 in. Pk./10.
710-1100

Butterflies
Create 10 butterflies with 20 wings, each 1.125 in. high x 0.625 in. wide. Pk./10.
710-7160

Red Roses
Small 0.75 in. Pk./12. 710-7152
Medium 1.25 in. Pk./8. 710-7151

White Roses
Small 0.75 in. Pk./12. 710-7155
Medium 1.25 in. Pk./8. 710-7154

Crowns with Hearts
0.75 in. x 1 in. Pk./12
710-6672

Cupcakes
1.25 in. x 1 in. Pk./12
710-2915

Bumble Bees
0.5 in. Pk./18
710-2916

Ladybugs
0.5 in. Pk./18
710-2917

Monkeys with Bananas
1 in. Pk./12
710-6671

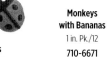

Bears with Gum Drops
1.25 in. x 0.75 in. Pk./12
710-2914

Candy Eyeballs
Perfect additions to faces on cupcakes, cookies, pops and more.

Large
0.75 in. dia.; 1 oz. Approx. 24 pieces
710-0133

Small
0.43 in. dia.; 0.88 oz. Approx. 62 pieces
710-0017

Knives
2 in. Pk./12
710-017

Bakeware

Having pans and tools you can count on makes a big difference in cupcake quality. Pick up all the essentials from the cupcake experts at Wilton!

ALUMINUM

Jumbo Muffin Pan
Make super-sized cupcakes and muffins. Six cups, each 4 in. dia. x 2 in.
2105-1820

Standard Muffin Pan
Most popular size for morning muffins, after-school cupcakes and desserts. 12 cups, each 3 in. dia. x 1 in.
2105-9310

Mini Muffin Pan
Great for mini cheesecakes, brunches, large gatherings. Each cup 2 in. dia. x 0.75 in.
12-Cup 2105-2125
24-Cup 2105-9313

Mini Ball Pan
Six cavities, each 3.5 in. x 3.5 in. x 1.5 in. deep.
2105-1760

6 in. x 2 in. Round Pan
2105-2185
8 in. x 2 in. Round Pan
2105-2193

Mini Wonder Mold
One cake mix makes 4 to 6 cakes. Pan is 10 in. x 10 in. x 3 in. deep. Individual cakes are 3.5 in. x 3 in.
2105-3020

Jumbo Sheet
Large batches of cookies slide off with ease.
14 in. x 20 in. 2105-6213

Insulated Sheet
Two quality aluminum layers sandwich an insulating layer of air for perfect browning without burning.
14 in. x 16 in. 2105-2644

Jelly Roll and Cookie Pans
Wilton pans are 1 in. deep for fuller-looking desserts.
10.5 in. x 15.5 in. x 1 in. 2105-1269
12 in. x 18 in. x 1 in. 2105-4854

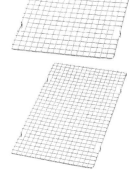

Cooling Grids
Chrome-plated.
10 in. x 16 in. Rectangle
2305-128
14.5 in. x 20 in. Rectangle
2305-129

NON-STICK

Standard Muffin Pan
Each cup 3 in. dia. x 1 in.
12-Cup 2105-954
6-Cup 2105-953

Standard Muffin Pan with Cover
12 cups, each 3 in. dia. x 1 in.
2105-1832

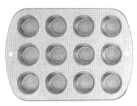

Mini Muffin Pan
Each cup 2 in. dia. x 0.75 in.
12-Cup 2105-952
24-Cup 2105-914

Jumbo Muffin Pan
Six cups, each 4 in. dia. x 2 in.
2105-955

Cookie/Jelly Roll Pans
17.25 in. x 11.5 in. 2105-968
15.25 in. x 10.25 in. 2105-967
13.25 in. x 9.25 in. 2105-966

Bar Pan
Make fun square cupcakes, brownies and more! 12 cups, each 2.75 in. x 2.75 in. x 1.5 in.
2105-0693

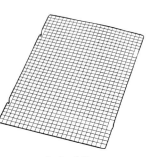

Cooling Grids
Cookies and cakes won't stick with our slick non-stick coating.
10 in. x 16 in.
2305-228
14.5 in. x 20 in.
2305-229

3-Tier Cooling Grid
Use individually or stack to cool batches of cupcakes at the same time. Individual grids are 13.5 in. x 9.75 in. x 3 in. high; stacked grids are 9.75 in. high.
2105-948

Wilton

SILICONE   DIMENSIONS NON-STICK

6-Cup Muffin
Six cups, each 2.75 in. dia. x 1.25 in.
2105-4802

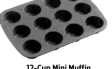

12-Cup Mini Muffin
12 cups, each 1.75 in. dia. x 1 in.
2105-4829

Round Pops
One 8 in. x 8 in. size brownie mix
makes 24 brownies. Eight cups,
each 1.75 in. dia. x 1.75 in. deep.
2105-4925

Standard Baking Cups
2 in. dia.; six red,
six blue. Convenient
fill line. Pk./12.
415-9400

Large Cupcake
Finished cake
8.25 in. x 7.5 in.;
10-cup total capacity.*
Pat. Nos. D575,097
and D591,552.
2105-5038

Multi-Cavity Mini Cupcakes
Finished cakes 3.8 in. x 4 in.;
6-cup total capacity.*
Pat. No. D577,535 and
Patent Pending.
2105-5043

* For cakes, fill pans ½ to ⅔ full.

Baking Tools

Choose Wilton products designed with features that make measuring, mixing and pan preparation easier.

Scoop-It Measuring Spoons
Set/5.
2103-325

Scoop-It Measuring Cups
Set/4.
2103-324

2-Cup Liquid Measure
Patent Pending.
2103-334

4-Cup Liquid Measure
Patent Pending.
2103-335

**Tilt-N-Mix
3-Pc. Bowl Set**
2103-306

Pastry Brush
Flexible silicone
bristles are great for
brushing on Cake
Release pan coating,
shortening or hot
glazes. More durable
than nylon bristles.
Comfortable
ergonomic handle.
8.5 in. long.
409-6056

Pastry Wheel
Comfortable handle
with finger/thumb
guard. 6.5 in. long.
2103-315

Cookie Spatula
Great for serving brownies
and bar cookies, too.
Comfortable ergonomic
handle with thumb rest.
Stainless steel. 9 in. long.
409-6054

Scoop-It Batter Spoons
Bake cupcakes exactly the same size with
portion-perfect spoons. Flexible edge helps
scrape batter from bowl. Cupcake-shaped plastic
ring holds spoons together. Nests for compact
storage. Jumbo spoon holds about 0.6 cup,
standard spoon holds about 0.25 cup, mini
spoon holds about 1.75 tablespoons. Set/3.
2103-1112

Cyclone Whisk
Pat. No. D582,223.
2103-317

**Silicone Spoon
Scraper**
Pat. No. D584,927.
2103-328

12 in. Rolling Pin
Has removable handles making it fully submersible and dishwasher safe.
2103-301

Non-Stick Parchment Paper
Oven-safe to 400°F, great for
conventional ovens, microwaves
and the freezer. Double roll is
41 square feet, 15 in. wide.
Certified Kosher.
415-680

Cake Tester
Reusable pick comes out
clean when cake is ready.
Includes storage cover.
2103-434

**Cake Release
Pan Coating**
Cakes release perfectly
every time without
crumbs, helping you
achieve a great surface
for decorating. In
convenient dispensing
bottle. 8 oz.
Certified Kosher.
702-6016

**Bake Easy!
Non-Stick Spray**
This convenient,
non-stick spray helps
your cakes release
perfectly with fewer
crumbs for easier
icing. 6 oz.
702-6018

**Perfect Fill
Batter Dispenser**
Built-in valve helps you
fill baking cups without
spilling batter onto your
pan. Makes filling mini
baking cups a breeze!
Just attach to a cut 16 in.
disposable decorating
bag, and squeeze to fill
cup ⅔ full with batter.
Available April 2013.
411-7369

Icings & Flavorings

Serve delicious iced cupcakes with convenient ready-to-use icings, mixes and flavors.

ICING MIXES & INGREDIENTS

Ice cupcakes with the perfect texture and taste with convenient mixes, ready-to-use icings and concentrated flavors.

Buttercream Icing Mix

Our convenient mix has the delicious taste and creamy texture of homemade buttercream icing. Makes about 1¾ cups—enough to ice a 1-layer 8 in. cake or cover 12 cupcakes with a tip 1M swirl. Certified Kosher Dairy.
710-112

Royal Icing Mix

A convenient mix for creating hard-drying flowers and other decorations! Makes 2 cups—enough icing for about 280 drop flowers or 88 small roses. Certified Kosher.
710-1219

Whipped Icing Mix

Our light, whipped icing provides the ideal texture for decorating in an easy-to-make, delicious mix. Light and delicate vanilla flavor. Makes about 7 cups—enough to ice and decorate one 2-layer 9 in. round cake or cover 36 cupcakes with a tip 1M swirl. Certified Kosher Dairy.
710-1241

READY-TO-USE ICINGS

Wilton makes the only ready-to-use icing that is the perfect consistency for decorating. The pure white color is best for creating true vivid colors using Wilton Icing Colors. Rich and creamy with a delicious homemade taste.

Creamy Decorator Icing

Ideal medium consistency perfect for icing borders and piped decorations. Has a great vanilla flavor and is easy to color. Yields 9 cups of icing, which will cover 60 standard cupcakes with a tip 1M swirl or cover three 2-layer 8 in. cakes or four 9 in. x 13 in. cakes. 4.5 lb. Certified Kosher.
704-680

Meringue Powder

Primary ingredient for royal icing. Stabilizes buttercream, adds body to boiled icing and meringue. Replaces egg whites in many recipes. Resealable top opens for easy measuring. 4 oz. can makes five recipes of royal icing; 8 oz. can makes 10 recipes. 16 oz. can makes 20 recipes. Certified Kosher.
4 oz. 702-6007
8 oz. 702-6015
16 oz. 702-6004

Color Flow Mix

Create dimensional flow-in designs for your cake. Great for covering and decorating cookies! 4 oz. can makes 10—1½ cup batches. Certified Kosher.
701-47

Piping Gel

Perfect for writing messages and adding decorative accents. Use clear or tint with icing color. 10 oz. Certified Kosher.
704-105

Decorator Icing

Ideal stiff consistency for making roses and flowers with upright petals. 16 oz. can.
White 710-118
Chocolate 710-119

FLAVORINGS

Wilton flavors are concentrated—only a drop or two adds delicious taste to icings, cakes, beverages and other recipes.

Imitation Clear Vanilla Extract

2 fl. oz. 604-2237
8 fl. oz. 604-2269

Imitation Clear Butter Flavor

2 fl. oz. 604-2040
8 fl. oz. 604-2067

Imitation Almond Extract

2 fl. oz. 604-2126

Pure Lemon Extract

2 fl. oz. Certified Kosher.
604-2235

Pure Vanilla Extract

Unmatched flavor and aroma enhances cakes, puddings, pie fillings, custards and more. 4 fl. oz. Certified Kosher.
604-2270

Edible Decorating Paper & Tools

Colorful *Sugar Sheets!* edible decorating paper adds excitement to cupcake tops and large cupcake sides.

Use edible, flexible *Sugar Sheets!* edible decorating paper to cut or punch virtually any shape or border design. There's no preparation, no mess. Just peel, punch or cut and place your decorations in minutes. The light, sweet flavor works with buttercream or fondant-covered treats. 8 in. x 11 in. Certified Kosher.

SOLID COLORS

PATTERNS

| Orange 710-2965 | Brown 710-2966 | Bright Yellow 710-2947 | Bright Pink 710-2952 | Bright Green 710-2958 | Damask 710-2941 |

| Red 710-2953 | Black 710-2961 | Purple 710-2949 | White 710-2960 | Bright Blue 710-2956 | Zebra 710-2943 |

Rotary Cutter

Hand cut accents from *Sugar Sheets!* edible decorating paper, fondant or gum paste! Easy to control with an ergonomic, soft-grip handle and smooth, easy-cutting stainless steel blade. Protective blade cover included. For food use only. 4 in. x 1.75 in.
1907-111

Dab-N-Hold Edible Adhesive

Spreads thin, attaches fast and easy! Use to apply *Sugar Sheets!* edible decorating paper pieces to fondant or crusted buttercream icing, create layered decorations and more! 2 fl. oz. Certified Kosher.
610-927

Decorating Tools

Keep Wilton basics on hand to add the perfect finishing touches to your cupcakes. Flexible spatulas, durable decorating bags and more make decorating easy.

DECORATOR PREFERRED SPATULAS

Icing your desserts, adding filling between cake layers and even filling your decorating bag is easier with premium Wilton Decorator Preferred Icing Spatulas.

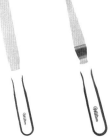

Cupcake
Round blade is perfect for icing cupcakes and small treats.
8.25 in. 409-7704

Straight Blade
9 in. 409-7703
11 in. 409-7701

Tapered Blade
9 in. 409-7699

Angled Blade
9 in. 409-7698
13 in. 409-7696

Wide
Square 90° corner of the blade edge works great for icing sides of a cake.
13 in. 409-7702

DECORATING BAGS

From parchment triangles to our convenient disposable or premium reusable Featherweight styles, Wilton bags are made to our strict specifications for consistent quality.

Featherweight Decorating Bags

The best quality bags for decorating with strong resilient seams to help them last for years! Featherweight bags feel soft and comfortable in the hand—the polyester material becomes softer the more the bags are used. Lightweight, strong and flexible, they'll never get stiff. Coated to prevent grease from seeping through. Dishwasher safe. Instructions included; sold singly.

8 in. 404-5087
10 in. 404-5109
12 in. 404-5125
14 in. 404-5140
16 in. 404-5168
18 in. 404-5184

Disposable Decorating Bags

Our proprietary blend of materials helps Wilton bags feel more comfortable and outperform other brands. Use with or without a coupler. Works great for microwave-melting and piping of Candy Melts candy. Strong flexible plastic; fits standard tips and couplers (sold separately). Instructions included.

12 in. Disposable Decorating Bags
Pk./12. 2104-358
Pk./24. 2104-1358

Dispenser Boxes
Convenient value packs make it easy to pull out one bag at a time. Instructions included.
Pk./50. 2104-1273
Pk./100. 2104-1249

16 in. Disposable Decorating Bags
Decorate longer without refilling the bag—great for piping borders on large cakes or icing cupcakes. Use with Cake Icer Tip 789. Pk./12.
2104-1357

Parchment Triangles

Make use-and-toss decorating bags ideal for small amounts of icing or brush striping. Excellent wet strength for candy or a variety of icings. Also great for smoothing iced cakes and transferring patterns. 15 in. Pk./100.
2104-1508

CAKE CONSTRUCTION

Essentials for proper support and presentation of cakes and treats.

Cake Boards

Strong corrugated cardboard, generously sized in rectangular shapes. Perfect for sheet and square cakes. For a batch of cupcakes or shaped cakes, use the pan as a pattern and cut out board to fit cake. Greaseproof coating.

10 in. x 14 in. Rectangle Pk./6.
104-554
13 in. x 19 in. Rectangle Pk./6. 2104-552

Fanci-Foil Wrap

Serving side has a non-toxic, grease-resistant surface. Continuous roll: 20 in. x 15 ft.

White 804-191
Gold 804-183
Silver 804-167

Cake Circles

Corrugated cardboard for strength and stability. Greaseproof coating.

6 in. Round Pk./10. 2104-64
8 in. Round Pk./12. 2104-80
10 in. Round Pk./12. 2104-102
12 in. Round Pk./8. 2104-129
14 in. Round Pk./6. 2104-145
16 in. Round Pk./6. 2104-160

Dessert Decorator plus

It's the easy-to-use tool for beautifully decorated desserts! One hand does it all: elegant shells, stars and leaves, beautiful script messages, pretty bows and flowers. Decorating instructions included.
415-0906

Includes:

2 Tip Couplers
Two sizes hold standard (small) and large tips.

5 Precision Tips
Produce perfectly shaped decorations every time.

| Round Tip | Star Tip | Petal Tip | Leaf Tip | Filling Tip |

DECORATING COUPLERS

Couplers make it easy to change decorating tips on the same icing bag.

Standard
Fits all decorating bags and standard tips.
411-1987

Coupler Ring Set
Attach Wilton standard-size metal decorating tips onto Wilton tube icings to create any technique. Set/4.
418-47306

DOWEL RODS

Provide support for all tiered cakes with our dowel rods.

Bamboo Dowel Rods
Made of eco-friendly bamboo, the renewable resource! Easy to cut. Length: 12 in.; dia.: 0.25 in. Pk./12.
399-1010

Plastic Dowel Rods
Heavy-duty hollow plastic provides strong, stable support. Cut with serrated knife or strong shears to desired length. Length: 12.25 in.; dia.: 0.75 in. Pk./4.
399-801

Decorating Tips & Accessories

Presenting high-quality tips, used by decorators throughout the world. Wilton tips are made to hold their shape and create precise decorations year after year. Dishwasher safe tips are tested for consistent performance in the Wilton Test Kitchen. All tips work with standard bags and couplers, unless otherwise indicated.

ROUND TIPS

Outline, lettering, dots, stringwork, balls, beads, lattice, lacework.

#1s
402-1009

#8
402-8

#1
402-1

#10
402-10

#2
402-2

#12
402-12

#3
402-3

#2A
Smaller version of 1A.
402-2001*

#4
402-4

#5
402-5

#1A
Bold borders, figure piping.
402-1001*

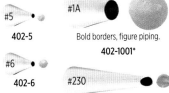

#6
402-6

#230
Fill cupcakes, eclairs and bismarcks.
402-230**

#7
402-7

OPEN STAR TIPS

Star techniques, drop flowers; use 6B and 8B with pastry dough, too. The finely cut teeth of 199 and 363 create decorations with many ridges.

#13
402-13

#21
402-21

#14
402-14

#22
402-22

#16
402-16

#32
402-32

#18
402-18

#199
402-199

#6B
402-6600**

#4B
402-4400**

#1M
(2110)
402-2110*

SPECIALTY TIPS

Shells, squares, curved ribbon, ropes and swirls.

#402
402-402*

#233
402-233

#79
402-79

LEAF TIPS

Ideal for shell-motion borders, too.

#352
402-352

#366
Makes leaves for larger flowers.
402-366*

*Fits large coupler.

**Tip does not work with coupler. Use with bag only or parchment. Cake Icer tip should be used with bags 16 in. or larger.

PETAL TIPS

Realistic flower petals, dramatic ruffles, drapes, swags and bows.

#59s/59s
402-594

#103
402-103

#126
402-126*

#97
402-97

#104
402-104

#127
402-127*

#101s
402-1019

#124
402-124*

#150
402-150

#101
402-101

#125
402-125*

#127D
Giant Rose**
402-1274

DROP FLOWER TIPS

Small (106-225); medium (131-194); large (2C-1G, great for cookie dough).

#129
402-129

#225
402-225

#1E
402-1005*

#2D
402-2004*

BASKETWEAVE TIPS

Tips 44, 45 make only smooth stripes; rest of basketweave tips and Cake Icer make both smooth and ribbed stripes.

#44
402-44

#46
402-46

#789

Cake Icer **
409-789

FLOWER MAKING ACCESSORIES

Start your icing flowers the right way. Pipe them on Wilton flower nails, convenient templates and pre-cut squares for consistent results.

Decorating Nail Set

A great selection of sizes for creating virtually any size nail flower! Includes 1.5 in., 2 in., 2.5 in. flower nails and 2.25 in. x 2.5 in. cupcake nail. Stems insert easily in nails to create a secure platform. Top-rack dishwasher safe. Plastic. Pk./4.

417-107

Flower Nail No. 7

For basic flower making. Provides the control you need when piping icing flowers. Stainless steel. 1.5 in. wide.

402-3007

Pre-Cut Icing Flower Squares

Perfectly sized waxed paper squares attach to flower nail with a dot of icing for easy piping and transfer of flowers. Pk./50.

414-920

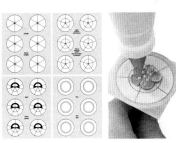

Flower Nail Templates

Convenient stickers guide you to create perfectly formed flowers! Includes four template styles used to create five popular icing flowers. Set/48.

414-1000

Colors

Create colorful special effects! Icing colors, gels and colored icing give you a rainbow of possibilities to fit celebration and seasonal color schemes.

ICING COLORS

Produce deep, rich color with just a small amount using this fast-mixing gel. Exclusive concentrated gel formula helps decorators achieve the exact shade desired without changing icing consistency. 1 oz. single bottles. Certified Kosher. **

Ivory 610-208
Buttercup Yellow 610-216
Golden Yellow 610-159
Lemon Yellow 610-108
Copper 610-450

Creamy Peach 610-210
Orange 610-205
Red-Red* 610-906
Christmas Red* 610-302
Red (no-taste) 610-998
Rose 610-401
Burgundy 610-698
Pink 610-256
Violet 610-604
Delphinium Blue 610-228

Cornflower Blue 610-710
Royal Blue 610-655
Sky Blue 610-700
Teal 610-207
Kelly Green 610-752
Leaf Green 610-809
Moss Green 610-851
Juniper Green 610-234
Brown 610-507
Black* 610-981

*Note: Large amounts of these colors may affect icing taste.
Use No-Taste Red for large areas of red on a cake. When using Black, start with chocolate icing to limit the amount of color needed.
**Sunlight and fluorescent lighting will alter colors on cakes and treats. Keep treats stored in a covered box and out of direct sunlight or fluorescent lighting.

COLOR MIST FOOD COLOR SPRAY

Easy-to-use spray gives the versatility and dazzling effects of an airbrush in a convenient can! Use it to transform plain iced cupcakes or cookies. No mess, taste-free formula. 1.5 oz. Certified Kosher. **

Silver 710-5521
Pearl 710-5522
Gold 710-5520

Green 710-5503
Red 710-5500
Blue 710-5501

Orange 710-5507
Violet 710-5504
Pink 710-5505

Black 710-5506
Yellow 710-5502

FOODWRITER EDIBLE COLOR MARKERS

Decorate on Wilton Cookie Icing, Fondant, Color Flow and royal icing designs. Or add dazzling color to countless foods, like toaster pastries, cheese, fruit slices, bread and more. Each set includes five 0.07 oz. FoodWriter edible color markers. Certified Kosher.

EXTRA-FINE TIP

FINE TIP

BOLD TIP

Extra Fine Tip Set 609-105
For fine detailing.
Fine Tip Neon Colors Set 609-116
Fine Tip Primary Colors Set 609-100
Bold Tip Primary Colors Set 609-115

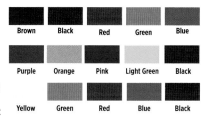

Brown | Black | Red | Green | Blue
Purple | Orange | Pink | Light Green | Black
Yellow | Green | Red | Blue | Black

DECORATING ICINGS & GELS

Perfect for adding small color details to cupcakes!

Decorating Icings

The same high-quality as our Ready-To-Use Icings, in a convenient tube. Ideal for small areas of color. Use with the Coupler Ring Set (p. 161) and any standard-size, Wilton metal tip (not included). Colors match Wilton Icing Colors. 4.25 oz. Certified Kosher.**

Red 704-218	Leaf Green 704-224
Violet 704-242	Kelly Green 704-227
Yellow 704-236	Chocolate 704-254
Orange 704-212	White 704-200
Pink 704-230	Black 704-206
Royal Blue 704-248	

Candy Melts & Tools

Top cupcakes with our easy-melting Candy Melts candy or add a fun molded candy accent! No one makes decorating with candy easier than Wilton.

CANDY MELTS

Delicious, creamy, easy-to-melt wafers are ideal for making candy accents for your cupcakes. Artificial vanilla flavor unless otherwise indicated. 12 oz. (unless otherwise noted). Certified Kosher Dairy.

Blue 1911-1352
Yellow 1911-1369
Orange 1911-1515
Red 1911-1364
Pink 1911-1361
Lavender 1911-1358
White 1911-1367

Dark Cocoa Mint 1911-1355
Light Cocoa 1911-1359
Dark Cocoa 1911-1353
Vibrant Green 1911-401
Black 10 oz. 1911-402
Peanut Butter 1911-1516
Dark Green 1911-1356

Peanut Butter Cups Mold
1 design, 11 cavities.
2115-1522

Truffles Mold
1 design, 14 cavities.
2115-1521

Dessert Dome Mold
Two-piece mold makes dome halves 1.2 in., 1.6 in. and 2.6 in. dia.; 3 designs, 6 cavities.
2115-2122

Dessert Accents Mold
Swirls, scrolls, zigzags, triangles and leaves add 5-star style. 5 designs, 10 cavities.
2115-2102

Lollipop Sticks
Sturdy paper sticks. Not for oven use.
4 in. Pk./50. 1912-1006
6 in. Pk./35. 1912-1007
8 in. Pk./25. 1912-9320
11.75 in. Pk./20. 1912-1212

Decorator Brush Set
Set/3.
2104-9355

Large Jewel Tone Foil Wraps
Wrap larger candies in beautiful, bright foil squares!
6 in. x 6 in. Pk./12.
2113-1119

CANDY COLOR SETS

Concentrated oil-based colors blend easily with Candy Melts candy.

Primary
Yellow, orange, red and blue 0.25 oz. jars. Certified Kosher. Set/4.
1913-1299

Garden
Pink, green, violet and black 0.25 oz. jars. Certified Kosher. Set/4.
1913-1298

Candy Melting Plate
Includes decorating brush.
1904-8016

Decorating Gels

Add colorful highlights to your decorating with these transparent gels. Create a beautiful stained-glass effect and add distinctive writing and printing. Colors match Wilton Icing Colors. 0.75 oz. Certified Kosher.

Red 704-318	Orange 704-312
Pink 704-330	Royal Blue 704-348
Violet 704-342	Kelly Green 704-324
Yellow 704-336	Brown 704-354
White 704-302	Black 704-306

Sparkle Gel

Squeeze on sparkling color effects with our ready-to-use gel. Great for dots, messages, water effects and fondant accents. Resealable 3.5 oz. tubes. Certified Kosher.

Orange 704-109
Black 704-1061
White 704-107
Gold 704-1060

Light Green 704-1019
Green 704-111
Pink 704-356
Light Blue 704-1013

Red 704-112
Yellow 704-108
Blue 704-110

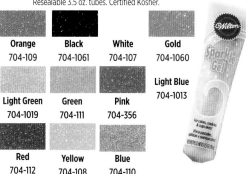

Fondant, Gum Paste & Tools

Flowers, figures and more make colorful and exciting cupcake accents! They are easy to do with these ready-to-use shapable icings and tools.

DECORATOR PREFERRED FONDANT

It's even easier to make smooth fondant cakes with impressive decorations that have a creamy texture and delicous taste. Wilton Decorator Preferred Fondant has an improved taste and texture without sacrificing the flexibility or ease of use.

White Fondant Packs

The 24 oz. package covers an 8 in. 2-layer cake plus decorations; the 80 oz. package covers a 2-layer 6 in., 8 in. and 10 in. round tiered cake plus decorations. Pure white. Certified Kosher.

24 oz. 710-2301
80 oz. 710-2300

Colored Fondant Packs

Pre-colored and ready-to-use. 24 oz. package. Certified Kosher.

Chocolate	710-2302
Black Vanilla	710-2303
Red Vanilla	710-2304
Purple Vanilla	710-2310
Pink Vanilla	710-2305
Blue Vanilla	710-2306
Green Vanilla	710-2307
Yellow Vanilla	710-2308

Colored Multi Packs

Each 17.6 oz. package contains four 4.4 oz. packets. Certified Kosher.

Primary Colors
Green, Red, Yellow, Blue.
710-445

Pastel Colors
Blue, Yellow, Pink, Green.
710-447

Neon Colors
Purple, Orange, Yellow, Pink.
710-446

Natural Colors
Light Brown, Dark Brown, Pink, Black.
710-448

GUM PASTE

Design breathtaking gum paste roses, daisies, apple blossoms, tulips and other flowers in advance for decorating cupcakes.

Ready-To-Use Gum Paste

Create beautiful hand-molded flowers right from the package. Just tint, roll out and cut to create incredible floral bouquets for your cakes. Easy instructions included. 1 lb. Certified Kosher.
707-130

Gum-Tex
6 oz. Certified Kosher.
707-117

Fondant Smoother

Smooths fondant-covered cakes to a beautiful surface. Contoured handle is comfortable to hold. Softly rounded base edge prevents marking fondant surface. The squared back helps to create a clean angle between sides and base of cake. 3.25 in. x 5.75 in.
1907-1016

Decorative Press Set

Squeeze with ease to make exciting decorations from gum paste or rolled fondant! Shapes include circle, basketweave, teardrop, three-hole, star and semicircle. Comes apart for easy cleaning. For food use only. Set/6.
1907-1116

Fondant Ribbon Cutter

Cut a variety of ribbon widths and designs in fondant and gum paste with our Fondant Ribbon Cutter. Includes:
• Three spacers: 1 in., ½ in. and ¼ in.
• Four cutting wheels: straight, wavy, zigzag.
• Two locks: ensures wheels and spacers do not shift. Set/25.
1907-1019

Three 1-in. spacers

Four straight cutting wheels

Four wavy cutting wheels

Three ½-in. spacers

Two locks

Four zigzag cutting wheels

Three ¼-in. spacers

Roller handle with easy-button release

20 in. Fondant Roller

The non-stick surface makes handling large pieces of fondant easy. 20 in. x 1.5 in. dia.
1907-1210

Roll-N-Cut Mat

For precise measuring, rolling and cutting of fondant or dough. Pre-marked circles for exact sizing. Square grid helps you cut precise strips. Non-stick surface for easy release. 20 in. square with circles from 3 in. to 19 in. dia.
409-412

Storage Board

Place cut pieces under flaps until you're ready to work. Ample space for storing multiple petals and leaves when making flowers. Use the back side to roll out fondant for small details. 8 in. x 10 in.
409-2544

Fondant Trimmer

Provides a clean cut for fondant and gum paste, and is safe to use on most surfaces. Wheel removes from handle for easy cleaning. Wheel: 3 in.; Handle: 7 in.
1907-1051

Detail Embosser

Add detail quickly with our Detail Embosser. Includes:
• Two easy-to-remove wheels; each wheel has three embossing designs.
• Six patterns: dash, bead, zigzag and wavy, stitch and dot.
• Roller handle with easy-button release and comfortable grip. Set/4.
1907-1018

20 in. Fondant Roller Guide Rings

Achieve the perfect thickness every time. Includes 1/16 in. (blue), 1/8 in. (orange) 3/16 in. (gold) rings. Set/3.
1907-1010

9 in. Fondant Roller

Just the right size for preparing small amounts of fondant. Perfect for use with fondant, gum paste and our variety of Cut-Outs fondant cutters. Includes 1/8 in. and 1/16 in. rings. 9 in. x 1 in. dia.
1907-1205

10-Pc. Gum Paste/Fondant Tool Set

Colored grips and numbered tip designs make tools easy to identify. Includes large/small veining tool, shell tool/knife, large/small dogbone tool, serrated quilting/cutting wheel, umbrella tool with five and six divisions, scriber/cone tool, large/small ball tool, palette knife, modeling sticks #1 and #2 and convenient case. Set/10.
1907-1107

Gum Paste Flower Cutter Set

Cutters are comfortable to hold, with a contoured top and precise cutting edges. Ejectors cut blossom and hydrangea shapes then imprint beautiful texture on both sides using the custom Impression Strip. The full-color trilingual instruction book includes step-by-step instructions for 13 of the most popular gum paste flowers. Set/25.
2109-0054

Flower Impression Set

This two-piece silicone mold set is the perfect complement to the Wilton Gum Paste Flower Cutter Set. On back, a wire stem groove creates a ridge for easy wire assembly on your flowers. Set/2.
409-2560

Wave Flower Former Set

Wave shape makes it easy to dry concave or convex shapes; large drying area is great for ribbons, bows and streamers. 14.5 in. x 9 in. assembled. Patent pending. Set/2.
1907-1320

Fondant Shaping Foam

Each square is 4 in. x 4 in.; thin is 0.0625 in. high, medium is 0.125 in. high, thick is 0.5 in. high. Set/3.
1907-9704

Stepsaving Rose Bouquets Flower Cutter Set

Cutters include large and small rose, rose leaf, calyx and forget-me-not. Set/6.
1907-1003

Calla Lily Former Set

Step-by-step instructions make it easy! Includes one cutter, six formers and complete instructions. Set/7.
417-1109

Flower Stamen Assortment

Includes 60 each pearl, fluffy and glitter. 2.5 in. long. Pk./180.
1005-410

Color Stamen Set

Includes 60 each yellow, white and orange. 2.125 in. long. Pk./180.
1005-4452

Flower Forming Cups

Includes 2.5 in. and 3 in. dia. cups. Set/6.
1907-118

Gum Paste Wire and Tape

Includes 32 wires (20-, 22- and 26- gauge) and 30 yds. of ½ in. wide tape.
1907-1113

CUT-OUTS FONDANT CUTTERS

With Cut-Outs Fondant Cutters, it's easy to make fun shapes for your fondant cakes and cupcakes. Just roll out fondant and/or gum paste, press down with the stainless steel Cut-Out and lift away. Remove shapes with a small spatula.

Crinkle
Circle, Square, Triangle, Heart. 1.25 in. Set/4.
417-444

Fancy
Flower, Leaf, Oval, Heart 1.5 in. to 2 in. Set/4.
417-445

Garden
Butterfly, Tulip, Bell, Flower 1.25 in. to 1.75 in. Set/4.
417-443

Water Brush

Just fill with water and brush to attach fondant and gum paste decorations. Perfect for rehydrating your *Sugar Sheets!* edible decorating paper. 7 in. x 0.75 in.
1907-1111

Ovals
0.625 in. to 2.25 in. Set/3.
417-438

Rounds
0.75 in. to 2.25 in. Set/3.
417-432

Hearts
0.75 in. to 2.25 in. Set/3.
417-434

Leaves
1 in. to 3 in. Set/3.
417-437

Funny Flowers
0.75 in. to 2.3 in. Set/3.
417-436

Flowers
0.625 to 2.1 in. Set/3.
417-435

Stars
0.625 in. to 2.1 in. Set/3.
417-433

Brush Set
Fine-bristle brushes in three tip designs (round, square and bevel). Set/3.
1907-1207

Deluxe Brush Set
Brushes are also ideal for attaching shapes using gum glue adhesive, striping decorating bags with color and more. Set/7.
1907-1112

COLOR DUST
Give flower decorations a deep matte finish, or create natural shading that adds depth. Certified Kosher (except Deep Pink and Purple). 0.05 oz. bottle.

White	Red	Deep Pink	Orange	Purple
703-100	703-101	703-103	703-104	703-105

Brown	Periwinkle Blue	Goldenrod	Spruce Green	Lime Green
703-106	703-107	703-108	703-109	703-110

PEARL DUST
Give your decorations a beautiful, glittering finish. Creates rich, lustrous highlights on flowers, bows, letters and more. Certified Kosher (except Orchid Pink and Lilac Purple). 0.05 oz. bottle.

Leaf Green	Lilac Purple	Sapphire Blue	Ruby Red	Gold
703-215	703-221	703-222	703-223	703-216

Yellow	Bronze	Orchid Pink	Silver	White
703-213	703-214	703-217	703-218	703-219

FONDANT & GUM PASTE MOLDS
Create amazing detail quickly with our theme silicone molds! Molds contain detailed impression areas, which imprint texture and dimension on gum paste or fondant shapes.

Letters/Numbers Set
409-2547

Baroque
409-2562

Fern
409-2548

Folk
409-2550

Macrame
409-2549

Global
409-2564

Jewelry
409-2551

Fabric
409-2563

Sea Life
409-2552

Nature
409-2565

Cookie Cutters

Cupcakes and cookies are the perfect combo! Whether you use our metal circle cutter to make a cookie cupcake base or our mini sets to make a fun animal accent, Wilton has the shapes and sizes you need.

COMFORT-GRIP

Easy-grip, stainless steel cutters with extra-deep sides are perfect for cutting cookies, brownies, sheet cakes and more. The cushion grip gives you comfortable control. Recipe included. Top-rack dishwasher safe. Each approx. 4 in. x 4 in. x 1.75 in.

Daisy
2310-619

Heart
2310-616

Star
2310-605

Round
2310-608

Flower
2310-613

METAL

Our metal cutters are built to last, cut cleanly and release with ease. Each approx. 3 in.

Daisy
2308-1007

Circle
2308-1010

Heart
2308-1003

Star
2308-1008

Gingerbread Boy
2308-1002

Bear
2308-1009

METAL SETS

Multi-piece sets add variety to the shapes you can cut. Recipe included.

6-Pc. Mini Romantic

Butterfly, heart, bell, crinkled heart, tulip, blossom.
Each approx. 1.5 in. Set/6.
2308-1225

6-Pc. Mini Geometric Crinkle

Square, circle, heart, diamond, triangle, oval.
Each approx. 1.5 in. Set/6.
2308-1205

6-Pc. Mini Noah's Ark

Lion, horse, ark, elephant, bear, giraffe.
Each approx. 1.5 in. Set/6.
2308-1206

6-Pc. Mini Harvest

Oak leaf, maple leaf, apple, pumpkin, elm leaf, acorn. Each approx. 1.5 in. Set/6.
2308-1217

6-Pc. Mini Halloween

Cat, pumpkin, bat, skull, ghost, moon. Each approx. 1.5 in. Set/6.
2308-1211

6-Pc. Mini Holiday

Candy cane, angel, tree, gingerbread boy, holly leaf, bell. Each approx. 1.5 in. Set/6.
2308-1214

7-Pc. Hearts

Seven different heart cutter designs. Sizes range from 1.5 in. to 3 in. Set/7.
2308-1237

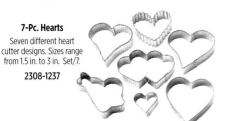

12-Pc. Mini Easter

Bunny face, egg, cross, flower, tulip, sun, carrot, chick, butterfly, bunny, umbrella, sprinkling can.
Each approx. 1.5 in. Set/12.
2308-1254

7-Pc. Coffin

Create ghoulishly good treats with our cookie cutter set packaged in a coffin container. Spider, cat, ghost, bat, pumpkin, coffin, tombstone. Each approx. 3 in. Set/7.
2308-0925

METAL NESTING SETS

Four graduated sizes up to 5 in. Set/4.

4-Pc. Circles
2308-0914

4-Pc. Blossoms
2308-1204

4-Pc. Stars
2308-1215

COLORED METAL SETS

Coated metal multi-piece sets represent popular themes. Recipe included. Each approx. 3 in.

3-Pc. Garden

Watering can, flower pot, spade. Set/3.
2308-0094

3-Pc. Flower

Tulip, daisy, butterfly. Set/3.
2308-0948

4-Pc. Football

Pennant, football, jersey, helmet. Set/4.
2308-1263

3-Pc. Trees

Classic fir, triangle tree, startop tree.
2308-1103

9-Pc. Halloween

Bat, ghost, cat, witch, moon, witch's broom, tombstone, house, pumpkin. Colored aluminum. Each approx. 3 in. to 3.75 in. Set/9.
2308-2501

PLASTIC NESTING SETS

Six graduated sizes up to 4.2 in. Set/6.

6-Pc. Hearts
2304-115

6-Pc. Stars
2304-111

PLASTIC SETS

Wilton has a wide variety of cutter shapes, and we've gathered your favorites in convenient sets. Great for cookies, brownies, gelatin treats, crafts and more.

A-B-C and 1-2-3
Great for learning games, too. Recipe included.
Average cutter size approx. 3.5 in. x 3.5 in. Set/50.
2304-1054

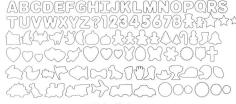

101 Cookie Cutters
Average cutter size approx. 3.5 in. x 3.5 in.
Recipe included. Set/101.
2304-1050

COOKIE TREAT STICKS

For fun cookie pops.

6 in. Pk./20.
1912-9319

8 in. Pk./20.
1912-9318

Presentation

Cupcakes make a big splash when served using our towering stands, colorful boxes and boards! Create a memorable party presentation or gift with ease.

CUPCAKE STANDS

Towering treat stands give your cupcakes a high profile at the party. Choose Cupcakes-N-More Dessert Stands with silver-finished wire spirals to securely hold cupcakes. Or, our Stacked Dessert Tower featuring stacking sections angled for the best view of decorated cupcakes. *Pat. No. 7,387,283. †Pat. No. D516,385.

24-Count Mini
Holds 24 mini-sized cupcakes.*
10.5 in. high x 9 in. wide.
307-250

13-Count Standard
Holds 13 standard-sized cupcakes.*
9.25 in. high x 9 in. wide.
307-831

23-Count Standard
Holds 23 standard-sized cupcakes.*†
12 in. high x 13 in. wide.
307-826

38-Count Standard
Holds 38 standard-sized cupcakes.*
15 in. high x 18 in. wide.
307-651

4-Tier Stacked Dessert Tower
Holds 36 standard-sized cupcakes. Sections easily disassemble and nest for storage; assembled tower is 16.25 in. high x 12 in. wide. Pat. No. D560,974.
307-856

Towering Tiers Cake Stand
Set includes: 2-pc. 18 in. plate; 2-pc. 16 in. plate; two plate supports (for use with the 18 in. and 16 in. plates); 14 in., 12 in., 10 in. and 8 in. plates; top nut; center post foot; five base feet; five (4.25 in. high) short center posts (for cupcake display); five (5.5 in. high) tall center posts (for cake display); Cake Corer; assembly instructions. Set/24.
307-892

DISPOSABLE CUPCAKE STANDS

Give cupcakes the perfect showcase for the party with easy-to-assemble, three-level stands. Securely holds 24 standard-sized cupcakes. Corrugated cardboard. Baking cups not included. 10.5 in. high.

White 1512-127

Black 1512-0860

FASHION CAKE BOARDS

Greaseproof cake boards show off your 10 in. cakes or treats in style. 12 in. dia. Pk./3.

Party Swirl 2104-5149

Zebra 2104-5150

Sweet Dots 2104-5152

3-in-1 Caddy
The 3-in-1 Caddy features an exclusive reversible cupcake tray which holds 12 standard-sized or 24 mini-sized cupcakes. Or, remove the tray to carry up to a 9 in. x 13 in. decorated cake on the sturdy locking base. 18 in. x 14 in. x 6.75 in. high. Pat. No. D572,539.
2105-9958

CUPCAKE BOXES

Display and give your cupcake creations with our window boxes. Each box includes an insert with recessed space to hold standard-sized cupcakes safely in place. Easy folding assembly; great for favors! Ribbon not included.

4-Cupcake Box
Holds four standard cupcakes. Pk./3.

Kraft
415-0953

Pastel
415-1361

White
415-1215

Silver
415-1359

1-Cupcake Box
Holds one standard cupcake. Pk./3.

Black & White Dots
415-0950

White
415-0436

Zebra
415-1897

CANDLES & TOPPERS

Just insert in your cupcakes for an instant celebration!

Celebration
2.5 in. high. Pk./24.
White **2811-207**
Pink **2811-213**
Red **2811-209**
Blue **2811-210**
Black **2811-224**

Hot Colors Rounds
2.5 in. high.
Pk./24.
2811-225

Rainbow Colors Rounds
2.5 in. high.
Pk./24.
2811-284

WARNING: Burn within sight. Keep away from things that catch fire. Keep away from children and pets. Always leave at least 2 inches (5 cm) between burning candles. Keep away from drafts.

Foil Pix
Looks like a dazzling fireworks display on your holiday treats! Great for cakes, cupcakes. 4 in. high. Pk./12.
2113-712

Mini Doll Pick Set
4.25 in. high with pick. Set/4.
1511-1019

Learn new skills 24/7!

TAKE WILTON METHOD CLASSES IN STORES NEAR YOU.

It's the easiest way to learn! Decorate using each technique with the help of a Certified Wilton Method Instructor. Create amazing cakes inspired by on-trend designs and exciting techniques.

LEARN THE WILTON METHOD ONLINE.

Enhance your skills with The Wilton Method at any time, on any device. Brush up on the techniques you learned in class or sign up for a fun online course. Learn whenever and wherever you want.

ACCESS CAKE IDEAS WHEREVER YOU ARE.

Discover exciting new ways to put your decorating techniques to work! Download the Wilton Cake Ideas & More App and connect with us on these social media sites.

Like us on Facebook.

Follow us on Pinterest.

Share ideas on Instagram.

Follow us on Twitter.

Subscribe to our YouTube Channel.